RICHARD III AND HIS EARLY HISTORIANS
1483-1535

Jean de Waurin presents his Chronicle to Edward IV (? in Bruges, 1470-1).
Richard of Gloucester may be the dark man in profile in the foreground, wearing
the Garter and with the 'short and sour countenance' described by Polydore
Vergil and others

RICHARD III AND
HIS EARLY HISTORIANS
1483–1535

by

ALISON HANHAM

CLARENDON PRESS · OXFORD
1975

Oxford University Press, Ely House, London W.1

GLASGOW   NEW YORK   TORONTO   MELBOURNE   WELLINGTON
CAPE TOWN   IBADAN   NAIROBI   DAR ES SALAAM   LUSAKA   ADDIS ABABA
DELHI   BOMBAY   CALCUTTA   MADRAS   KARACHI   LAHORE   DACCA
KUALA LUMPUR   SINGAPORE   HONG KONG   TOKYO

ISBN 0 19 822434 6

ⓒ *Oxford University Press 1975*

*Printed in Great Britain
by Billing & Sons Limited, Guildford and London*

Prefatory Note

EXCEPT in the appendix, where the exact spelling of a text is sometimes important to the argument (though even here I have disregarded earlier conventions with regard to the use of *u* and *v*, *i* and *j*, and have usually printed y^e and y^t as *the* and *that*), I have modernized spelling, capitalization, and punctuation in all English quotations. This decision was taken on the ground that the syntax of late fifteenth- and early sixteenth-century English prose often proves a sufficient barrier to the modern reader without the further complication of unfamiliar or misleading spellings; for example *farder* for 'more afraid', which even expert editors of More have misunderstood, or *then* for 'than' and vice versa. The decision to modernize was made easier by the facts that all but one of the English writings quoted are available in editions which preserve the early spelling, with varying degrees of accuracy, and that in many instances the spelling is that of a copyist or printer, not the author himself. William Rastell's practices, for example, are very different from More's own. Although the documents I have used are in print, not all can be readily obtained by the reader with no access to the major libraries. It is hoped therefore that this volume may have some use as a source-book. Wherever possible, edited texts have been compared with the original manuscripts, and a number of new readings are here offered.

Some quotations from Polydore Vergil are taken from the excellent anonymous sixteenth-century English translation published in part by the Camden Society in 1844 and 1846. This probably reflects Vergil's native style and habits of thought better than a modern version would be apt to do. Otherwise I have preferred to make my own translations from Latin, and from the Spanish of Diego de Valera in chapter two, even when entirely acceptable English renderings are in existence. It was more fun to do so, and the translator's exploration of the range of possible connotations in his original is a useful exercise for the historian. It was a necessary exercise in the case of the *Crowland Chronicle*. At the time of writing, the only English translation in print was that by H. T. Riley, published in 1854, which was too unreliable to employ.

While in no way holding them responsible for anything here said, I should like to express my thanks to a number of friends and colleagues who very kindly read and commented on drafts of various chapters, or allowed me to pick their brains on particular problems. I am especially grateful for such help, at different stages, from L. H. Butler, John Clive, H. J. Hanham, G. L. Harriss, Denys Hay, Maurice Keen, Ann Kettle, Zeph Stewart, and S. E. Thorne.

The tentative identification of Richard Duke of Gloucester with one of the two courtiers who wear the Garter in an illumination to Jean de Waurin's *Chronicle* (Plate I) was put forward by Dr. Pamela Tudor-Craig in her catalogue for the Richard III Exhibition at the National Portrait Gallery in 1973.

Contents

List of Plates

I   The Usurpation and Reign of Richard III

Fʀᴏᴍ the gossips of England and France in the summer of 1483 to modern writers and readers of historical romance, people have been fascinated by the actions and character of King Richard III. For a long time the dominant portrait of him was that furnished by Shakespeare: a coolly diabolical plotter driven by furious ambition, owning affection to no man, and redeemed by little save a streak of cynical humour. The monster thus brought to birth was by Sir Thomas More out of the Machiavel of the Elizabethan stage and had theatrical ancestry on both sides. Successive generations of actors kept it before the public with unabating gusto, at the same time as sceptical scholars were joining forces with romantic Yorkists to demolish it as a myth. The second group have been successful to the extent that no one now accepts Shakespeare's Richard as historically valid, and few find More's wholly convincing. Unfortunately, the admirers of Richard have not succeeded in producing any more credible figure.

To some extent, this book investigates and seeks to re-evaluate the historical evidence about Richard's deeds and intentions. It is chiefly concerned, however, with the question of how the literary Richard came into being; to examine, that is, the way in which Richard's story was treated by the historians who wrote about him between 1483, the year in which he seized the throne, and the date of More's death. This will involve principally an examination of the near-contemporary description of Richard's usurpation by the Italian, Mancini; of the 'second continuation' of the *Crowland Chronicle* (based, as I shall hope to show, on an account by someone who was on the inside of events throughout the reign); of the history put together by the humanist historian, Polydore Vergil, and the relation of his work both to More's and to the *Crowland Chronicle*; and finally of More's own work. I shall also look more briefly at other chronicle accounts, and at some of the difficulties which contemporary documentary evidence from the reign can itself present for the modern historian.

But in order to describe the development of the story, it is necessary first to attempt an outline of the basic facts of Richard's reign and of its principal events, as far as they can now be reconstructed.

When Edward IV lay dying in the early days of April 1483, after an eventful but on the whole notably successful reign of just over twenty-two years, his heir's prospects must have looked reasonably well assured. The worst difficulties for his government were likely to be caused by relations with Scotland, and with France and Burgundy, which had suddenly worsened alarmingly with the Treaty of Arras in December 1482. Edward himself, by strenuous effort, had put royal finances into an order which few medieval English monarchs had achieved; efficient government had been re-established after the disorders of Henry VI's reign and the Earl of Warwick's interventions in national affairs; the Lancastrian opposition had been largely eliminated or absorbed after Barnet and Tewkesbury, and the remaining source of serious sedition, Edward's own brother George, Duke of Clarence, had finally been removed in 1478.

Ever since the announcement of his secret marriage to Elizabeth Woodville, widow of the Lancastrian Sir John Grey, Lord Ferrers of Groby, which had taken place in 1464, Edward had held a balance between the queen's large family and their rivals among the 'older nobility' and those men like William, Lord Hastings, who had themselves risen through his recognition of their activities in his cause. Both factions provided the king with boon companions, and since the king was the pivot of the balance between them, he may not have appreciated the full extent of their mutual hatred. They in turn had been careful, on the whole, not to offend the king by open aggression. One ugly portent of things to come had been a bitter quarrel between Hastings on the one hand and on the other Anthony, Earl Rivers, the queen's brother, and Thomas, Marquis of Dorset, her son by her first marriage. Rivers and Hastings had been rivals for the captaincy of Calais, which went to Hastings in 1471, and Dorset and Hastings (whose step-daughter was Dorset's wife) were said to have quarrelled over mistresses. A row blew up in 1482, when it would appear that Hastings and Rivers accused each other (but only through informers) of plotting to surrender Calais to the French. For a short time Hastings apparently had the worst of it, and Thomas More reports that he was in serious danger before he contrived to gain the king's ear and clear himself.[1] Bad blood between Hastings and the Woodvilles remained, and one of Edward's last actions was to demand and receive a formal act of reconciliation between Hastings and Dorset.[2] He had reason to suppose that both would be loyal to his son.

There was still more reason for Edward to trust his remaining brother, Richard Duke of Gloucester, whose political allegiance, unlike that of Clarence, had never wavered. Gloucester's popularity with the country was high as a result of his striking (if ephemeral) success in the war against Scotland of the previous summer, and Edward's last parliament, in which the speaker was a supporter of Gloucester's, had made him lavish grants of lands and power in the north-west marches.[3] There is evidence that among the codicils which Edward hastily added to his will was one expressing his desire that Richard should be protector of his children and kingdom.[4] The effective tutelage of the young heir was, however, vested at the time of Edward's death in Earl Rivers, who had charge of the prince and his household at Ludlow.

[1] Thomas More, *History of King Richard the Third*, ed. R. S. Sylvester, *The Complete Works of St. Thomas More*, II (New Haven, Conn., and London, 1963), p. 51 (both English and Latin versions). There seems little reason to date Hastings's disgrace to 1477 (ibid., p. 173 n. and references there). To the account of E. W. Ives, 'Andrew Dymmock and the Papers of Antony Earl Rivers, 1482–3', *Bulletin of the Institute of Historical Research* XLI (1968), 221, it may be added that the affair seems to have concluded when Hastings expelled the servants of Robert Radcliffe from Calais in August 1482, after rumours that the keys of the city had been counterfeited (Cely Letters, P.R.O., Anc. Corr. (S.C.1) 53/138, 20 August 1482, and *A Chronicle of London from 1089–1483*, ed. N. H. Nicolas and Edward Tyrrell (1827), p. 147), and when John Edward (not Edwards, as Ives has it), Hastings's informer against the Woodvilles, and one Guillaume Vambar were condemned to execution at Tyburn for conspiracy, sedition, and treason early in December (S.C.1 44/60).

[2] C. A. J. Armstrong, ed. [Dominic Mancini], *The Usurpation of Richard the Third* (Oxford, 2nd edn., 1969), p. 68.

[3] Cora L. Scofield, *The Life and Reign of Edward the Fourth* (London and New York, 1923), II. 359. [4] Armstrong, *Usurpation*, notes 7 and 63.

The Prince of Wales was not an infant: he was twelve, and while he could not yet be expected to reign unaided, there was not the prospect of a long minority such as England had seen under Henry VI. It is sometimes forgotten now that the capacities of a twelve-year-old youth were much more highly rated, and extended, in medieval times, and Henry VI himself had, nominally at least, taken over the reins of government at the age of fifteen. Indeed, it may have been less the prospect of conciliar rule, and squabbling, that alarmed the anti-Woodville faction than the fact that the new king was already of an age to give effective support to his maternal relatives in the struggle for power.

✳One curious and, as it turned out, most unfortunate feature of events was that many of those to be involved in the coming struggle for power were not present at Edward's death-bed or even at his funeral. When the king died early on 9 April the new king was at Ludlow with his maternal uncle Rivers, his half-brother Richard Grey, and other members of his household as Prince of Wales. News of his father's death reached him only on 14 April.[1] Two of his leading subjects were also absent from the funeral ceremonies at Windsor. The Duke of Gloucester was on his estates in Yorkshire, and Henry Stafford, Duke of Buckingham, the other magnate who played an important part in succeeding events, was also in the country, probably in Wales. Buckingham was a member of the royal family by right both of his illegitimate Beaufort descent from John of Gaunt (shared with Henry Tudor), and of his direct descent from Thomas of Lancaster, youngest son of Edward III.

Among those left in London, the chief members of the Woodville party were the queen herself, Dorset, and Sir Edward Woodville (who was, possibly, already engaged in preparing a fleet to deal with French pirates in the Channel), Lionel Woodville, Bishop of Salisbury (not, apparently, a member of the royal council),[2] and Thomas Rotherham, Archbishop of York and Lord Chancellor. Lord Hastings held

---

[1] James Gairdner, *History of the Life and Reign of Richard the Third* (rev. edn., Cambridge, 1898), p. 48.

[2] J. R. Lander, 'Council, Administration and Councillors 1461–85', *B.I.H.R.* XXXII (1959), 138–80.

a watching brief for those who distrusted the queen's party.[1] Chief among the neutral councillors should probably be counted Thomas Bourchier, Cardinal Archbishop of Canterbury, and John Russell, Bishop of Lincoln and Keeper of the Privy Seal. Although there was evidently a majority of the queen's party on the council, there is no evidence that she herself made any attempt to act as regent for her son,[2] and P. M. Kendall's suggestions that the council acted illegally in providing temporary government at this period seem quite unbased.[3]

According to later record, those of Edward IV's councillors who were in London at his death or had assembled there afterwards debated two important questions. In the view of contemporaries, on both issues the opposing sides were actuated by fear for themselves if the other party gained power.[4] The Woodville faction were believed in particular to fear Gloucester's vengeance for the death of Clarence, for which they were held responsible.[5] First, as reported by Mancini, the question arose of the form of government to be adopted during the minority of the new king.[6] The minority opinion on the council (supported, however, by the country at large) was that Gloucester should become protector, in the customary manner and in the terms apparently proposed in the late king's will.[7] The majority—the queen's party—voted for a conciliar form of government: 'that the government should be carried on by a number of people, from whom Gloucester should not be excluded; indeed, he was to be described as chief councillor.' It is possible that Mancini's expressions *administrare* and *administratio* here obscure an argument like that which occurred over the status of Humphrey Duke of Gloucester during the minority of Henry VI. At that time Duke Humphrey had vainly demanded the 'governance' of the realm and the title of *Rector regni Anglie* (abrogating the addition of *rector regis*—

[1] He was intimate with John Morton (*Paston Letters and Papers of the Fifteenth Century*, Part I, ed. Norman Davis (Oxford, 1971), p. 618), but Morton's position at this time is not known,

[2] Despite James H. Ramsay, *Lancaster and York* (Oxford, 1892), II. 476.

[3] Paul M. Kendall, *Richard the Third* (1955), pp. 165 ff.

[4] Mancini, ed. Armstrong, p. 70. [5] Ibid. [6] Ibid.

[7] 'Because Edward had directed so in his will, and because by law the governance was due to him,' p. 71.

governor of the king—which he claimed that William Marshal had had in the minority of Henry III).[1] In fact both Humphrey and Edward IV's father, Richard Duke of York, during his two short protectorates, had to be content with the title of 'protector and defender', and 'not the name of tutor, lieutenant, governor nor of regent, nor no name that should import authority of governance of the land'.[2] But it is also possible that the Woodvilleite council were reluctant to grant Richard of Gloucester even this status, which chiefly conferred responsibility for military defence and internal order. Certainly he does not seem to be termed 'protector' at this stage.[3] They may also have hoped that once Edward V was crowned they could argue, like the lords in 1429, that the king's coronation oath did away with the need for any other protector and defender.[4]

Having settled the question of government to its satisfaction, the council fixed the coronation for 4 May and wrote to Rivers to get the king to London three days beforehand.[5] When the moderates pointed out that it was impolitic to move so fast in Gloucester's absence, Dorset is reported to have said 'We are so important that we can legislate and execute by ourselves, regardless of the king's uncle.'[6] Such arrogance cannot have helped his cause, and even the moderates, according to the *Crowland Chronicle*, became wary of entrusting the king to the guardianship of his mother's family. Hastings and his friends said more bluntly that base blood unfitted them for such a task.[7] The second difference arose over the size of the

[1] S. B. Chrimes, 'The Pretensions of the Duke of Gloucester in 1422', *English Historical Review*, XLV (1930), 101–3.

[2] J. S. Roskell, 'The Office and Dignity of Protector of England', *E.H.R.* LXVIII (1953), 193–233; *Rotuli Parliamentorum*, IV. 326.

[3] The two documents which style Richard Protector of England before 4 May have every appearance of being misdated. They are a commission of the peace entered on the patent roll and dated 21 April (no other commission of the reign of Edward V is earlier than 14 May), and an entry in B.M. MS. Harleian 433 disposing of certain of Earl Rivers's forfeited lands, dated improbably 2 May.

[4] *Rot. Parl.* IV. 336–7. This document gives little support to the idea (held by Gairdner and others) that coronation *per se* would dissolve a protectorate automatically.

[5] 'Crowland Chronicle', ed. W. Fulman, *Rerum Anglicarum Scriptorum Veterum*, I (Oxford, 1684), p. 565; Mancini, p. 72.   [6] Mancini, p. 74.

[7] Mancini (p. 78) says 'many people' felt that it was fairer and more advantageous to have the Duke of Gloucester as guardian. The extant version of the

(Woodville) escort to be provided for the king on his journey to London. Here Hastings and his supporters were apparently successful in getting a limitation agreed. Hastings reported both issues to Gloucester, with his own advice to take prompt measures to retrieve the position; a counsel of expediency which would later cause him bitter regret. Gloucester wrote diplomatically to the queen and the council assuring them of his loyalty, and after a solemn funeral service for the late king at York, himself headed the northern nobles in taking an oath of allegiance to Edward V.[1]

Meanwhile he was also in communication with the Duke of Buckingham. Persuading the young king's advisers to join forces with them for a ceremonial entry into London, the two dukes arranged for a rendezvous at Stony Stratford. C. A. J. Armstrong suggests that to effect this meeting the king's party must have made a considerable detour from the direct route between Ludlow and London.[2] Perhaps their earlier suspicions had been lulled by Gloucester's amenability, or they thought it unwise to incur his enmity by a further rebuff at this stage. They were in a strong political position; with a working majority on the council, *de facto* tutelage of the king, a favourable settlement of the question of the protectorship, a fleet about to put to sea, and control of the Tower and its treasury, held by Dorset. As nominal warden of the marches of Wales, the young king (in practice, Rivers on his behalf) had effective troops at his disposal at Ludlow. There was therefore nothing to gain by discourtesy to Gloucester. Alternatively, Richard's charge that they set up an ambush for him was true.[3] In any event, Gloucester and Buckingham did not propose to waste time in fencing with the niceties of protocol. While maintaining all proper deference to their sovereign, when the two parties came together they arrested Rivers, Lord Richard Grey, and Sir Thomas Vaughan (chamberlain to the king as Prince of Wales), and dismissed his

---

Crowland Chronicle says of Hastings that later, when the Woodvilles were overcome and Richard had been made protector, 'he was bursting with joy at the new state of affairs, and said that all that had happened was that the governance of the king had been transferred from two of the queen's line to two more noble representatives of the royal blood' (p. 566).

[1] *Crowland Chron.*, p. 565.   [2] Mancini, n. 44.   [3] Ibid., pp. 76, 84.

retinue of attendants.[1] They accused the king's entourage of misguidance and incompetence, and of plotting to ambush and kill Gloucester to deprive him of his rightful position as protector.[2] The prisoners were escorted to some of Gloucester's strongholds in Yorkshire, and the king and his new guardians went to Northampton *en route* for London.

This coup took place early on Wednesday, 30 April. The news of it reached London by the following night.[3] The queen fled to sanctuary at Westminster, taking with her the king's younger brother and his sisters. Dorset and others of her party made a quick attempt to gather troops and support, met hostility or indifference, and then joined her, possibly with part of the royal treasure.[4] The queen's brother, Sir Edward Woodville, had just put to sea with his fleet. According to a story unique to Thomas More, Archbishop Rotherham took it upon himself to give the great seal into the queen's hands in sanctuary.[5] Whether for such political ineptitude or because (as Mancini suggests) he supported the queen's faction in general, he was dismissed from office by the new regime and Bishop Russell of Lincoln was appointed chancellor. Gloucester meanwhile wrote to the council and the mayor and aldermen of London, putting forward a reasoned and convincing account of his actions. He backed this up by an exercise in practical propaganda, sending four wagons of captured Woodville arms to be paraded through the city.[6] The

---

[1] Ibid., pp. 74–8; *Crowland Chron.*, p. 565. Haute is added to the list of prisoners in some later sources.   [2] Mancini, p. 76; *Crowland Chron.*, p. 565.

[3] Probably 1 May rather than 'during the night 30 April–1 May', as Armstrong says (Mancini, nn. 51, 52). Stony Stratford is 52 miles from London, and at this period the usual distance covered by a messenger on horseback appears to be about 30 to 35 miles per day.

[4] I have here tried to reconcile Mancini and the *Crowland Chronicle*. Both suggest that some attempt was made to recruit forces. The latter says (p. 565), 'The following night [*nocte sequenti*, not *ea nocte*, 'that night'], when these rumours had reached London, Queen Elizabeth moved into the sanctuary of Westminster. On the next morning the supporters of either party were to be seen gathering round one side or the other; some whole-heartedly, others dissimulating because uncertain how things would turn out. Some collected their forces and made their headquarters at Westminster in the queen's name, and the others at London under the aegis of Lord Hastings.'

[5] Ed. Sylvester [Yale *Works*], pp. 21, 22–3.

[6] Mancini, p. 82. Mancini states that the claim aroused distrust among the more knowledgeable, who knew the arms had been stored long before during the war with Scotland.

king, with his uncle and the Duke of Buckingham, made his state entrance into the capital on Sunday, 4 May, the date originally set for his coronation. Oaths of allegiance were taken in the city, but Lord Rivers's failure to march promptly to London had in fact lost Edward the throne.

When a council had been convened, Gloucester was appointed protector. According to the *Crowland Chronicle*:

The said Richard Duke of Gloucester took on him the customary office,[1] which had formerly come to Humphrey Duke of Gloucester during the minority of King Henry, so that he was named protector of the realm. That authority, by the agreement and acceptance of all the lords, conferred the right to order and forbid in all matters like another king, as conditions required.[2]

This brief definition seems to suggest powers far more sweeping than those accorded to either Duke Humphrey or Richard's own father under Henry VI. Mancini says rather vaguely that on the authority of the council Richard was declared *protector* or *administrator* of the king and kingdom,[3] but the chancellor's projected speech to parliament in June refers to 'the defence of the realm and *tutele* and oversight of the king's most royal person during his years of tenderness . . . to be his tutor and protector'.[4] Tutelage had been expressly denied to Humphrey.

Other points of council business recorded are the decision, reached after some debate, to transfer the king's temporary residence from the Bishop of London's palace to the royal apartments in the Tower, and an order to Sir Edward Woodville to disband his fleet under pain of treason (he got away with two of the ships, the others being recovered for the government).[5] The protector failed, however, to persuade the council that Rivers and his associates should be attainted of treason, and indeed the council seems to have voiced its concern at his treatment of them.[6] The grounds for refusal were first that it was by no means clear that they had prepared any ambush for Gloucester, and secondly that, in any case,

[1] *Illum solennem magistratum*: either 'customary' or 'high' office.   [2] p. 566.
[3] pp. 82–3. On Richard's probable status at this time see further Roskell, 'The Office . . . of Protector', pp. 227–8.
[4] *Grants, etc. from the Crown during the Reign of Edward the Fifth*, ed. J. G. Nichols (Camden Society, 1854), pp. xlvii–xlviii.
[5] *Crowland Chron.*, p. 566; Mancini, p. 84; *Grants*, pp. 2, 3 (10 and 14 May).
[6] Mancini, p. 84; *Crowland Chron.*, p. 566.

Gloucester could not accuse them of treason for an attack on
his person that had taken place before he had been confirmed
as protector. Finally the council fixed a new date for the king's
coronation: Sunday 22 June. (The *Crowland Chronicle*'s 'the
feast of the Nativity of St. John the Baptist was fixed as the
time at which the coronation was to be performed without
fail' does not necessarily mean 24 June itself.[1]) Writs dated
13 May were issued to summon parliament for 25 June, and on
20 May letters were addressed to sheriffs ordering those eligible
for knighthood to come to London by 18 June.[2] The date
chosen for the coronation does not seem, however, to have
been publicly proclaimed until some time after 9 June.[3]

By 9 June councillors had in mind the awkward fact that the
king's mother, brother, and sisters were obstinately skulking
in sanctuary. When repeated blandishments had failed to
persuade the queen to emerge,[4] the council, under Gloucester's
influence, finally sent a deputation under the Archbishop of
Canterbury to obtain the presence at least of the young Duke
of York at the forthcoming coronation, and ominously backed
their delegation with an armed force which surrounded the
sanctuary.[5] The confrontation occurred on the morning of
Monday, 16 June, and the queen eventually agreed to surrender the boy, perhaps on Canterbury's personal assurance
that he would be returned to her after the ceremony.[6] The
boy was welcomed by Gloucester and Buckingham and then
joined his brother at the Tower.[7] At about the same time the
young Earl of Warwick, son of the attainted Duke of Clarence,
was brought to London and lodged in Gloucester's household,
under the care of the duchess, his maternal aunt.[8] About 16
June also, a writ was strangely sent to York cancelling the
summons of their representatives to parliament.[9]

---

[1] p. 566; 'statutoque . . . pro die certo', but *dies* could mean loosely 'term'.
[2] Mancini, n. 94; Thomas Rymer, ed., *Foedera* (20 vols., 1704–35), XII. 181.
[3] *Stonor Letters and Papers, 1290–1483*, ed. C. L. Kingsford (Camden Soc., 3rd
Ser., 1919), No. 330. (See below, pp. 35, 150.)
[4] Ibid., and Mancini, n. 74.
[5] Mancini, p. 88; *Crowland Chron.*, p. 566.
[6] Mancini, p. 88.
[7] *Stonor Letters*, No. 331, and below, p. 42.
[8] Mancini, p. 88.
[9] *York Civic Records*, I, ed. Angelo Raine (Yorkshire Archaeological Society,
Record Ser. XCVIII, 1939), 75, and below, pp. 38–40.

It soon became clear that with the seizure of the Duke of York a new train of events had been set in motion. Three days later, on Thursday 19 June, the protector arranged for the council to meet next morning in two divisions, one at Westminster and the other at the Tower.[1] Accordingly, about 10 a.m. on 20 June Lord Hastings, Archbishop Rotherham of York (the recently deposed chancellor), John Morton Bishop of Ely, and others assembled at the Tower, where Richard himself was in attendance. When they reached the council chamber in the private apartments, Richard gave a pre-arranged signal and some of Buckingham's retainers rushed in. Accusations of treason were made; Hastings was hustled out and beheaded on a makeshift block on Tower Green, and the two bishops were taken into custody. The incident caused general horror and confusion, but the people of London, who started to rush to arms, were quieted by prompt action on the part of the mayor,[2] and by official reassurances from the protector, who announced that an attempt on the king's person, part of a wider conspiracy, had been frustrated and the chief rebel executed.[3]

In the meantime, the news was around London that huge numbers of troops were on their way to the capital on behalf of Gloucester and Buckingham.[4] Part of this contingent came from York, to whose mayor Richard had addressed a request for troops as early as 10 June.[5] The reason advanced was the dangerous machinations of the queen and her affinity (or those of them not in prison) against Gloucester, Buckingham, and others of the old noble blood of the realm and their northern supporters. These troops joined others at Pontefract under the command of the Earl of Northumberland and Ralph Lord Neville, heir of the Earl of Westmorland, on 25 June. They did not reach London until July,[6] when everything was over bar the crowning, but Gloucester and Buckingham and

---

[1] The arguments for restoring this traditional order of events, which has been controverted by recent historians, are discussed below, pp. 24–9.

[2] *Acts of Court of the Mercers' Company, 1453–1527*, ed. Laetitia Lyell (Cambridge, 1936), p. 155.

[3] Mancini, p. 90.   [4] *Stonor Letters*, No. 331.

[5] *York Civic Records*, I. 73, and below, pp. 35–8. Mancini thought they had been summoned only as the day of Richard's coronation approached (p. 98).

[6] *Acts of Court*, p. 155.

other supporters like John Howard had among them enough private forces for such tasks as guarding the king, watching the sanctuaries, and, about this time, mounting a full-scale search for the Marquis of Dorset who had none the less managed to escape from sanctuary.[1] After 20 June Buckingham's retinue was swelled by the accession of Hastings's retainers, who transferred their allegiance after their lord's death.[2] The threat, moreover, of a large force of northern troops descending on the capital was sufficiently potent. The fear engendered by the undisciplined northerners of Queen Margaret's army in 1461 had not yet been forgotten in the south.

Saturday 21 June was devoted partly to mopping-up operations; the houses of those arrested the previous day were occupied, and more arrests occurred.[3] By now the coronation must have been cancelled again. Certain trustworthy London preachers were given instructions about the content of their sermons next day, and the mayor, Edmund Sha, later incurred suspicion of complicity because the most notable of these preachers was Ralph Sha, his brother. It is not clear how far members of the council knew what was going on at this point. Mancini heard later that Buckingham had previously tested the loyalties of Hastings, Rotherham, and Morton, and had concluded that they would be implacably opposed to a seizure of power by Richard.[4] (Thomas More, on uncertain authority, cast William Catesby in this role.[5]) Subsequently, no contemporary doubted that Hastings had been killed for this reason, but it is impossible to say whether this was obvious to his fellow councillors on 21 June. The position must, however, have become clear on 22 June, when, in place of the cancelled coronation, there was a sermon from Ralph Sha at Paul's Cross alleging that the late king had been conceived in adultery and his sons had no claim on the throne. (Improbable as this may seem, it was what Mancini was given to understand at the time, and Polydore Vergil later heard stories to the same effect.) The theme seems to have been pursued from other pulpits

---

[1] Mancini, p. 90.   [2] *Stonor Letters*, No. 331.
[3] Ibid. (but see also below, pp. 24–9).   [4] Mancini, p. 90.
[5] Yale *Works*, II. 45–6; see further J. S. Roskell, 'William Catesby, Counsellor to Richard III', *Bulletin of the John Rylands Library*, XLII (1959), 145–74.

as well,[1] and was taken up and added to by Buckingham in an address, or addresses, to the lords who had assembled at London (with diminished retinues, by the protector's instructions),[2] and representatives of the city. The three estates who convened for the expected parliament on 25 June instead met 'out of parliament' and subscribed to an elaborate petition which asserted Richard's title to the throne and the disability of his nephews, who were now said to be illegitimate on the grounds of their father's precontract with Eleanor Butler, a daughter of the late Earl of Shrewsbury.[3] This petition was then presented to Richard, and he took title by occupying the King's Bench in the Hall of Westminster on Thursday 26 June and performing the usual ceremonies of accession. On the previous day Rivers and his associates had been executed at Pontefract, possibly after some form of trial.[4] The greatly feared troops under Northumberland and Neville reached London only about 3 July, in time for the coronation of Richard and his queen Anne Neville on 6 July. They were then sent home again.

Before the coronation of the new monarch, the previous king and his brother had gradually disappeared from public view. Their attendants had been changed after the Hastings affair (perhaps on the excuse that their negligence had exposed their charges to danger on that occasion), and the boys were confined to the innermost reaches of the Tower.[5] The last of the king's servants to be allowed access, his physician Dr. Argentine, reported that the young king was in daily fear of death. On Mancini's evidence, the popular view, even before Richard's coronation, was that this fear had been all too well founded, but Mancini could learn nothing of his fate.

---

[1] Mancini (p. 94) mentions several preachers. More (pp. 58–9) refers to a later sermon by Thomas Penketh, provincial of the Augustinians.   [2] Mancini, p. 94.

[3] *Rot. Parl.* VI. 240–2; below, pp. 45–8; *Crowland Chron.*, pp. 566–7. B. Wilkinson, *Constitutional History of England in the Fifteenth Century* (1964), p. 162, seems to have overlooked this explicit statement when he says that there is no description of the presentation of a bill of petition from the three estates by 'the chroniclers'.

[4] Mancini, n. 85; *Crowland Chron.*, p. 567, 'at the order of Richard Ratcliff'. John Rous says Northumberland acted as their chief judge (*Joannis Rossi Antiquarii Warwicensis Historia Regum Angliae*, ed. Thomas Hearne (Oxford, 1716), p. 213). Later opinion apparently blamed Sir Richard Ratcliff and William Catesby, as much as the protector, for this action (*Crowland Chron.*, p. 572).

[5] Mancini, p. 92.

Neither could any other reliable chronicler. The scientific evidence strongly suggests, however, that the remains now entombed in Westminster Abbey as those of Edward V and his brother are indeed the bones of two children of an age similar to that reached by the princes in 1483.[1] It is highly improbable that two other children of these ages were ever buried together in unconsecrated ground in the vicinity of the royal apartments at the Tower.

After his coronation Richard made a gradual progress north to York, where he created his only son Edward Prince of Wales, amid splendid ceremonies.[2] But already disaffection had begun, and there were conspiracies in the south and west, aimed initially at rescuing the rightful king and his brother. Some of the Woodville faction, perhaps more pessimistic about the fate of the princes, were said to be plotting to take their sisters from sanctuary and send them to safety abroad.[3] As conspiracy started to develop into a rising, it acquired a surprising leader in Henry Duke of Buckingham. The exact reasons for his volte-face are unknown, but the defection of this former friend and collaborator evidently came as a shock to the king. Nor is it quite clear at what point the rebels abandoned the cause of Edward V and switched their allegiance to Henry Tudor. The *Crowland Chronicle* ascribes the decision to the spread of a rumour that the boys had been murdered, by some means unspecified. On the whole, the context makes it likely that the writer means to imply that this rumour was encouraged by the king.[4] At this stage, Henry Tudor must have

[1] L. E. Tanner and W. Wright, 'Recent Investigations regarding the Fate of the Princes in the Tower', *Archaeologia*, LXXXIV (1934), 1–26; Kendall, *Richard III*, Appendix I, pp. 406–7, and for rebutting evidence by doctors who had not themselves seen the remains, ibid., pp. 497–8.

[2] *Crowland Chron.*, p. 567.   [3] Ibid., and below, p. 49.

[4] p. 568: 'When at length the people around London, with those of [many of the Home and south-west counties] had undertaken to avenge [the princes'] cause, and it had been publicly proclaimed that the Duke of Buckingham, repenting the deed [i.e. the usurpation], would be the chief leader in this action, it was spread about that the said sons of King Edward had perished (by what violent means is unknown). For this reason, all those who had started this movement, seeing that all would soon be lost if they could not find a new leader for their enterprise, bethought themselves of Henry, Earl of Richmond.' Vergil was in no doubt: 'King Richard . . . kept the slaughter not long secret, who, within few days after, permitted the rumour of their death to go abroad, to th'intent (as we may well believe) that after the people understood no issue male of King Edward to be now

seemed an unlikely candidate for the throne. It may well have been John Morton, Bishop of Ely, who was Buckingham's prisoner at Brecknock, who suggested to his host and warder the advisability of joining forces with Henry. It appears that simultaneously Henry's mother Margaret Beaufort, now wife of Thomas Lord Stanley, and Queen Elizabeth Woodville were scheming together to make a match between Henry and the Princess Elizabeth of York.[1] Buckingham and Morton adopted this proposed match as a condition for supporting Henry. According to the *Crowland Chronicle*, Richard's spies kept him accurately informed about the course of the plot, at least as far as its English side was concerned.[2] Nevertheless, as Chrimes points out, Richard's proclamation of 23 October 1483, against Dorset, Buckingham, the Bishops of Ely and Salisbury, and other rebels, did not yet mention Henry as an enemy.[3]

The rebellion was a disastrous failure, except in so far as many of its leaders escaped for renewed plotting abroad. Buckingham was captured and beheaded on 2 November, and Henry, arriving too late, returned hastily to Brittany. According to a lost source, Henry was proclaimed king in absentia at Bodmin.[4] If this is true, the action may have encouraged him to use the royal style.[5] Richard pursued Dorset, Peter Courtenay, Bishop of Exeter, and other leaders to Exeter. The first two got away to Brittany; some eventually found refuge in sanctuary, but Sir Thomas St. Leger (widower of Richard's sister) was among those caught and executed.[6] A large

---

left alive, they might with better mind and good will bear to sustain his government' (*Three Books of Polydore Vergil's English History*, ed. Henry Ellis (Camden Soc., 1844), pp. 188–9). Kendall, however, probably relying on Riley's translation of the *Crowland Chron.* (H. T. Riley, *Ingulph's Chronicle of the Abbey of Croyland with the Continuations* . . . (1854), p. 491), argued strongly that it was Buckingham who spread the rumours (*Richard III*, pp. 267–8, 412).

[1] For this side of the conspiracy, see S. B. Chrimes, *Henry VII* (1972), pp. 22–3, based largely on Polydore Vergil, whose information about Henry s activities at this point is the best we have.

[2] p. 568. This would help explain 'the slowness with which he took overt action to mobilize men and resources against the rebellions', on which Chrimes comments (p. 24).

[3] *Calendar of Patent Rolls, 1476–85*, p. 371.

[4] Cited in A. L. Rowse, *Tudor Cornwall* (Bedford Historical Ser., 1957), p. 111 and n. 3.

[5] Gairdner, *Richard III*, pp. 213–15.   [6] *Crowland Chron.*, p. 568.

number of gentry, like Sir William Stonor, had been involved and were in due course attainted. The widespread outbreak had been disruptive and expensive. It also sent valuable recruits to Henry, like Giles Daubeny, John Cheyney, William Brandon the younger, and Edward Courtenay, Earl of Devon.

Richard's first and only parliament was first summoned for 6 November 1483, but had to be postponed until January 1484.[1] The commons elected William Catesby as their speaker. Having confirmed Richard's title and the petition presented to him in June 1483, parliament proceeded to deal with the attainders caused by the rebellion. These totalled about a hundred. The Bishops of Ely, Salisbury, and Exeter forfeited their temporalities, and Margaret Beaufort's lands were transferred to her husband, Lord Stanley, for life with remainder to the king. Bishop Morton, like others, was later pardoned but not enticed back to England. The *Crowland Chronicle* says that Richard distributed the profits and forfeited estates among his northern supporters, whom he established throughout the kingdom and especially in the south, where their oppression was bitterly resented.[2]

As Gairdner said, 'The public Acts of this Parliament have always been noted as wise and beneficial',[3] but how far the ordinary legislation of this (or any) parliament was initiated by the king in person is a debatable point.[4] So much has been made of Richard's good government that it ought to be said that he was in no position to enact oppressive measures, even had he wished to do so; that the abolition of benevolences was probably a concession to popular feeling; and that specific acts dealing with commerce are likely to have been inspired (as usual) by discussions between the council and interested parties among the merchant community. More generally, no study has yet been published which would test the claim that the day-to-day administration of justice and government during the reign was unusually fair and efficient: many of the ordinary legal records of the reign are in fact

[1] Ramsay, *Lancaster and York*, II. 515 and n.

[2] p. 570; cf. B. P. Wolffe, *The Crown Lands, 1461–1536* (1970), pp. 63–4.

[3] *Richard III*, p. 160.

[4] H. G. Hanbury, 'The Legislation of Richard III', *American Journal of Legal History*, VI (1962), 95–113, carries very little conviction.

lost. Equally, there is nothing to show any notable perversion of justice beyond the summary executions of Hastings and Rivers and his associates, the former of which has recently been described as an unparalleled travesty of legal form.[1]

During this parliamentary session Elizabeth Woodville was persuaded, by threats and promises, to send her daughters to the king's court, where they were honourably treated. The former queen herself was given a generous annual sum 'for her exhibition and finding'; which was, however, to be paid to John Nesfield, esquire of the body, to attend upon her.[2] Nesfield was the man who had been set to guard the sanctuary to prevent escapes in 1483,[3] and Gairdner may have been wrong in suggesting that Elizabeth herself left sanctuary so soon.[4] By February Richard felt strong enough to plan a campaign against the Scots for the following May,[5] and about the same time he imposed a special oath of allegiance to his son, which was subscribed by nearly all the lords spiritual and temporal, together with the knights banneret and esquires of the household.[6] The boy's death less than two months later, not far off the anniversary of Edward IV's death in April, was inevitably seen as divine retribution on a usurper. Richard had no hope of another heir by his ailing wife. The only immediate heirs were Clarence's son, the Earl of Warwick (theoretically debarred by his father's attainder), and the Earl of Lincoln, another nephew by Richard's sister Elizabeth Duchess of Suffolk, whose claims Richard eventually preferred. A further blow to his dynastic ambitions occurred in the summer of 1484 when Henry Tudor, warned in time, narrowly escaped from the hands of Pierre Landois, treasurer of Brit-

[1] J. G. Bellamy, *The Law of Treason in England in the Later Middle Ages* (Cambridge, 1970), p. 215. But cf. also B. P. Wolffe, *The Royal Demesne in English History* (1971), pp. 192–3; '[After October 1483, the rebels'] lands were seized and redistributed to [Richard's] loyal supporters on a scale unprecedented in English history since Richard II disinherited his opponents in 1398. Moreover, this confiscation and redistribution proceeded without the normal delaying safeguards of legal inquisition as laid down in several statutes, and parliament subsequently legalized this arbitrary procedure.' This was the same parliament that enacted that the goods of suspected felons were not to be taken before their owner was convicted or attainted (Hanbury, pp. 106–7).
[2] The text of the agreement is in Gairdner, *Richard III*, pp. 165–6.
[3] *Crowland Chron.*, pp. 567–8.   [4] *Richard III*, p. 167.
[5] J. C. Halliwell, *Letters of the Kings of England* (1846), I. 156–7.
[6] *Crowland Chron.*, pp. 570–1.

tany, who proposed to hand him over to Richard.[1] Instead
Henry escaped to the more hospitable soil of France. It was
perhaps later in the same year that the Lancastrian
John de Vere, Earl of Oxford (again just missing an emissary
of Richard's) made a spectacular escape from Hammes Castle
near Calais, together with his gaoler James Blount, its captain,
and Sir John Fortescue, gentleman porter of Calais.[2]

Although he had started his reign 'with ample resources to
satisfy his overweening ambitions', Richard was now becoming
short of money.[3] In parliament he had declared illegal the
'benevolences' or forced gifts exacted by Edward IV, but he
now had recourse to forced loans, which were little more
popular, even though they were secured by pledges or letters
of payment.[4] The Crowland chronicler speaks darkly of other
means of money raising as well:

He had recourse to the exactions of King Edward, which he had openly
condemned in parliament, although he was careful to avoid any use of the
word 'benevolences'. [The rubric here runs 'Exaction of malevolences'.]
And he sent out specially chosen men, 'the children of this world, wiser
in their generation than the children of light', who with supplications and
threats, by right and by wrong, were to scrape up huge sums out of the
records relating to almost all kinds of property-holding in the kingdom.[5]
I shall dwell on this no further, nor add to the tale of abuses, which were
so many they can scarcely be reckoned. They furnish such a dangerous
precedent that it is better not to put such a thing into the heads of the unscrupulous.[6] And there are many other matters as well, which are not
written down here, for shame.[7]

If the Crowland chronicler is to be believed, the king's
personal reputation was sinking along with his reserves.
At the Christmas festivities in 1484 gossip was caused by the
king's indiscreet attentions to his eldest niece.[8] When the

[1] Chrimes, *Henry VII*, pp. 29–31.
[2] Ibid., p. 34. But a reference to news at Calais on 23 April 1484 which the
writer dare not put on paper (Cely Letters, S.C.1 53/171) may possibly refer to
this incident, which is not clearly dated by Vergil. Lady Blount and the garrison
of Hammes received a pardon on 27 January 1485 (*C.P.R. 1476–85*, p. 526).
[3] *Crowland Chron.*, p. 567.   [4] Gairdner, *Richard III*, pp. 196–7.
[5] *Qui ... maximas pecuniarum summas de omnium pene statum regni archivis abraderent*—
apparently an attempt to define 'financial feudalism'. Riley's translation 'to
scrape up immense sums of money, after examining the archives of the realm,
from persons of nearly all conditions' (p. 498) is not an accurate translation of the
Latin as it stands.
[6] This rather suggests that Richard's exactions did, in the event, set a pattern
for the officials of Henry VII.   [7] pp. 571–2.   [8] p. 572.

queen fell seriously ill shortly afterwards rumours flew, and her death in March 1485 caused the usual tales of poisoning. The sequel was bizarre. Richard was forced to counter both these stories of murder and the persistent belief that he meant to marry his niece by denying them in person to the mayor, aldermen, and commons of London,[1] and by sending letters, much less explicit, to such towns as York and Southampton.[2] The Crowland chronicler, however, gives a circumstantial behind-the-scenes account which, if true, must mean that the king had seriously entertained the marriage scheme and was now lying.[3] And recent work on Sir George Buck's unpublished defence of Richard, while it cannot substantiate Sir George's claim to have seen and copied a letter from Elizabeth of York to the Duke of Norfolk, expressing her desire for the marriage, shows that Sir George's quotations from the lost letter are far more convincing than the printed version offered by his great-nephew, which is couched impossibly in seventeenth-century English.[4]

At the same time Richard was facing the increasingly real threat of an invasion by the Earl of Richmond. The first proclamation against him was issued on 7 December 1484.[5] It was reissued on 23 June 1485, in similar terms save that Thomas, Marquis of Dorset, was no longer mentioned, his position having become ambiguous.[6] Richard's accusation that Henry had taken the royal title is borne out by Henry's letters to supporters within the kingdom, with their references to

[1] *Acts of Court*, pp. 173–4; below, pp. 51–2.
[2] *York Civic Records*, I. 115–16; Southampton Record Office, SC 2/9/1/20, and *11th Report Hist. MSS. Comm.*, Appendix III, p. 106.   [3] Below, pp. 52–3.
[4] George Buck, Esq., *The History of the Life and Reigne of Richard the Third* (1646), p. 128. Dr. Arthur Kincaid, whose edition of the elder Buck's MS. awaits publication, kindly drew my attention to the striking differences between the two texts. Sir George's original citation, now damaged, is in B.M. MS. Cotton Tiberius E. X f. 238ᵛ. Buck's testimony has some ring of truth, in that the document was embarrassing to his thesis that Richard had no real desire for the marriage. The letter could not have been written by Elizabeth Woodville, as Gairdner suggested (p. 204 n.), since it contained a reference to the love 'the kinge [the writer's] father' bore to Howard. If it was genuine, Vergil's strongly emphasized assertions of the princess's repugnance for her uncle become very interesting (*The Anglica Historia of Polydore Vergil, A.D. 1485–1537*, ed. Denys Hay (Camden Soc., 1950), pp. 2*, 3).   [5] Chrimes, *Henry VII*, pp. 35–6 and n.
[6] His mother, Elizabeth Woodville, had written advising him to make peace with Richard, and he attempted to desert Henry, but was foiled: Vergil (1844), p. 214; Chrimes, *Henry VII*, p. 38.

'our loving and true subjects' and 'the odious tyrant Richard, late Duke of Gloucester, usurper of our . . . right', which show Henry curiously treating the anointed king as a rebel against him.[1] In case Richard should succeed in his reported plans to marry Elizabeth, Henry mooted a marriage with a sister of Sir Walter Herbert. Herbert's other sister was the wife of Henry Percy, Earl of Northumberland, and Henry's messengers to Northumberland may not have been frustrated so completely as historians have claimed.[2] Certainly, before attempting a landing in 1485 Henry seems to have received promises of support from Thomas, Lord Stanley, with his paramount influence in Cheshire and Lancashire, and his brother Sir William Stanley, the chamberlain of North Wales; Gilbert Talbot, Rhys ap Thomas, and Sir John Savage. Reynold Bray and John Morgan of Tredegar were assiduously working in his interest in Britain.

Richard's spies reported Henry's movements and it was widely said that he intended to land at Milford, i.e. Milford Haven in Pembrokeshire. This accurate information was, however, misinterpreted by advisers, who insisted (whether from malice or excessive ingenuity) that the small port of Milford at the entrance to the Solent was meant.[3] Good espionage having thus been nullified at headquarters, Richard commissioned his chamberlain, Francis Lord Lovel, to watch the sea at Southampton, and strengthened the south-coast defences. He himself took up a strategic midland position at Nottingham. On 22 June he sent out commissions of array to mobilize the country.[4] Despite the suspicious nature of the request, he permitted Thomas Lord Stanley, steward of the household, to remove to his estates in the north-west, insisting, however, on taking his son Lord Strange as a hostage.[5]

Henry landed on 7 August 1485. His subsequent movements (for which Vergil is the main authority) are discussed in detail by Chrimes[6] and Gairdner.[7] Shrewsbury opened its gates to him, and when he reached Stafford, perhaps on 17 August, he apparently had a meeting with Sir William

---

[1] Gairdner, *Richard III*, pp. 214–15.

[2] Ibid., p. 208; Chrimes, p. 39; but see below, pp. 55, 57 fn. 4.

[3] *Crowland Chron.*, p. 573.   [4] Gairdner, *Richard III*, p. 210.

[5] *Crowland Chron.*, p. 573.   [6] *Henry VII*, pp. 40 ff.

[7] *Richard III*, pp. 215 ff.

Stanley. His steadily increasing band of supporters was enlarged at Tamworth by the accession of Sir John Savage, Brian Sanford, and Simon Digby with their retainers. Richard had definite news of the landing on 11 August.[1] He immediately summoned his supporting commanders, John Howard, Duke of Norfolk, and his son the Earl of Surrey, the Earl of Northumberland, Lord Lovel, Lord Stanley, and Sir Robert Brackenbury, to meet him at Leicester. Some of those called, like Brackenbury's friends Sir Thomas Bourchier and Sir Walter Hungerford, instead went over to the invader,[2] and it soon became clear that Richard's first line of defence, Sir Walter Herbert and Rhys ap Thomas in Wales, had betrayed him, and that Sir William Stanley in North Wales had done nothing to check Henry's progress. Thomas Stanley answered the king's summons with the reply that he was incapacitated by the sweating sickness.[3] Lord Strange, his son, was caught attempting to escape from the king's party, and confessed to conspiring with his uncle, Sir William Stanley, and Sir John Savage, who were forthwith proclaimed traitors.[4] Strange threw himself on the king's mercy and made every effort to convince him of his father's continuing loyalty. His father's subsequent movements will be left for consideration at a later point.[5]

The king took up his headquarters at Leicester, where he was reinforced by substantial numbers of troops. Henry by this time was encamped at Lichfield, which the Stanleys had evacuated. Accounts of the disposition of forces in the ensuing battle are divergent,[6] and Henry VII's first official historian, Bernard André, declined to give any account, preferring to leave a blank page. In these circumstances, it is understandable that the reconstructions of more modern historians agree no better than the narratives of fifteenth- and sixteenth-century writers. The *Crowland Chronicle*[7] relates that on the morning of the battle matters in the royal camp were in such confusion that there was no chaplain available to say mass, nor any breakfast prepared. It was reported afterwards that Richard confessed to passing the night in terrifying dreams, and that he prophesied that the outcome of the battle, which-

---

[1] Ibid., p. 226 and n. 3.   [2] Vergil (1844), pp. 219, 220.
[3] *Crowland Chron.*, p. 573.   [4] Ibid.   [5] Below, pp. 133–4.
[6] Below, pp. 55–8.   [7] p. 574.

ever way it went, would spell the destruction of the realm. In much the spirit of his earlier proclamations and letters, he declared further that if he won he would exterminate all rebels, while his adversary would similarly wreak vengeance in the event of victory. As the enemy advanced, Richard gave orders for the execution of Lord Strange as scapegoat for his father and uncle, but his lieutenants prudently postponed the matter until the outcome of the battle became clear. Northumberland's troops failed to engage on either side. Sir William Stanley's held off for a time, then entered the battle on behalf of Henry. The king's intimate supporters fought fiercely and most were killed on the field with Richard himself, to whose courage all sides pay tribute. It was generally reported that when defeat seemed certain he was urged to flee and answered that he would rather die a king than live in defeat. Many of his army, however, were less committed to his cause.

Of the survivors on Richard's side, Francis Lord Lovel and Humphrey and Thomas Stafford escaped, later to carry on the fight against Henry VII with persistence but ill success. Thomas Howard, Earl of Surrey, was captured and eventually received into favour when his loyalty had been proved; Northumberland made peace more easily.[1] Among those executed by the victor were two West Country gentlemen, father and son, named Bracher,[2] and William Catesby who, with Ratcliff and Lovel, was considered to be a prime shaper in Richard's policies. The Crowland chronicler observes, with unusual venom, that Catesby had been pre-eminent among all the advisers of the late king, and was beheaded at Leicester 'in final payment for such surpassing service'.[3] His will suggests that in his need Catesby, like Richard, expected succour from the Stanleys which did not come: 'My Lords Stanley, Strange, and all that blood, help and pray for my soul, for ye have not for my body as I trusted in you.'[4]

---

[1] But see below, pp. 55–7.

[2] *Crowland Chron.*, p. 575; grants to William Bracher, king's servant, yeoman of the crown: *C.P.R., 1476–85*, pp. 366, 373, 390.

[3] 'Cujus caput . . . pro ultima remuneratione tam excellentis officii sui abscisum est', p. 575.

[4] Prerogative Court of Canterbury (P.R.O.), 15 Logge (ff. 114ᵛ–115), 25 August 1485.

Was it Catesby who had stayed the execution of Lord Strange?

The foregoing short account of Richard's usurpation and rule follows, as far as possible, documentary sources and the two most nearly contemporary (and most reliable) narratives: that of Dominic Mancini, which covers April to July 1483, and that of 'the second continuator' of the chronicles of Crowland Abbey, who deals rather succinctly with the whole period. The bulk of this study will be devoted to discussing these and later works in an attempt to discover how much the writers really knew, and to show what individual shape they imposed on their material. But before assessing the validity of their evidence some of our other sources of knowledge must be examined. These variously help to illuminate some aspects of the reign, and raise new questions of their own.

Excursus A note on the dating of
Lord Hastings's execution

In an article in the *English Historical Review* in 1972[1] I argued that
Lord Hastings was arrested at the Tower and executed on Friday
20 June 1483, not Friday 13 June as had been assumed, initially on
the authority of the *Crowland Chronicle*, backed up by Fabyan,
Polydore Vergil, and later writers. The evidence for this redating
is briefly:

1. That the minutes of a meeting of the London Mercers'
Company held on Sunday 15 June[2] show that John Morton, Bishop
of Ely (who was arrested at the same time as Hastings, on the
evidence of the *Crowland Chronicle*[3] and Mancini),[4] was still at
liberty on that day. The mercers' meeting had been called to discuss
a reported conversation between Hastings, Morton, and Russell,
and there is no suggestion whatever that Hastings was now dead.

2. That Mancini and all the early Tudor chroniclers place the
execution of Hastings after the delivery of the Duke of York from
sanctuary, an event known to have occurred on Monday 16 June.
This sequence makes far more sense than that given in the *Crowland
Chronicle*, which alone, and in an unreliable text, reverses the two
events. It might be added that, since Mancini's account was written
quite independently, if both Mancini and the English chroniclers
were wrong, it is a very remarkable coincidence that they should
all fall into the same error.

3. That the date of the execution given in a letter from Simon
Stallworth to Sir William Stonor, written on 21 June,[5] is ambigu-
ously expressed as 'Friday last', and that this is more likely to imply
20 June than 13 June.

4. That 13 June is part of an erroneous time scheme which (as is
well known) put all the events leading up to Richard's accession,
and the accession itself, a week too early.

Dr. B. P. Wolffe has rejected this thesis, in an article which
appeared too late for full discussion here.[6] His four main points are
that the entry in the Mercers' Book belongs more probably to
1482 or 1479, and that the accounts of the controller of Calais give
the date of Hastings's death as 13 June, confirmed by the returns of
inquisitions post mortem as 'consolidated' by a family lawyer, and
by the description of the arrest of John Forster in the register of
the Abbey of St. Albans. The argument about the mercers' minute
is unconvincing. It is a desperate remedy to suggest that this entry

---

[1] 'Richard III, Lord Hastings and the Historians', *E.H.R.* LXXXVII (1972),
233–48. [2] *Acts of Court*, pp. 154–5. [3] p. 566. [4] p. 90. [5] *Stonor Letters*, No. 331.
[6] 'When and Why did Hastings Lose his Head?', *E.H.R.* LXXXIX (1974),
835–44.

alone was silently displaced when the volume was copied in the 1520s, and far from being out of place in June 1483, it fits remarkably closely. Payment of subsidy had lapsed after the death of Edward IV, and the merchants were now fighting a forlorn action against any grant to Edward V in the parliament due to meet on 25 June. They were naturally delighted when they heard, on 15 June, that private support might be forthcoming from three influential councillors. When the same situation arose in 1510, they sought the patronage of three councillors on their own initiative, and were rebuffed.[1]

On Dr. Wolffe's second point, an enrolled government account would be likely to contain an 'official' date, if, as I was reluctantly forced to postulate, official falsification has occurred. Interestingly enough, the copies of returns of inquisitions post mortem reveal some alteration in just this direction.

In at least four of the ten Chancery documents the official who copied the original return appears to have erased his first date and substituted *terciodecimo* (or *tredecimo*) ['thirteenth'] *die Junii* for a shorter numeral. This appears most clearly in the copy of the return from York (P.R.O. C. 141 1/11), where the date of death now reads 'di[e] veneris tredecimo die Junii anno regni Regis Edwardi quinti bastardi primo'. *Die* has been interlineated before *Junii*, and *tredecimo* is substituted for some other numeral. Similarly, the date given in the returns for Sussex, Rutland, and Derbyshire (C. 141 3/32 Nos. 1, 4, 11) shows clear signs of alteration, and in those for Lincolnshire, Nottinghamshire, and Warwickshire (Nos. 7, 12, and 14) the date is written in a rather cramped way. In the returns for Northamptonshire and Yorkshire no alteration is detectable, and that for Leicestershire is illegible at this point, being badly rubbed. The Exchequer returns (E. 149 248/9 Nos. 1–5, from Northumberland, Northamptonshire, Rutland, Nottinghamshire, and Derbyshire) all give the date 13 June without visible sign of disturbance. It therefore seems likely that the original returns in some of these cases put Hastings's death at some date other than 13 June, and that somebody first copied this date and then corrected it.

The most damaging evidence on the other side of the argument is that relating to the arrest of John Forster, who was seized and imprisoned about the same time as Hastings and his associates. In the article cited I unfortunately failed to make the correct identification of this man, although Professor Roskell had done so in his article 'William Catesby, Counsellor to Richard III' published in 1959.[2] John Forster (or Foster) was a man of similar type to William Cates-

---

[1] *Acts of Court*, pp. 326–7, 346–50.
[2] *Bulletin of the John Rylands Library*, XLII (1959), 145–74.

by, an administrator with a legal training. It may have been his career in the service of Edward IV and his queen that initially brought him into association with Lord Hastings and John Morton and his family. He was a son of Stephen Forster, mayor of London in 1454, and his wife Agnes,[1] and married a daughter of Sir Thomas Cook.[2] After imprisonment in France with Philip Malpas (his wife's grandfather), Thomas Vaughan, William Hatcliff, and other Yorkists,[3] he became receiver-general of Queen Elizabeth in 1465;[4] served as provost of the English army in France in 1475;[5] and is described as marshal of the Marshalsea in 1476.[6] He was sheriff of Huntingdonshire, Cambridge, Bedford, and Buckinghamshire at various periods and commissioner of the peace for Hertfordshire 1477–82.[7] His latest commission at the period in question (and before he was reinstated by Henry VII) was to assess the alien subsidy for Hertfordshire, 27 April 1483.[8] When he died in 1488 his heir was his niece Agnes (Forster), wife of Robert Morton junior, a relative of Bishop Morton.[9]

There are two surviving accounts of Forster's imprisonment in June 1483. The first is in the Register of Abbot Wallingford of St. Albans,[10] where it follows the rehearsal of an indenture conferring the stewardship of lands of the abbey jointly upon Forster and Lord Hastings. The entry reads, in translation:

It should be observed that the above letters patent to William Lord Hastings and John Forster, armiger, were of no effect, because a short time after their concession William Lord Hastings suffered capital punishment, as his offences demanded (as it was stated) within the Tower of London on 12 June, that is, the day of St. Basilides and his companions, 1483 . . . by order of King Richard III, at the beginning of the first year of his reign. And the said John Forster was committed to the Tower on the orders of our lord the king on 13 June of that year, and remained a prisoner there from the said 13 June until the 10th day of March next following, that is for three-quarters of a year less four days. And being thus kept in custody in prison, in the hope of obtaining remission of his punishment he released all the title and interest which he had in the said office of steward of St. Albans to William Catesby, then of the great council of our lord King Richard. And that office was conceded to this William within two days after the arrest of the said John Forster, and afterwards conceded to him in the

[1] *Calendar of Close Rolls, 1476–85*, No. 1341.
[2] Ibid., Nos. 1316, 1478; *Inquisitions Post Mortem Henry VII*, I, No. 94.
[3] Scofield, *Edward IV*, I. 188, 210.   [4] Ibid., p. 378.   [5] Ibid., p. 188 n. 3.
[6] *C.C.R., 1468–76*, No. 1561.   [7] *C.P.R., 1476–85*, p. 561.   [8] Ibid., p. 354.
[9] Writ of *diem clausit extremum* 16 June 1488; *Cal. Fine Rolls Henry VII, 1485–1509*, p. 155; *Victoria County History, Hertfordshire*, II. 247.
[10] Bodleian MS. Rawlinson B. 332 f. 59ᵛ; edited H. T. Riley, *Chronica Monasterii S. Albani*, II (*Registra Johannis Whethamstede, Willelmi Albon, et Willelmi Walingforde*, Rolls Ser., 1873), pp. 265–7.

PLATE I

Register of the Abbot of St. Albans: in left margin, fanciful drawing of Lord Hastings's head

document which follows [a formal grant made by the abbot on 1 August 1483, when Forster was still in prison].[1]

It seems to be true that Forster was released on or about 10 March 1484 after relinquishing other property to nominees of the king, but the other dates so elaborately given in this note—the execution of Hastings on 12 June, the accession of Richard III, the imprisonment of Forster, and his release of the stewardship on 14 or 15 June—are all quite eccentric, and it is not clear whether the note was composed during the reign of Richard III or that of Henry VII.[2] There are also peculiarities about the grant that immediately precedes it in the register. As originally copied, it bore no date of any kind: '1482' (in arabic numerals, not written out in full in Latin as in Riley's edition) has been subsequently added in another hand. This grant closely parallels another grant of the stewardship to Hastings and Forster jointly and in survivorship, which bears the date 8 February 1482 (i.e. 1483 new style, only four months before Hastings's death).[3] But there is one difference. In the grant allegedly revoked by Forster there is a new clause confining the emoluments of the stewardship to Forster alone. Only after his death are they to pass to Hastings. Read together with the report of Catesby's haste to grab the stewardship ('within two days'), the whole thing looks suspiciously like an attempt to show that Hastings was dead at the time of Forster's surrender, and the emoluments wholly at Forster's disposal.

The St. Albans record fails, moreover, to agree with Forster's own version of affairs (or more strictly, that of his lawyers) in a petition to the first parliament of Henry VII.[4] This, while similarly saying nothing of the grounds for Forster's arrest beyond a vague reference to an allegation of treason, gives a different date for the arrest itself, and makes no mention of Hastings. According to Forster's petition, he was seized at his country residence of Weld Hall, Herts., and taken to the Tower on Saturday 14 June. He was deprived of food and drink 'fro the said Saturday of his first bringing to the Tower till the Monday next following', so that he was 'like to have perished', kept in fetters and daily threatened with beheading

---

[1] This entry was annotated in the margin (in Latin), probably some time after 1486, 'William Lord Hastings was beheaded in the Tower of London without trial. John Forster, learned in the law, was thrown into the Tower and deprived of the office of Steward of the Liberty of the monastery of St. Alban.' It has been adorned, rather unkindly, with a grotesque head wearing a startled expression (Plate I).

[2] 'Our lord King Richard' suggests that he was still on the throne, but Catesby was '*then*' of the great council'. The abbots' registers are, of course, only compilations from the original documents.

[3] MS. Rawlinson B. 332 f. 58ʳ; ed. Riley pp. 255–7.   [4] *Rot. Parl.* VI. 332.

for treason and forfeiture of all his property, so that, 'hearing of the cruel and rigorous disposition showed in the behalf of the...late King Richard' and 'by the advice of the council of the said late King Richard', he entered into a bond (on 9 March 1484) to cause his feoffees to grant his manor of 'Mawdelyn', Herts., to Sir Robert Brackenbury, by then Constable of the Tower, and other nominees.[1] He also, it would seem, paid Richard one thousand marks in jewels and money.[2]

There appear to be three possibilities with regard to this evidence.

1. That the date of Forster's arrest given in his petition is correct, and the statements in the St. Albans register approximately so; that is, that Forster was imprisoned as the result of an association with Hastings, and that Hastings was executed, all other evidence to the contrary, on 13 June.

2. That, as the St. Albans register states, Forster was arrested on the day after the execution of Hastings, but that the register and Forster's petition to parliament are both wrong in placing the arrest variously on 13 or 14 June, the writers having been misled by the widespread later conviction that the execution had occurred on 13 instead of 20 June.

3. That while Forster's petition may be correct in stating that he was arrested on 14 June, the note in the St. Albans register is wrong in placing his arrest after the execution of Hastings. Because the stewardship of the abbey lands had been granted to Forster and Hastings in survivorship, it might have seemed legally convenient to William Catesby (or to some subsequent holder of the office) to represent that Forster had agreed to surrender the stewardship at a time when it was his alone, that is, after and not before the death of Hastings. Why, too, is there so much stress laid on the fact that the bribe was allegedly offered in the first forty-eight hours of Forster's imprisonment? Both the erratic dating in the note and the discrepancies in the two recitations of the grant to Forster and Hastings help cast suspicion on the transaction as recorded.

Stallworth's letter of Saturday 21 June does not necessarily conflict with Forster's own evidence.[3] Writing to Sir William Stonor,

---

[1] At Forster's request, his feoffee Thomas Holbache, also in the service of Elizabeth Woodville (Wolffe, *Crown Lands*, p. 125), had on 1 March 1483 demised the manor to Thomas Rotherham, Archbishop of York, John Morton, Bishop of Ely, Robert Morton, Keeper of the Rolls, John Cheyney, John Fortescue, Robert Morton, and others: B.M. Cart. Harl. 51 F. 35.

[2] It is not clear whether the money was actually paid, or whether the sum represents merely the stated penalty for non-observance of his bond to surrender the manor.   [3] For paraphrase, see below, p. 42.

Stallworth refers to the execution of Hastings, the surrender of the Duke of York (on 16 June), and the imprisonment of Bishop Morton and Archbishop Rotherham, and then says, 'As for Foster, he is in hold and men fear his life.' This bald statement tends, in fact, to exclude the likelihood that Forster's arrest had occurred on the very day on which Stallworth wrote, that is the day after the probable date of Hastings's death on 20 June. It sounds rather as though Stonor, in Oxfordshire, had previously heard of Forster's arrest. Forster is now not merely arrested at his home but 'in hold', that is, being kept in custody, and his friends are alarmed that a capital charge may be in preparation. In this case, if Forster had already been in the Tower for a week, no doubt the news of Hastings's summary beheading on 20 June would be one of the proofs of the 'cruel and rigorous disposition' of Richard and his associates which frightened Forster into submitting to the second of his captors' demands. But if so, on what grounds was he accused of treasonable activity so early as 14 June? Could his arrest have been intended as a warning to Hastings and to Forster's connection, Morton? On the other hand, is it Forster's previous service with Elizabeth Woodville that is significant? Was he (rather than Mistress Shore) the link between two mutually hostile groups who were now uniting, or suspected of uniting, in opposition to Richard's plans?

The further fact remains that, for reasons which are unclear, at least two of the events between 16 and 26 June 1483 were assigned wrong dates at an early period. The death of Hastings was dated 13 June in the copies, but apparently not all the originals, of the returns by various juries of inquisition in October 1484, and may have been assigned to 12 June at St. Albans about the same time. The death of Anthony Earl Rivers is dated 20 June (instead of 25 June) in inquisitions post mortem of 1486.[1] It is probably sheer coincidence that persistence of this last error could explain More's certainty that Rivers and Hastings were killed on the same day (to which More nowhere puts a precise date).[2] But for what it is worth, More, often well informed about background details, appears to take it for granted that Hastings was executed, on a Friday, just before the date set for the coronation of Edward V (in fact Sunday 22 June). He makes play with the statement that at the time of the execution preparations were going on night and day, and much meat had been killed in readiness for the coronation.[3] This hardly points to 13 June, since meat would not keep in summer for ten days or more. But it will be demonstrated in due course that all More's evidence must be approached with the greatest circumspection.

[1] *Inq. P.M. Henry VII*, I, No. 33 (2 Nov. 1486).
[2] Yale *Works*, II. 52, 57.   [3] Ibid., pp. 46–7.

2   Some documentary evidence and
       modern problems of interpretation

I F Vergil and More cannot be unreservedly followed by a
historian, even the best early account of Richard's career—
that in the *Crowland Chronicle*—falls far short of modern
historical standards. When it came to writing down events,
Mancini and the 'Crowland' chronicler often failed to exploit
their advantages as onlookers as fully as we should wish.
As historiographers, they are superior to other chroniclers
largely because there is reason to believe them acute and reliable observers of the contemporary scene, for their narratives
do not differ greatly in nature from those of the 'City' chroniclers or Vergil, in the sense that they take a very selective view
of events and leave much unsaid. The modern historian, even
when dealing in the same limited way with personalities and
battles, would ask many more questions.[1] His curiosity must
often remain unsatisfied because the evidence has disappeared, but in compensation he has certain documentary
sources, most of which were not used by historians of the
fifteenth and sixteenth centuries. These may often throw new
light on events or their backgrounds, or serve to modify the
chroniclers' assumptions. They also give a means of checking
their accuracy at certain points. The modern historian therefore has some strong advantages over his predecessor in the
period under discussion. But his documentary sources are
sadly few, and often create new problems. Many of the
sources which supplement chronicle accounts have survived
by chance, and their importance in any reconstruction of
events shows how precariously based many of our interpretations must be, and how dangerous any argument from silence.
It is worth stressing that there are exactly two private letters
which throw really useful light on Richard's usurpation, both
in the Stonor collection, and both preserved by the merest

---

[1] Recently his most valuable contributions to knowledge of the period have been
in the fields of economic and administrative history, which are outside the scope of
the present study.

accident. But even if more letters of the period survived, they might not tell us a great deal: writers were habitually discreet about domestic politics. In general it would be safe to say that our picture of English history in the late fifteenth century is often deceptively clear because there are so few details to confuse the eye. It would seem that the Tudor historians were often no better informed, and so were forced to rely largely on dubious oral traditions, or on each other. When they found it difficult to ascertain the truth of a matter they were often, in turn, in the same position as contemporary observers had been. It is a crashing truism that the modern news media enable us to arrive quickly, if not at the truth, at least at a generally accepted and standardized version of the news. This does not happen when news travels informally from mouth to mouth. In some cases rumours recorded in the contemporary documents of Richard's reign were soon proved false; in others the truth could never be established and stories put about in his reign lingered on, to be embroidered in later times which also added their own tales.

Some of the most reliable information on important points may occur incidentally in unexpected sources. The information that John Morton was still at liberty on Sunday 15 June 1483, which is clearly implied in a minute of the Mercers' Company, supports the chronology given in all but one of the early historians' accounts, and careful examination of conflicting documents and of the dissenting *Crowland Chronicle* reveals good grounds for discounting their contrary statements. In this case it is the tangential nature of the mercers' evidence that makes it so convincing. When their clerk recorded that a deputation was to call on Morton that same afternoon, he was entirely preoccupied with the company's commercial interests, and the date held no political importance for him. Similarly, most historians would be inclined to accept Lord Derby's evidence before an ecclesiastical court (below, p. 134) because the question put to him was not 'Had you met Henry Tudor before the Battle of Bosworth?' but 'How long have you known the parties to this intended marriage?'

If non-chronicle evidence sometimes answers such questions, it may also raise new ones untouched by the chroniclers, and prove inadequate to answer them. For example, when and how were the two projected coronations of Edward V announced and then cancelled? There is no reason to doubt the chroniclers' statement that the coronation of the young king was first fixed for Sunday 4 May. It would be interesting, but not perhaps very important, to know who cancelled or postponed the ceremony; when; and how the news was made public. During Richard's protectorship a new ceremony was arranged for a date which can be identified with reasonable certainty as Sunday 22 June. It is not clear when public proclamation was made to this effect, but the announcement seems to have been left very late: it had not taken place when Stallworth wrote to Sir William Stonor on 9 June. A question of still greater moment is 'When was the ceremony put off again?' The cancellation must have occurred after the surrender of the Duke of York on the morning of 16 June, which had the ostensible object of allowing him to attend his brother's crowning. And it may be deduced that by 21 June Stallworth knew that Stonor no longer expected to come up to London for the ceremony. Certainly, none did take place on 22 June. This leaves at most four and a half days during which a cancellation could have been announced, and in the very tight schedule of Richard's successful usurpation the timing of the announcement, ominous in import and surely accompanied by some sort of excuse and explanation, takes on great significance. It cannot, however, be established. In the sweep of their story, the chroniclers pass over this detail,[1] and such scraps of evidence as have come to light are confused and even misleading. At first sight it appears that a representative from New Romney was paid for attendance at Edward's coronation, and so must have been already in London when its cancellation became known.[2] But analysis of the complete unpublished chamberlains' account[3] suggests that 'paid John Cheynew for riding to the coronation of our lord King Edward V for eight days at 2s. the day—16s.' merely reflects confusion and clerical error, and that Cheynew was really paid, along

---

[1] Mancini seems to suggest that the cancellation occurred after Hastings's death (below, p. 69). This is plausible.

[2] Relying on the very incomplete extract in the *5th Report Hist. MSS. Comm.* (1876), p. 547, I took this to be so in my article, *E.H.R.* (1972), p. 241 n. 2.

[3] Kent County Record Office, NR/FAc 3, ff. 96–96a. There is also a typescript translation, TR 1020/11 (pp. 521–33).

with Romney's other three barons, for attending the coronation of Richard III in July.[1]

The whole testimony of the accounts of New Romney and Lydd[2] on the subject of the one actual and two abortive coronations of 1483 well shows the limitations of such documents, where entries for payments are undated and often unchronological. It was probably in April that New Romney received, at the hands of sentries from Dover Castle, 'a commission for the coronation of our Lord King Edward' (i.e. for 4 May?), and another 'for parliament'. There is then the entry 'paid to a certain man of the Lord Arundel [Constable of Dover Castle and Warden of the Cinque Ports] bringing a commission for the coronation of our lord the king [which and when?], in reward—20*d.*' After this there is 'paid for a mandate from Dover Castle countermanding coronation and parliament'. This may refer to a *supersedeas* issued in April when it became apparent that Edward V would not reach London in time for the ceremony set for 4 May, because the next entry but one refers to the hire of a horse when Richard Fullar, the common sergeant, rode to Hythe to find out how many barons they had chosen for the coronation of Edward V. There follows immediately the entry about the wages of John Cheynew, and much further on, after a group of entries which are wildly disordered, payments to Romney's other three barons of the Cinque Ports for Richard's coronation.

The evidence about parliamentary sessions (also a matter of some importance) is equally vague. In all, the New Romney accounts for 25 March 1483 to 25 March 1484 contain seven different entries relating to coronation ceremonies, and seven to parliamentary sessions, whether actual or abortive. In the course of the period, two coronation ceremonies and accompanying sessions of parliament were planned for Edward V (on 4 May and 22 June), and some sort of representative assembly took place on the second occasion, despite the issue of a *supersedeas* to York, and possibly other places. Richard III was crowned on 6 July and summoned a parliament to meet

[1] The four of them are named as doing so in a contemporary report: *A Calendar of the White and Black Books of the Cinque Ports, 1432–1955*, ed. Felix Hull (Hist. MSS. Comm. and Kent Arch. Soc., 1966), App. I, pp. 641–2.

[2] *Records of Lydd*, ed. Arthur Finn (Ashford, Kent, 1911), pp. 309–18.

on 6 November, which had to be postponed until January. It is clear that John Cheynew and William Gregory were Romney's representatives at Richard's parliament of January 1484.[1] It is not, unfortunately, clear whether a payment to John a Forde 'for his wages at the parliament that was held at Westminster, for seven days at 2*s.* the day—14*s.* 'was in respect of the 'parliament' which petitioned Richard to take the throne on 26 June (in which case, why did Romney send only one member?), or whether Forde was receiving arrears from the previous year's account for attendance at Edward IV's last parliament in January–February 1483. The accountants of Lydd do not help solve the problem by recording, among payments between 22 July 1482 and 22 July 1483, that they paid 'John a Forde of the town of New Romney for tidings of the parliament'. They also contributed 24*s.* to New Romney 'for the parliament of the lord the king this year', and this second entry almost certainly refers to Edward IV's parliament.[2]

These casual reflections of confused events, together with much coming and going in Kent at the time of the risings in autumn 1483, do serve, however, to emphasize the background of uncertainty against which Richard's usurpation took place. The confusion is rather suggested than made apparent in the historical accounts, which necessarily give an over-tidy impression.

Information of a different kind is furnished by Prebendary Simon Stallworth, the correspondent of Sir William Stonor, who was in London in June 1483 as a member of the staff of John Russell, Bishop of Lincoln, who had succeeded Archbishop Rotherham as chancellor early in May. Stonor and Stallworth seem to have been in regular contact at this time, but unfortunately there survive only two of Stallworth's letters and none of Stonor's side of the correspondence. The sort of news that Stallworth relayed is shown in the first of his letters, written on Monday 9 June.[3] He starts unhelpfully by saying that there is no news since he last wrote. The

---

[1] This is confirmed in the accounts of Lydd. It is of some incidental interest that, to judge by the sums paid them, they remained at Westminster for at least one calendar month after the official business of parliament concluded on 20 February, attending for something like fifty-eight and forty-six days respectively.

[2] *Records of Lydd*, pp. 310, 311.

[3] *Stonor Letters*, No. 330.

queen, with her brother the Bishop of Salisbury, her youngest
son the king's brother, and others of her party, is still in sanctuary at Westminster and 'will not depart as yet'. Wherever
goods of the Marquis of Dorset can be found they are seized,
and the Prior of Westminster has been, and still is, in great
trouble on account of certain goods which the Marquis handed
over to him. (Dorset, the queen's eldest son by her first marriage,
had probably been accused by the protector of seizing the royal
treasure in the Tower.[1]) The protector, the Duke of Buckingham, and all the other lords, both temporal and spiritual,
had met in the council chamber at Westminster from 10 a.m.
to 2 p.m., but none of them spoke with the queen (that is,
probably, no further attempt was made to persuade her to
leave sanctuary).[2] Great preparations are in hand for the coronation, 'which shall be this day fortnight, as we say'.[3] At that
time Stonor will no doubt be in London and 'know all the
world', i.e. get all the news for himself. The king is lodged at
the Tower. The Duchess of Gloucester came to London last
Thursday (5 June). And 'my lord' (Chancellor Russell)
sends a message about a man of Stonor's district, and
will consult further with Stonor when he comes to London.

The day after this was written (and so the day after the
meeting with the lords spiritual and temporal), Richard wrote
to the mayor, aldermen, and commons of York, begging them
to come to him at London as speedily as possible with as large
a force of armed men as they could raise, to assist him in frus-
trating the devious plots of the queen and her faction.[4] His
rather dramatic epistle reached York on Sunday 15 June. The
bearer, Sir Richard Ratcliff, added the verbal message that
the city should send a force of horse and foot to join the Earl
of Northumberland at Pontefract and proceed under him to
London. It was agreed to send a sizeable force of 300 men.[5]
Ratcliff also bore a similar message to [?Ralph] Lord Neville
with a request for troops, written at London on 11 June.[6]
The clerk who recorded the 'credence' or confidential verbal

[1] Mancini, p. 80; More, Yale *Works*, II. 19.

[2] Not, as Ramsay thought, 'not a single lord had taken the trouble to call on the
Queen': *Lancaster and York*, II. 483.

[3] That is, 14 days hence inclusive of 9 June: 22 June.

[4] *York Civic Records*, I. 73–4.   [5] Ibid., p. 74.

[6] Quoted from the *Paston Letters* by Kendall, *Richard III*, p. 206.

instructions which Ratcliff gave York, wrote that the York contingent was to be at Pontefract on 'Wednesday at even next coming', but this seemingly meant not Wednesday 18 June (impossibly soon, when troops had to be collected), but Wednesday 25 June.[1] It was not until 17 June that the city council decided on the rates of pay for the four captains and their troops. (The two aldermen who had the supreme command had already been elected parliamentary representatives for the city, so that they were to receive 'the parliament wages').[2] The protector's summons was publicly proclaimed only on 19 June,[3] and it was not until 21 June that the council decreed what cognizances their forces should display on the march.[4] Their arrival at Pontefract on 25 June must have coincided very nearly with the executions of Rivers and his associates. The protector's proclamation, which echoed the terms of his letter, is a narrow appeal to prejudices of region, class, and faction:

Richard, brother and uncle of kings, Duke of Gloucester, protector, defender, great chamberlain, constable, and admiral of England, straitly charges and commands that all manner of men, in their best defensible array, incontinent after this proclamation made, do rise and [come] up to London to his highness, in the company of his cousin the Earl of Northumberland, the Lord Nevill, and other men of worship by his highness appointed, there to aid and assist him to the subduing, correcting, and punishing of the queen, her blood, and other her adherents. Which hath intended and daily doth intend to murder and utterly destroy his royal person, his cousin the Duke of Buckingham, and other of [the] old royal blood of this realm, and also the noblemen of their companies; and as it is notably known, by many subtle and damnable ways forecasted the same,[5] and also the special destruction and disherison of them and of all other the inheritors and men of haviour

---

[1] The solution to this problem of chronology may be that 'Wednesday next' meant in fifteenth-century Yorkshire what it means in modern Scotland; that is, not what the Scots term 'Wednesday first' and the English 'this coming Wednesday', but 'two Wednesdays hence'. So, according to *Y.C.R.* I. 54, on Tuesday 14 May 1482 the city heard that the Duke of Gloucester would invade Scotland on 'Wednesday next coming after this present date' and decided to send him 80 men, and on Saturday 13 July (ibid., p. 59) they ordered another force to muster 'of Monday next coming' at 9 a.m.—evidently these troops were not expected to assemble fully equipped the next day and within two days respectively. On Wed. 9 Oct. (ibid., p. 63) the captains were asked to account for the money they had expended and asked 'day to Monday next coming'. The accounts were approved on Wed. 23 October—a fortnight later.

[2] *Y.C.R.* I. 74–5.   [3] Ibid., p. 75.   [4] Ibid.
[5] Is there already a hint of witchcraft charges here?

[i.e. landowners and substantial persons], as well of these north parts as of other countries that belongen them. And therefore in all diligence prepare yourselves and come up, as ye love their honours, weals, and sureties, and the sureties of yourselves and the common weal of this said realm.[1]

Why did Richard send these demands at this particular time? The northern troops eventually reached London about 3 July, in time for Richard's coronation on 6 July, but the Londoners were already expecting their arrival on 21 June, when Stallworth mentions to Sir William Stonor an exaggerated figure of 20,000 men for the combined forces of Gloucester and Buckingham. Was the threat from the queen's relations the alleged conspiracy of Dorset and Lisle mentioned in the chronicle of John Rous?[2] There is at least one difficulty about such a view. According to Mancini, Dorset escaped from sanctuary only about 20 June.[3] Stallworth's letter of 9 June might be taken to imply that he had escaped before the date of writing, but further doubt is cast on Rous's story by the fact that Lisle shortly went over to Richard's party, and received a viscountcy in the first week of the new reign.[4] In the light of subsequent events, and the fact that the northern troops played a purely passive role in them, the most obvious deduction is that Richard wanted these troops to assist his attempt on the throne, and used a story about Woodville plots as a convenient excuse to summon them. But it may be unsafe to argue from hindsight, and it is possible that Richard had some cause to fear a counter-coup in early June. According to Mancini, Richard had imprisoned Rivers and his companions on a charge of attempted ambush,[5] and some time in May he tried unsuccessfully to persuade the council to find Rivers and his associates guilty of treason (that is, this is related between the appointment of Russell as chancellor and the breaking-up of the Woodville fleet).[6] Mancini also seems to suggest that Richard made further attempts to obtain the council's condemnation, and resorted to private measures only when these had failed.[7] Was his last such attempt made at the full meeting of 'the lords spiritual and temporal' described

---

[1] *Y.C.R.* I. 75.   [2] Below, p. 119.   [3] p. 90.
[4] *Stonor Letters*, No. 331; G. E. Cokayne, *Complete Peerage* (13 vols., 1910–59), VIII. 60.
[5] p. 76.   [6] p. 84.   [7] p. 92.

by Stallworth on 9 June, and did their resolute opposition cause him to summon the York troops next day to dispose of Rivers and the rest and then frighten the obdurate among the council at London? Was it, in other words, less a concrete Woodville plot than ominous criticism from the council which looked like upsetting his plans?[1] Or had he detected a *rapprochement* between Hastings and his friends and the Woodville party?[2] Nothing of the kind is hinted by Mancini or the 'Crowland' chronicler, however, and More introduces the suggestion only to say it is false.

Still more mysterious is the *supersedeas* of parliament received by the city of York on 21 June.[3] On 6 June a writ had been received for the election of their representatives to attend a parliament at Westminster on 25 June.[4] On 13 June it was decided to send the chosen men, Aldermen Thomas Wrangwish and William Wells, up to London eight days before parliament opened, instead of the customary six days, so that they might attend the coronation and 'commune with the lords for the weal of the city' (i.e do some lobbying).[5] The usual six days' allowance probably meant five days' riding and a sixth for recuperation or unexpected delays. The two extra days allotted on this occasion suggest that Wrangwish and Wells would leave York on the morning of 17 June and arrive on the evening of 21 June, in time for the coronation next day. It has not been previously noted that they must therefore have been nearly at their destination when, on 21 June, the city sheriffs received the new writ to cancel their attendance at parliament. Wrangwish and Wells had already been given the (?nominal) command of the city's contingent of soldiers,[6] so since it was much too late to countermand their journey, the council now agreed to pay them the wages due from the time they left York, not as parliamentary representatives, but military leaders.[7]

---

[1] The *Crowland Chron.* (p. 566) says that 'one great cause for doubt was the continued imprisonment of the king's relations and servants, and that the protector did not take fitting care of the honour and safety of the queen'.

[2] For the arrest of Forster, ?on 14 June, see above, pp. 26–9.

[3] *Y.C.R.* I. 75.

[4] Ibid., p. 72. This strangely required four, not the usual two, representatives. The matter seems, however, to have been adjusted and the clerk does not comment on the discrepancy.

[5] p. 72.   [6] p. 74.   [7] p. 76.

A *supersedeas* which reached York during the morning of 21 June (the council met at 1 p.m.) must have been issued on 17 June at latest, and more probably on 16 June. There are two points of significance about this. In the first place, the date may mean that it was issued shortly after Richard had obtained custody of his younger nephew on Monday 16 June. In the second, even if it was not known in London that the York M.P.s planned to arrive two days early, a message dispatched on 16 or 17 June would plainly be too late to catch men who had to travel from York to reach London by 25 June. Unfortunately, it is not clear whether York was peculiar in receiving such a *supersedeas*.[1] Gairdner suggested that the writ to York was issued by Richard's enemies on the council to exclude his known supporters from a parliament which he had called chiefly to confirm him in the office of protector.[2] The new dating of Hastings's execution to 20 June instead of 13 June removes one obstacle in the way of Gairdner's theory—Richard's potential opponents were still at liberty on 17 June. But if the writ was really issued to keep Gloucester's friends from parliament, the move came much too late. An alternative suggestion was touched on by Gairdner, in the course of a rather confused discussion of the problem, namely that the parliamentary session was countermanded by the protector himself in his own interests. This, although rejected by Gairdner, bears further examination.

A usurper's relations with parliament were highly ambiguous. Like Edward IV and Henry IV before him (and Henry VII afterwards), Richard well knew that his claim to the throne must have popular acknowledgement and be regularized by some form of parliamentary acceptance. The monarchy was in no sense elective, however, and a purely 'parliamentary' title would be as impossible constitutionally as it was undesirable politically. Henry IV had solved the problem by confronting parliament with the abdication of his predecessor, so that the assembly which proceeded to approve his claims had no status as a legally constituted body. On 16 June 1483

---

[1] For the *supersedeas* recorded at New Romney, see above, p. 33. It is unsafe to assume that this referred to the parliament of 25 June.
[2] Gairdner, *Richard III*, pp. 84–7.

Richard's position was more delicate. He had obtained both heirs to the throne, and this with the support of the council. It is very likely that he had already formed the design of seizing the crown for himself and had acquired control of the Duke of York to this end. It is equally likely that he had not yet mentioned his further plans to any but his closest associates. How much support he would receive when the subject was finally broached could not be known, but loyalist opposition was not likely to be negligible, either in council or parliament. If his gamble for the throne failed, as it easily might, he would need at all costs to retain his position as protector, secured by parliamentary approval. If by 25 June his schemes looked like succeeding, he would also require some quasi-official support. On the other hand, if things went badly, a hostile parliament swayed by the powerful interests which might oppose him would be disastrous. On balance, it would probably seem to Richard and his advisers on 16–17 June that whether his usurpation succeeded or he was forced to fall back on his position as protector, it was in Richard's interest to ensure that some kind of parliamentary assembly met on 25 June as arranged. It would be possible, however, to secure one that was representative of the kingdom at large but not possessed of sufficient legal authority to frustrate his aims, and a favourable decision from an unconstitutional assembly could always be properly ratified later. To issue a *supersedeas* to his loyal city of York, too late to prevent its representatives from reaching London, would neatly invalidate parliament without hindering the assembly of its delegates. If they fawned, so much the better: their teeth had been drawn.

By the time that the delegates did meet—informally indeed, though by then the informality was probably due to doubts about the status of the king in whose name they had been summoned—Richard's intentions were clearly known and his position had been immeasurably strengthened by one further action. Either this was a coup of impeccable timing, modelled on his previous arrest of Rivers, or on both occasions Richard's enemies played into his hands in a most opportune way. Two private documents convey the effects of the incident.

The wool merchant George Cely was a hoarder who left family correspondence and a mass of highly unsystematic memoranda to be taken into Chancery in the course of a posthumous lawsuit. The spare leaf of one of his memoranda[1] contains these notes:

There is great rumour [i.e. uproar] in the realm. The Scots has done great in England. Chamberlain [Lord Hastings] is deceased in trouble. The chancellor is disproved and not content. The Bishop of Ely is dead. If the king, God save his life, were dec[eas]ed; [if] the Duke of Gloucester were in any peril; if my lord prince, [which] God defend, were troubled; if my lord of Northumberland were dead or greatly troubled; if my lord Howard were slain.
De Monsieur Saint Johns.

The reference to the death of the lord chamberlain, Lord Hastings (well known to the Celys as captain of Calais), and the false news of the death of John Morton, Bishop of Ely, suggest that these rumours were communicated in the first panic on 20 June, after news had spread of arrests at the Tower and the execution of Lord Hastings. The man who apparently passed on the news—'Monsieur Saint Johns'—is almost certainly the Celys' patron Sir John Weston, Prior of the order of St. John in England, who had been a member of Edward IV's council[2] and was very probably a member of Edward V's at this time.

The extreme brevity of the note may be due to discretion. Or the writer may have intended it only as an *aide-mémoire*. Certain markings suggest that perhaps the news was to be encoded, with agreed ciphers representing particular words or phrases, to be sent on to someone else; or else that the ciphers represent additional information intelligible only to Cely and Weston. It is unfortunately not clear whether these rumours were spontaneous or had received some official countenance from Richard's supporters; in a proclamation, for instance, or in the explanation that was given to the mayor of London. What is clear is that they implicated Hastings and his friends in a widespread and dangerous conspiracy, which somehow threatened the life of the king and the safety of his brother. The suggestion would seem to be that the conspiracy which Richard had foreseen on 10 June had now come to a head. Whether it ever had a more than imaginary existence is another, insoluble, question. The Cely note is rare and most interesting

[1] P.R.O., S.C.1 53/19.
[2] J. R. Lander, 'Council, Administration and Councillors', p. 179.

first-hand evidence of the sort of stories—true and false—which spread about the country after an event like the arrests at the Tower, and the kind of doubt and confusion that attended Richard's coup and helped make his usurpation possible,

Next day, on 21 June, the faithful Stallworth wrote again to Stonor.[1] By then some of the smoke had cleared and Stallworth could give a collected account. The tone, and rather abrupt opening, suggest either that Stonor had sent to ask Stallworth for reliable information, or that Stallworth had already dispatched one hasty message and was now enlarging on it. This important letter has often been printed, both in modern spelling and in slightly erroneous versions of the original. It has as often been misunderstood, so that I shall here give a complete paraphrase.

[*In the hand of a secretary:*] Worshipful sir, I commend me to you. As for news, you are lucky to be out of everything—things here are in a pretty mess and everyone distrusts everyone else. This Friday[2] the chamberlain was beheaded somewhere about noon. On Monday a crowd of armed men assembled at Westminster and the Duke of York was handed over [from sanctuary]. He was given to the cardinal [Archbishop of Canterbury], the chancellor, and a group of temporal lords. The Duke of Buckingham then goes to meet him in the middle of Westminster Hall, and the protector receives him in the Star Chamber with many affectionate greetings, and after that he went to the Tower with the cardinal, where, thank God, he is in good spirits. Lord Lisle [the queen's brother-in-law] has come to join the protector. It is said that 20,000 men, belonging to the protector and the Duke of Buckingham, will be in London this week—why, I don't know, unless as a peace-keeping force. My lord [chancellor] has a lot to do, and more than he is happy about, if any other course were open to him. The Archbishop of York and the Bishop of Ely are still in the Tower with Master Oliver King. (Though I suppose they will be let out again. *Cancelled.*) Men have been sent to keep their [town] houses safe. [*In Stallworth's hand:*] And I suppose some of the [*change in character of writing, but still Stallworth's hand:*] protector's men will be sent to their places in the country. They are not likely to be released from prison yet. As to Foster, he is in custody and we fear for his life. Mistress Shore is in prison, and what will become of her I don't know. Please excuse me from writing anything more; I am so sick I can scarcely hold my pen. Jesus keep you. At London, 21 June. [*Added in Stallworth's normal hand:*] All the lord chamberlain's men are switching allegiance to the Duke of Buckingham. Simon Stallworthe.

---

[1] P.R.O., S.C.1 46/207 (ed. Kingsford, *Stonor Letters*, No. 331).
[2] 'As on Fryday last': for the interpretation of this see Hanham, *E.H.R.* (1972), p. 237.

Evidently Stallworth started to dictate this letter to an amanuensis, setting down the various startling events of the past few days and referring to his preoccupations: the accession of the queen's brother-in-law to the protector's party, the threatened arrival of troops, the dismay of his master, the chancellor, at the turn of events, and the fate of the two bishops —clergy and civil servants like Stallworth himself—whose cloth would presumably be respected, but whose property was firmly in the hands of the protector. Much more may have been entrusted verbally to the messenger. Stallworth seems to take it for granted that Stonor already knows that the bishops have been arrested and Hastings executed, just as it is clear that sometime between 9 June and 21 June Stonor must have cancelled his visit to London for the intended coronation. Stallworth's secretary laid down his pen after mentioning that the bishops' town houses had been occupied. Stallworth then added a few words of a new sentence, and was in turn interrupted. (Kingsford, in his Camden edition of the Stonor letters, did not recognize that this phrase is in Stallworth's hand, not that of the amanuensis.) When Stallworth resumed, it was with a slow and feeble hand and in writing larger and more angular than usual. By now he had apparently heard more news, because he crossed out his previous supposition that the bishops would be released shortly, and now says this is unlikely. Again, it is likely that Stonor had asked about Forster, or that Stallworth had mentioned him earlier, but the introductory phrases 'as for' and 'as to' did not necessarily imply previous mention of the subjects they introduced. Stallworth did not sign and dispatch the letter as soon as he had dated it. Either he was interrupted once more, or he waited for further news or a remission of illness, because he appends his signature in paler ink and in his normal handwriting, together with a postscript about the disposition of Hastings's retainers. The original says that these 'be come' my lord of Buckingham's men. This does not mean 'have become' (which would be 'be [or 'are'] become' in fifteenth-century English)—it is present tense and means 'are going over to Buckingham'. This minor point of translation has a certain importance, because of the dispute about the date of the events referred to.

The next document to be put in evidence is a copy of the instructions given to Lord Mountjoy, Dr. John Cook, and Sir Thomas Thwaites, who were sent to Calais shortly after Richard's accession on 26 June (possibly on 28 June), to ensure the loyalty of Lord Dynham, the acting captain of Calais since Hastings's death, and the rest of his council there.[1] Shortly before, Dynham had written to Richard, under the title of protector, about four matters. His first and most important object was to point out that as soon as news of the death of Edward IV had reached Calais, members of the government there had taken a solemn oath of loyalty to his son Edward V, and sworn to hold the town for him and his lieutenant Lord Hastings. Now evidently (although the 'instructions' do not rehearse this) they found themselves in grave embarrassment because they had received news that Hastings had been executed for treason and that Richard had claimed title to the throne. Richard's delegates were told to explain that a similar oath to Edward V had been taken 'in diverse places in England by many great estates and personages, being then ignorant of the very sure and true title which our sovereign lord that now is, King Richard the Third, hath and had the same time to the crown of England', so that notwithstanding that unfortunate mistake,

now every good true Englishman is bound upon knowledge had of the said very true title, to depart from the first oath so ignorantly given to him to whom it appertained not. And thereupon to make his oath of new and owe his service and fidelity to him that good law, reason, and the concord assent of the lords and commons of the realm have ordained to reign upon the people: which is our said sovereign lord, King Richard the Third, brother to the said King Edward the Fourth. . . . Whose sure and true title is evidently showed and declared in a bill of petition which the lords spirituals and temporals and the commons of this land solemnly porrected unto the king's highness at London the 26th day of June. Whereupon the king's said highness, notably assisted by well near all the lords spiritual and temporal of this realm, went the same day unto his palace of Westminster, and there in such royal[ty] honourably apparelled within the great hall there took possession and declared his mind that the same day he would begin to reign upon his people. And from thence rode solemnly to the cathedral church of London, and was received there with procession, with great congratulation and acclamation of all the people in every place, and by the

---

[1] Ed. (from B.M. MS. Harl. 433) by James Gairdner, *Letters and Papers Illustrative of the Reigns of Richard III and Henry VII*, I (1861), 11–16.

way that the king was in that day. The copy of the which bill [of petition] the king will to be sent to Calais, and there to be read and understanded, together with these presents. Desiring right effectuously all manner persons of the said three jurisdictions,[1] what estate, degree or condition that they be of, and also them of Guisnes and Hammes, to make their faiths and oaths to him as to their sovereign lord, like as the lords spirituals and temporals and many other noble men in great number being in England, freely and of good heart have done for their parts.

This official statement, carefully underlining the manifestations of popular support for Richard, and failing to mention that parliament was not lawfully constituted, barely conceals the comic elements in the situation. It is difficult to estimate the date of Dynham's letter because the speed of communication between Calais and England depended on weather and the availability of ships. Since he addressed Richard as protector and not king, Dynham had evidently not had official notification of the change in status on 26 June. He may, however, have heard of the intended offer of the crown by the lords and commons, which would mean that he had been sent a message on 25 June.

The petition is rehearsed in the 'Act for the Settlement of the Crown' of 1484.[2] It is a very interesting document, which needs to be quoted at length, because its arguments are more diffuse than cogent. The petition, contained in a roll of parchment presented to Richard by persons representing the three estates 'out of parliament', had in 1484 to be enrolled and ratified by the estates now duly meeting 'in form of parliament'. The enrolled copy runs:

Please it your noble grace to understand the considerations, election, and petition underwritten, of us the lords spirituals and temporals and the commons of this realm of England, and thereunto agreeably to give your assent to the common and public weal of this land, to the comfort and gladness of all the people of the same.

First, we consider how that heretofore in time passed this land many years stood in great prosperity, honour, and tranquility, which was caused for so much as the kings then reigning used and followed the advice and counsel of certain lords spirituals and temporals, and other persons of

---

[1] The three jurisdictions were those of the captain of Calais as commander-in-chief of the town and garrison, the mayor of Calais, and the mayor of the Staple.

[2] *Rot. Parl.* VI. 240–2.

approved sadness, prudence, policy, and experience; dreading God and having tender zeal and affection to indifferent ministration of justice, and to the common and politic weal of the land. Then our Lord God was 'dred, luffed, and honoured';[1] then within the land was peace and tranquility, and among neighbours concord and charity; then the malice of outward enemies was mightily resisted and repressed, and the land honourably defended, with many great and glorious victories; then the intercourse of merchandises was largely used and exercised. By which things above remembered the land was greatly enriched, so that as well the merchants and artificers, as other poor people labouring for their living in diverse occupations, had competent gain to the sustentation of them and their households, living without miserable and intolerable poverty.[2] But afterward, when that such as had the rule and governance of this land, delighting in adulation and flattery, and led by sensuality and concupiscence, followed the counsel of persons insolent, vicious, and of inordinate avarice, despising the counsel of good, virtuous, and prudent persons, such as above be remembered, the prosperity of this land daily decreased, so that felicity was turned into misery, and prosperity into adversity, and the order of policy and of the law of God and man confounded, whereby it is likely this realm to fall into extreme misery and desolation (which God defend) without due provision of covenable remedy be had in this behalf in all goodly haste.

Over this, amongst other things, more specially we consider how that the time of the reign of King Edward IV, late deceased, after the ungracious pretensed marriage (as all England hath cause so to say) made betwixt the said King Edward and Elizabeth, sometime wife to Sir John Grey, knight, late naming herself and many years heretofore Queen of England, the order of all politic rule was perverted; the laws of God and of God's church, and also the laws of nature and of England, and also the laudable customs and liberties of the same, wherein every Englishman is inheritor, broken, subverted, and contemned, against all reason and justice, so that this land was ruled by self-will and pleasure, fear and dread, all manner of equity and laws laid apart and despised. Whereof ensued many inconvenients and mischiefs—as murders, extortions, and oppressions, namely of poor and impotent people, so that no man was sure of his life, land nor livelihood, ne of his wife, daughter ne servant, every good maiden and woman standing in dread to be ravished and defouled. And besides this, what discords, inward battles, effusion of Christian men's blood, and namely by the destruction of the noble blood of this land, was had and committed within the same, it is evident and notary through all this realm, unto the great sorrow and heaviness of all true Englishmen.

---

[1] Too much weight cannot be placed upon this point, but one or two spellings like *luffed*, *thaym*, and *thair*, which occur in the copy of the petition but not in the rest of the Act which embodies it, could support the contemporary claim that the petition was drawn up by a northerner. It should be remembered that to a fifteenth-century Londoner, 'the north' might include Leicestershire and Northamptonshire.

[2] No exact date is given for this golden age, and one wonders what period the author had in mind.

This preamble is the kind of thing standard in the conventional process of deposition, which meant showing that the reigning monarch was incompetent by reason of his persistent reliance on evil counsellors. But that the misgovernment of the previous king made his son unacceptable as a ruler would, if meant seriously, be a startlingly new constitutional theory. More relevantly:

And here also we consider how that the said pretensed marriage betwixt the above-named King Edward and Elizabeth Grey was made of great presumption, without the knowing and assent of the lords of this land, and also by sorcery and witchcraft committed by the said Elizabeth and her mother Jaquet Duchess of Bedford, as the common opinion of the people and the public voice and fame is through all this land; and hereafter, if and as the case shall require, shall be proved sufficiently in time and place convenient. And here also we consider how that the said pretensed marriage was made privily and secretly, without edition of banns, in a private chamber—a profane place and not openly in the face of the church after the law of God's church, but contrary thereunto and the laudable custom of the church of England. And how also, that at the time of contract of the same pretensed marriage, and before and long time after, the said King Edward was and stood married and troth plight to one Dame Elianore Butteler, daughter of the old Earl of Shrewsbury, with whom the same King Edward had made a precontract of matrimony, long time before he made the said pretensed marriage with the said Elizabeth Grey, in manner and form abovesaid. Which premises being true, as in very truth they been true, it appeareth and followeth evidently that the said King Edward during his life and the said Elizabeth lived together sinfully and damnably in adultery against the law of God and of his church, and therefore no marvel that, the sovereign lord and the head of this land being of such ungoodly disposition and provoking the ire and indignation of our Lord God, such heinous mischiefs and inconvenients as is above remembered were used and committed in the realm among the subjects. Also it appeareth evidently and followeth that all the issue and children of the said King Edward been bastards and unable to inherit or to claim anything by inheritance by the law and custom of England. . . .

This conclusion may not be self-evident to the modern mind. It will be noted that, with all the petitioners' anxiety to establish Richard's firm right to the throne, they made no offer to furnish proof for their most substantial argument for the illegitimacy of his nephews—the claim that Edward's marriage was invalidated by precontract with Eleanor Butler. The matter that is common knowledge and 'hereafter, if and as the case shall require [!], shall be proved sufficiently in time and place convenient' is simply that the Woodville marriage occurred without the assent of the council and was contrived by sorcery. The first was indeed common knowledge. Not surprisingly, no proof of the latter charge is on record.

After referring to the attainder of George Duke of Clarence, which disabled and barred his issue, the petition continues:

> Over this, we consider how that ye be the undoubted son and heir of Richard late Duke of York, very inheritor to the said crown and dignity royal, and as in right King of England by way of inheritance, and that at this time, the premises duly considered, there is none other person living but ye only, that by right may claim the said crown and dignity royal by way of inheritance, and how that ye be born within this land; by reason whereof, as we deem in our minds, ye be more natural inclined to the prosperity and common weal of the same, and all the three estates of the land have, and may have, more certain knowledge of your birth and filiation abovesaid.[1] We consider also the great wit, prudence, justice, princely courage, and the memorable and laudable acts in diverse battles which (as we by experience know) ye heretofore have done for the salvation and defence of this same realm, and also the great noblesse and excellence of your birth and blood, as of him that is descended of the three most royal houses in Christendom, that is to say England, France and Hispanie. . . .
>
> For certainly we be determined rather to aventure and commit us to the peril of our lives and jeopardy of death, than to live in such thralldom and bondage as we have lived long time heretofore, oppressed and injured by extortions and new impositions, against the laws of God and man, and the liberties, old policy, and laws of this realm, wherein every Englishman is inherited. . . . [And] albeit that the right title and estate which our sovereign lord the king Richard the Third hath to and in the crown . . . been just and lawful . . . the court of parliament is of such authority, and the people of this land of such nature and disposition (as experience teacheth), that manifestation and declaration of any truth or right made by the three estates of this realm assembled in parliament, and by authority of the same, maketh, before all other things, most faith and certainty, and, quieting men's minds, removeth the occasion of all doubts and seditious language. . . .

When a legal parliament finally gave its authority to this remarkable document, considerable doubt, disquiet, and sedition had indeed shaken the country.

One of the first hints of opposition to Richard after his coronation comes in a newly noticed letter which has occasioned some controversy. It was written from the king at Minster Lovell to his chancellor, Bishop Russell, on 29 July [1483], as Richard was setting out on progress. It runs:

[1] The petition thus 'touched aslope craftily' (as More phrased it) allegations that Richard's brothers, who were born abroad, were illegitimate.

Right reverent father in God, right trusty and well beloved, we greet you well. And whereas we understand that certain persons of such as of late had taken upon them the fact of an enterprise, as we doubt not ye have heard, be attached and in ward, we desire and will you that ye do make our brief of commission to such persons as by you and our council shall be advised for to sit upon them and to proceed to the due execution of our laws in that behalf. Fail ye not hereof, as our perfect trust is in you.[1]

It has been argued by Mrs. Tudor-Craig that this letter is a covert reference to the murder of Edward V and his brother, carried out to the king's displeasure by persons acting on the instructions of somebody else, perhaps the Duke of Buckingham.[2] Analysis of the language does not, however, confirm her main contention in support of this theory, namely that the crime had been successful. The conspirators '*had* [past subjunctive in an otherwise present-tense letter] taken upon them', that is, 'would have attempted' to embark on a dangerous scheme, had they not been detected. And in the fifteenth century, *fact* did not have its modern sense, but meant 'enterprise' or 'crime'. If anything more than a minor piece of sedition was at the root of this, Mrs. Tudor-Craig's rejected suggestion that it concerned a project to rescue some of the princesses from sanctuary deserves consideration. The *Crowland Chronicle* reports that while Richard was on progress and the princes were still thought to be alive in the Tower,

It was also spread about that those men who had fled to sanctuary aimed at removing some of the king's daughters from Westminster in disguise to send them overseas. . . . When this was discovered, Westminster Abbey and all the area around was turned into a fortress and put under the care of very tough men appointed by King Richard, whose captain was a certain John Nesfeld.[3]

The chancellor's instructions would certainly fit some such frustrated plot, about which discretion was necessary, and if some of the conspirators were in sanctuary, that explains why only some had been arrested.

In September, Thomas Langton, who had just been consecrated Bishop of St. David's in Wales, had his head full of intrigues of a different sort. He was in favour with the new

---

[1] P.R.O., Chancery Warrants for the Great Seal (C.81) 1392/1.

[2] Pamela Tudor-Craig, *Richard III* (catalogue for an exhibition at the National Portrait Gallery, June–October 1973), pp. 54–5 and App. 4.

[3] pp. 567–8.

king, and confidently expected to move shortly to a more magnificent office. From York he sent an exuberant letter to the Prior of the Cathedral Church of Canterbury,[1] giving him some advice about shipping wine from Bordeaux and then continuing:

> I trust to God ye shall hear some tidings in haste that I shall be an Englishman and no more Welsh, *sit hoc clam omnes* ['but mum's the word'].[2] The King of Scots hath sent a courteous and a wise letter to the king for peace,[3] but I trow ye shall understand they shall have a sit-up or ever the king depart from York. They lie still at the siege of Dunbar, but I trust to God it shall be kept from them. I trust to God soon—by Michaelmas—the king shall be at London. He contents the people where he goes best that ever did prince, for many a poor man that hath suffered wrong many days have be relieved and helped by him and his commands now in his progress. And in many great cities and towns were great sums of money give him, which all he hath refused. On my troth I liked never the conditions of any prince so well as his: God hath sent him to us for the weal of us all.

Langton then breaks discreetly into Latin, and unfortunately time and damp have abetted him, so that the opening of the sentence is almost illegible and has to be guessed from the few letters still visible. It appears to read: 'Ne*que* exc*epti*onem do voluptas ali*qualiter* regnat in augm*entatia*'['Sensual pleasure holds sway to an increasing extent, but I do not consider that this detracts from what I have said'].[4] The bishop's stricture fits well enough with the Crowland chronicler's comments on Richard's court, but does not chime with the view, offered in derision by More and made fashionable by Kendall, that Richard was a dour and earnest puritan.

[1] Cathedral Archives and Library, Canterbury: Christ Church Letter 88.

[2] Langton had been granted the temporalities of the see of St. David's on 21 May 1483, and the grant was confirmed on Richard's coronation day. It is not clear what English bishopric Langton now had his eye on. He in fact succeeded Lionel Woodville at Salisbury after Woodville's death the following year. The Bishop of Durham died 24 Nov. 1483, and was succeeded by John Shirwood, who had been Edward IV's proctor to the Roman Curia, an office then conferred on Langton. Death cheated him of the Archbishopric of Canterbury five days after his election on 22 Jan. 1501. (A. B. Emden, *Biographical Register of the University of Cambridge to 1500* (Cambridge, 1963), pp. 352–3.)

[3] Misread as 'for [h]is cace' in J. B. Sheppard, ed., *Christ Church Letters* (Camden Soc., 1877), p. 46.

[4] Miss Anne M. Oakley, the Cathedral archivist, very kindly looked at the MS. under ultra-violet light for me, but reported that it failed to reveal more than appears on a photocopy of the document. From the traces visible on this I have reconstructed the word *exceptionem*.

Later in the reign some 'doubts and seditious language' had to be countered by official action, and so were brought into the open. The report in the minutes of the London Mercers' Company contrasts with the impression of general popularity conveyed by some of the documents previously quoted.[1] On 31 March 1485 the recorder of the Mercers' Company noted that the previous day the king had summoned the mayor and aldermen to the great hall of the Knights of St. John at Clerkenwell. He then in person addressed a large assembly of lords and citizens on the subject of certain rumours spread by malicious people, and issued a refutation of them. Richard complained that, to his very great displeasure, there had been persistent gossip and silly rumour spread among the people by ill-disposed persons, to the effect that the queen had been poisoned by his own consent to enable him to marry his niece Elizabeth. The king expressed great sorrow and annoyance about this, and said it had never occurred to him to make such a marriage: 'It never came in his thought or mind to marry in such manner wise, nor willing or glad of the death of his queen, but as sorry and in heart as heavy as man might be, with much more in the premisses spoken.' Then he ordered everyone to cease such false talk, on pain of incurring his displeasure, and said that from henceforth anyone who repeated these lying tales would be imprisoned until the person from whom he had heard them was produced.

The entry in the accounts of the Mercers' Company (published only in 1936) strikingly confirms the report in the *Crowland Chronicle* that Richard denied such rumours at a meeting at Clerkenwell, and shows that the stories about Anne being poisoned, rehearsed by the priest Rous and others, were really current soon after her death and not invented by Tudor historians. It also confirms, if confirmation were needed, the accounts of how Richard strove throughout his reign to establish good relations with his subjects. Unfortunately it does not make clear whether Richard's denials carried conviction with his hearers, and still less whether they were sincere or whether, as the Crowland chronicler claims, Richard had been forced to renounce ideas of marrying Elizabeth by the representations of his advisers. The words used are standard

[1] *Acts of Court*, ed. Lyell, pp. 173–4.

clichés of the period, which would be used equally by a man gripped with grief and a man anxious to give a convincing suggestion of sorrow. The utmost that can be concluded from the report is that the recorder reported the substance of the speech faithfully. Whatever the truth about his plans for remarriage, Richard's distress and indignation were probably genuine enough as regards the accusation of poisoning Anne, which seems unlikely to be true. But once again, authentic evidence serves to raise a cloud of conjecture. Richard may have been totally innocent of any desire for his wife's death or for marriage with his niece, and have expressed sincere distaste for such suggestions. He may have been guilty on both counts, and staged a histrionic rebuttal when political considerations forced him to change his plans. He may, thirdly, have attempted to hasten his wife's death by the psychological means suggested by Vergil[1] and the Crowland chronicler,[2] in which case unfounded accusations of poisoning might well strike him as peculiarly unjust.

Although it does not resolve all such ambiguities, the account of the affair in the *Crowland Chronicle* is remarkably detailed:

It must be mentioned that at this Christmastide immoderate stress was laid [at the court] on dancing and festivity, frivolous [or perhaps 'deceptive']³ new clothes, identical in colour and design, being given out to Queen Anne and the Princess Elizabeth, eldest daughter of the dead king.

At this people began to talk, and the lords and prelates were horrified. It became common gossip that the king was bent on marrying Elizabeth at all costs, either in expectation of the queen's death, or after divorce, for which he thought he had sufficient grounds. He could see no other way of confirming himself as king, nor of putting down the hopes of his rival.

Shortly after this, the queen became seriously ill, and her weakness was supposed to get ever worse as the king entirely shunned his wife's bed. It was his doctors' advice to do so, he declared. Little more need be said. About the middle of March, on the day that there occurred a great eclipse of the sun, Queen Anne died and was buried at Westminster, not without the proper funeral pomp due to a queen.

In the end the king's earnest intention of marrying his niece Elizabeth reached the ears of people who wanted no such thing, and the king was forced to summon the council and exculpate himself by denying profusely that the idea had ever entered his head. But there were men present at that

---

[1] (1844), p. 211.   [2] p. 572.

[3] *Vanisque mutatoriis vestium.* The supposition that the clothes were for a 'disguising' would lend point to the chronicler's strictures.

council meeting who well knew the contrary. In point of fact, those who were most strongly against this marriage were two men whose views even the king himself seldom dared oppose: that is, Sir Richard Ratcliff and William Catesby, esquire of the body. These told the king to his face that if he would not relinquish the project (and what is more, personally issue an authoritative denial before the mayor and people of London), the northerners on whom he most relied would rise in a body against him. They would accuse him of killing the queen—the daughter and heiress of the Earl of Warwick, through whom he had first won their regard—in order to indulge an incestuous lust for his brother's daughter, a thing abominable to God. For good measure they brought in more than a dozen doctors of theology, who stated that the pope could not grant a dispensation within this degree of consanguinity.[1] It was widely assumed that these two, and others like them, raised so many obstacles out of fear, because if Elizabeth became queen it would be in her power sooner or later to avenge the deaths of her uncle Earl Rivers and her [half-]brother Richard on those who had been the leading advisers in the matter. And so, a little before Easter, in the great hall of St. John's, and before the mayor and citizens of London, the king made a total repudiation of the whole scheme in a clear and loud voice. But more, people thought, at his advisers' desire than his own.[2]

Although the chroniclers, apart from the 'Crowland' writer, make little of it, this episode is the best-recorded, and corroborated, one of Richard's career. The concluding act of his tragedy has been fully described, but there is much less unanimity about the details. Bernard André, writing about 1502—some twelve years before Vergil completed the earliest extant draft of his *Historia*, and seventeen years after the event—says,

I have heard something of the battle by oral report, but the eye is a safer judge than the ear in such a matter. Therefore I pass over the date, the place, and the order of battle, rather than assert anything rashly; for, as I have said before, I lack clear sight. And so until I obtain more knowledge of this debatable field, I leave both it and this page a blank.[3]

[1] Contemporary opinion on the point is investigated by H. A. Kelly, 'Canonical Implications of Richard III's Plan to Marry his Niece', *Traditio*, XXIII (1967), 269–311. (I am grateful to Professor Charles Wood for this reference.) Kelly concludes that a dispensation might not have been thought impossible by all authorities. But I do not think the Crowland writer, whom Kelly identifies with Bishop Russell, 'disassociat[es] himself from the doctors of theology who advised Richard that the pope could not allow the marriage [and] seems to indicate that he holds the contrary opinion' (p. 273). The full context makes clear that it was Ratcliff and Catesby, not the theologians, who 'raised so many obstacles out of fear'.

[2] p. 572. According to Vergil (ed. Hay, 1950, p. 2*), they still got blamed for the marriage scheme.

[3] *Historia Regis Henrici Septimi*, ed. James Gairdner (Rolls Ser., 1858), p. 32: 'Hoc ego bellum quamvis auribus acceperim, tamen hac in parte certior aure

André's reticence may in fact have been due more to political discretion than scholarly scruple. Others were less reluctant to give an account of affairs, and it so happens that we have a very interesting record of some of the oral reports that did circulate soon after Bosworth. This, which contains the earliest description of the battle that can be certainly dated,[1] was compiled in Spain on 1 March 1486, when the historian Diego de Valera wrote out for Ferdinand and Isabella of Castile the detailed news just brought to Puerto de Santa Maria by merchants 'worthy of credit' who had been in England at the time of the battle and 'saw all the things that happened' between then and the end of January 1486.[2] If Bernard André's expressed distrust of oral history was genuine, such accounts would amply justify his attitude. The Spaniards' report is a fine concoction of fact, or possible fact, and palpable fiction. According to them, for instance, Richard had poisoned his nephews while their father was fighting in Scotland [*sic*] and Richard himself was in England.[3] But the description of Bosworth itself claims to derive from the Spanish adventurer Juan de Salazar who fought on Richard's side.[4]

According to this account, Henry landed in Wales with 5,000 men, both French and English,[5] and made a victorious

---

arbiter est oculus. Diem, igitur, locum, ac belli ordinem, quia ut dixi sum privatus hac luce oculorum, ne quid temerarie affirmum, supersedeo. Et pro tam bellico campo, donec plenius instructus fuero, campum quoque latum hoc in albo relinquo.' There is a pun here on *campus* 'field of battle', 'subject of debate', and 'blank space in a manuscript'.

[1] Since the date at which the 'Crowland' account was composed is unknown.

[2] Spanish versions are printed in *Epístolas y otros varios tratados de Mosén Diego de Valera*, ed. José A. De Balenchana (Madrid, 1878), pp. 91–6, and in *Biblioteca de autores españoles*, CXVI: 'Prosistas Castellanos del siglo XV', I, ed. Mario Penna (Madrid, 1959), 32–4. An English translation appeared in the *Bulletin of Spanish* (later *Hispanic*) *Studies*, IV (1927), 34–7, and was reprinted with commentary by Elizabeth M. Nokes and Geoffrey Wheeler, 'A Spanish Account of the Battle of Bosworth', *The Ricardian*, March 1972, pp. 1–5. (I am indebted to Mr. Wheeler for a copy of this, and for bringing the account to my notice.) For a fuller discussion, see Anthony Goodman and Angus Mackay, 'A Castilian Report on English Affairs, 1486', *E.H.R.* LXXXVIII (1973), 92–9.

[3] When Valera adapted this letter for his *Crónica de los reyes católicos* he added that Richard had also poisoned Edward IV: Goodman and Mackay, p. 94 n. 3.

[4] Salazar was a well-known soldier of fortune, who spent much of his career in the service of Maximilian. There are references to his period in England in B.M. MS. Harl. 433: Nokes and Wheeler, pp. 4–5.

[5] All figures are undoubtedly much exaggerated.

progression as far as Coventry [*sic*], near which town King Richard had as many as 70,000 troops encamped.[1] Before crossing to England, Henry had an assurance that 'milort Tamorlant' (Northumberland),[2] one of the principal noblemen of England, and several other leaders who had sworn fealty to him, would aid him when they came to do battle, and fight against King Richard, and so they did. Although Henry's followers did not know this beforehand and were dispirited by the reported size of Richard's army, Henry stirred up their courage for battle.

Richard drew up his forces, giving the van of 7,000 men to his great chamberlain.[3] 'Lord Tamorlant' with Richard's left wing of 10,000 men left his position and passed in front of the king's vanguard, then turned his back on Henry's forces and engaged in fierce combat with the king's van, and so did all the others who were sworn to Henry.[4] When little Salazar your subject, who was then in the service of King Richard, saw their treason, he said to the king, 'Sir, seek safety. You cannot hope to win this battle, for your followers have openly betrayed you.' But the king answered, 'Salazar, God forbid that I yield one foot. This day I will perish as a king or have the victory.' Then he placed the crown over his helmet (which they value at 120,000 crowns [i.e. roughly £25,000 stg.]), and donning his coat-armour set himself to fight fiercely, so inspiring the loyal remnant that his efforts long sustained the battle. But finally the king's army was defeated and he himself killed. More than 10,000 on both sides are said to have died. Salazar fought very well but managed to escape. Most of the king's loyal servants died there, and all the king's treasure, which he had brought to the field, was lost there. After his victory, Henry was acclaimed king by all. He had the dead king exposed to public view for three days at a little hermitage near the battle-field, covered from the waist down with a piece of poor black cloth.

After this, Henry was received at London with the joyful demonstrations usually accorded a conqueror, and summoned all the magnates, both lay and spiritual, who unanimously did homage to him as king and rightful lord. But because he was told that Northumberland, despite his aid in the battle, had not really intended Henry to be king but planned for a son of

[1] The *Crónica* assigns Richard 40,000 men.

[2] Northumberland is much the most likely identification on phonetic grounds. Neither Stanley nor Westmorland, who have also been proposed, would be likely to produce *Tamorlant* in a Romance language.

[3] The Great Chamberlain was in fact Northumberland. Francis Lord Lovel was chamberlain of the household, and Lord Stanley steward. Vergil (p. 222) says that Norfolk commanded a company of archers in the van, but this conflicts with the *Crowland Chron.*, which gives him command of a wing.

[4] It is very likely that the account here confuses current stories about the parts played by Northumberland and Sir William Stanley.

the Duke of Clarence to become king and marry one of his own daughters, the king had him arrested and imprisoned until he handed over Clarence's son and swore perpetual allegiance to Henry, together with two other earls[1] of his family.

The story about Northumberland's project of playing king-maker to the young Earl of Warwick is interesting. Goodman puts the arguments for it persuasively, and perhaps dismisses it too lightly, on the ground that if Northumberland had plotted to keep Henry off the throne in August 1485 it is surprising to find him trusted and fighting for Henry against the northern rebels at Easter 1486.[2] The objection is weighty, but not totally compelling. It is one thing to support one pos-sible claimant against an unconsecrated usurper, and another to engage in armed rebellion against the anointed king, and both sides could have recognized this difference, especially when, in 1486, Henry badly needed Northumberland's aid in the north. Further, Northumberland's coup, if he did intend one after the death of Richard, existed only *in posse* and not *in esse*: Henry's emissary got to Warwick first, apparently, and it is unlikely that Henry could have proved much against Northumberland. Vergil[3] says Henry sent for Warwick to be brought from Sheriff Hutton (one of Richard's castles, not a Percy stronghold) before he left Leicester. His speedy action is interesting, and so is Vergil's treatment of the question. In the earlier manuscript Vergil said 'For indeed, Henry, not unaware of the mob's natural tendency always to seek changes, was fearful lest, if the boy should escape, and given any altered circumstances, he might stir up civil discord.' In the edition printed after Henry's death this becomes: 'He feared, not without cause, that ruthless men might use this boy to harm him, and having suffered from many oppressors from an early age, his greatest desire was now for peace.' Vergil further-more conceals that Northumberland was imprisoned after the battle: 'Among [those who submitted] the chief were Henry Earl of Northumberland and Thomas Earl of Surrey. This man [Surrey] was committed to ward, where he re-mained long [i.e. until 1489]; he [Northumberland], as

---

[1] *Condes*, the word also used for Richmond's title.
[2] 'A Castilian Report', pp. 95–8.
[3] Ed. Hay (1950), pp. 2*, 3.

friend in heart, was received into favour.'[1] Whether or not there was any substance in them, the circulation of stories against Northumberland helps explain his later reputation in York,[2] and perhaps Bernard André's rather uncharacteristic reticence about the battle.

The Spanish account of Bosworth may be compared with those of the Crowland chronicler and Polydore Vergil, both also written at second-hand. The *Crowland Chronicle* runs:[3]

> The Earl of Richmond, with his troops, moved straight against King Richard; while the Earl of Oxford, a most valiant soldier and his second-in-command, surrounded by a great force as much French as English, held the wing facing the Duke of Norfolk. But where the Earl of Northumberland stood, with a troop of a size and quality befitting his rank, no opposing force was visible, and no blows were exchanged in anger.[4]
>
> In the end, providence gave a glorious victory to the Earl of Richmond, now sole king,[5] together with the precious crown which King Richard had formerly worn. For during the battle, and not in flight from it, the said King Richard fell pierced with many deadly wounds, like a very spirited prince and one most daring in the field. Further, the said Duke of Norfolk, Sir Richard Ratcliff, Sir Robert Brackenbury, constable of the Tower of London, John Kendall, the king's secretary, Sir Robert Percy, comptroller of the royal household, and Walter Devereux, Lord Ferrers, were killed in that fury of battle, and many, for the most part those northerners in whom King Richard had so trusted, took flight before it came to hand-to-hand fighting, so that no worthy or able foe remained against whom the glorious victor Henry VII might gain some further experience of warfare. When out of this battle peace had come to the whole country, the body of King Richard was found among the slain [lacuna in MS.], and many other insults were heaped upon it, and it was removed to Leicester, with unbecoming contumely, a halter being put about the neck. The new king, adorned with the crown so notably won, proceeded to Leicester. Meanwhile, many lords and others were taken into captivity, first among them Henry Earl of Northumberland and Thomas Howard, Earl of Surrey, eldest son of the dead Duke of Norfolk. William Catesby was also captured . . . [6]

Vergil's account[7] may be summarized as follows:

---

[1] (1844), p. 225.   [2] Below, p. 63.

[3] This translation differs in a number of respects from that of H. T. Riley.

[4] If this account is correct, it furnishes further reason for Henry's imprisonment of Northumberland. Henry fulfilled his side of the bargain by holding off from Northumberland's troops, but Northumberland failed to turn them against Richard as expected (and as wrongly reported by the Spanish merchants).

[5] The chronicler has previously said that Henry's followers styled him King Henry VII before the battle.

[6] pp. 574–5.   [7] (1844), pp. 222–4.

Richard arrayed his forces with a very long vanguard of footmen and horse, with archers in front led by John Duke of Norfolk. The king came behind with his bodyguard. Shortly before battle engaged, Henry sent a message to call in Lord Stanley and his troops (to join, that is, the 3,000 who were already with him under the command of Sir William), and was dismayed to receive the prevaricating answer that in the meantime Henry should array his own force and that Stanley would come with his army well appointed. Nevertheless, Henry kept only a small force about him in the battle, 'trusting to the aid of Thomas Stanley'.[1] Henry had a small vanguard, because he was very short of men, led by archers under the Earl of Oxford. On the right wing of the vanguard was Gilbert Talbot and on the left John Savage. With Henry there was a troop of horse and a few foot. After the first onslaught Oxford halted by his standards and drew his men together in close order, whereupon the other side also held off, fearing a trap (and some very willingly, because they 'rather coveted the king [Richard] dead than alive and therefore fought faintly'). Then Oxford and others made a fresh charge in wedge-shaped formation. Richard saw Henry and made a detour round the embattled vanguards to attack him, killing his standard-bearer and over-throwing Sir John Cheyney. At the last minute Sir William Stanley came to Henry's rescue and Richard's soldiers fled. 'King Richard alone was killed fighting manfully in the thickest press of his enemies.' In the meantime Oxford had also put Richard's van to flight, and many were killed during the pursuit. Others failed to fight at all.

This notably omits all reference to the Earl of Northumberland.

News in the immediate aftermath of the battle was vague and inaccurate. The sergeant to the mace of the city of York, who had been sent to get news and perhaps met another messenger on his way, galloped back to deliver, on 23 August (the day after the battle), information that Richard had been killed on 'the field of Redemore' 'through great treason of the Duke of Norfolk [*sic*] and many other that turned against him'.[2] York, in a panic at the loss of their 'good lord' and the likelihood of retaliation by his conqueror, turned to the Earl of Northumberland for protection, and having heard that he was at Wressel, sent there for his advice and assistance 'at this woeful season', but Sir Henry Percy then informed them that he was 'with the king at Leicester for the weal of himself

[1] Later, discussing Sir William's execution for treason against Henry VII, Vergil says plainly that Thomas did send troops to the battle, but remained himself in his camp: ed. Hay (1950), p. 77.

[2] *Y.C.R.* I. 118–19; York City Library, House Books 2–4, f. 169b, wrongly supposed by Raine to be missing. Mr. O. S. Tomlinson kindly informs me that the deletion has in fact occurred between the present ff. 169b and 170.

and this city'.[1] On 25 August the city agreed to send a deputation to the new king himself for confirmation of their liberties, and to write letters seeking the help of Lord Stanley and Northumberland, being still unaware that he was a prisoner.[2] But Henry's own intelligence just after the battle was scarcely more accurate. He issued a proclamation bidding his new subjects keep the peace and interfere with no soldiers returning home from the battlefield,

And moreover, the king ascertaineth you that Richard Duke of Gloucester, late called King Richard, was slain at a place called Sandeford, within the shire of Leicester, and brought dead off the field unto the town of Leicester, and there was laid openly, that every man might see and look upon him. And also there was slain upon the same field, John late Duke of Norfolk, John late Earl of Lincoln, Thomas late Earl of Surrey, Francis Viscount Lovell, Sir Walter Deveres, Lord Ferrers, Richard Ratcliff, knight, Robert Brachenbury, knight, with many other knights, squires and gentlemen, of whose souls God have mercy.[3]

This casualty list was wrong in three cases (Lincoln, Surrey, and Lovel). An emissary of Henry's, furthermore, had been sent to York with warrants for the arrest of the dead Richard Ratcliff as well as Bishop Stillington of Bath.[4] Nobody at the time seems to have agreed on the name of the battle site.

Abroad, the news travelled slowly and uncertainly. On 20 October 1485, some two months after Bosworth, the Bishop of Imola wrote from Mayence to Pope Innocent VIII: 'according to common report which I heard on my way here, the king of England has been killed in battle. Here, some people tell me he is alive, but others deny it.'[5] As this, and much else in this chapter, may demonstrate, to approach more nearly to the historical event does not always bring us closer to certainty. Conflicting rumours, misunderstood news, wishful thinking, and deliberate falsification may all play a part in distorting the record at any stage. The historian's first task is often therefore to impose order on confusion. The various concepts of order which shaped the accounts of Richard's early biographers, and, to a lesser extent, the various kinds of further confusion which they introduced, will be a theme of the succeeding chapters.

[1] *Y.C.R.* I. 120. [2] Ibid. [3] Ibid., p. 121. [4] p. 122.
[5] *Cal. State Papers, Venetian*, I. 156.

Excursus Richard's relations with the city of York

There is no doubt that the Common Council of York regarded Richard's death as a disaster for the city. He had, after all, done much for them, and they for him. They lent him troops at their own expense and gave places to his protégés, and his secretary and the clerk of his council received their fees or gifts. In return he remitted their taxes, upheld their privileges and granted new ones, and protected them from their enemies.[1] No doubt they wrote sincerely that 'King Richard, late mercifully reigning upon us, . . . with many other lords and nobility of these north parts, was piteously slain and murdered, to the great heaviness of this city',[2] and in October 1485 their clerk (the same John Harington who had been clerk to Richard's council) referred to a grant to the city made by 'the most famous prince of blessed memory, King Richard, late deceased'.[3] But the ordinary citizens of York were never unanimous in his praise. It is difficult to tell how deep their criticism went because some of the remarks which reached the ears of the city council, and were found sufficiently shocking to record, may have been aimed as much at the city establishment—an oligarchy of wealthy merchants whose power was resented by the members of the crafts[4]—as at the person of the prince from whom it derived support. For instance, one Thomas Watson, dyer, accused Alderman Thomas Wrangwish in 1483 of stealing a horse of his, and added that if he gave Wrangwish his deserts, Wrangwish would have been hanged by the neck, and could in vain 'have sought all his friends that he had'.[5] More outspoken talk was reported on 13 February 1483. On 31 January the forthcoming mayoral election came under discussion at a tavern. Steven Hoghson said, 'Sirs, one thing: and it please the commons, I would we had Master Wrangwish, for he is the man that my Lord of Gloucester will do for.' The parties could not agree on how Robert Rede, girdler, had answered. For some purpose of his own, William Wells spread it about that Rede had said, in effect, 'No. The commons would not vote for Gloucester's man—the mayor was chosen by the commons "and not by no lord".' But numerous witnesses said that Rede's comment was in fact that

---

[1] Thus in September 1483 the mayor was rewarded for his support with appointment as the king's chief Sergeant of Arms at the annual salary of £18 5s.; tolls were remitted to the annual value of £58 11s. 2d., and the mayor and commonalty were granted £40 in perpetuity: *Y.C.R.* I. 82.

[2] York City House Books 2–4, f. 169b. Raine (p. 119), following Drake, reads 'lawfully' for 'mercifully'.   [3] *Y.C.R.* I. 126.

[4] For this see further Edward Miller, 'Medieval York' in *V.C.H., City of York* (1961), pp. 25–113.   [5] *Y.C.R.* I. 69.

'My Lord of Gloucester would not be displeased whom some ever it pleased the commons to choose for their mayor.'[1] The extent of Gloucester's patronage was generally taken for granted, as a fact of political life. In the previous year one scandalous remark reported at third hand had merely questioned its utility: 'What may my Lord of Gloucester do for us of the city? Nothing but grin of us.'[2]

The citizens of York were far from docile in their relations with their rulers. In the summer of 1482, just as a contingent of soldiers from the city was about to join the Duke of Gloucester's army to invade Scotland, three ringleaders insisted on being paid a whole month's wages in advance, instead of the agreed instalment for fourteen days; 'whereupon the remnant of the soldiers took a courage and would not go without they had their whole wages for twenty-eight days', and the council had to pay them to avoid holding up the whole expedition.[3] The returned soldiers groused about the lack of action on the campaign. Some were reported to grumble that they did nothing but wait on the ordnance and baggage train, and one man had been so bored that he threatened to take the string off his bow and use it to whip on his horse.[4]

At home there were rows about rights of commonage. One with Lord Lovel was eventually settled in Lovel's favour when he had become chamberlain to Richard III.[5] More seriously, in 1484 the king's direct action caused a major riot, when he asked the city council to surrender rights of common over land belonging to St. Nicholas's Hospital, and the council complied 'if the commons will agree to the same'.[6] The commons, and three 'gentlemen' (Roger Laton, John Hastings—later made mace-bearer at the king's request[7]—and Thomas Wandesford) signified their disagreement by staging a disturbance on 4 October. On 6 October twelve of the council (including Laton, Hastings, and Wandesford) were deputed to pacify the mob.[8] The worst-disposed of the leaders were clapped in prison and the council then sent anxious letters to the king and members of his household to deprecate his anger. He was not appeased. The city was in disgrace, and a furious letter came from the Earl of Northumberland, whose authority as a member of the Council for the North had been affronted:

Whereas I am informed that now lately a great riot is committed within the city of York and the franchises thereof, which without brief remedy is like to grow to great inconveniencies; if thus it be (my Lord of Lincoln

---

[1] pp. 68–9. [2] p. 56. [3] p. 62. [4] p. 67. [5] pp. 81–2.
[6] p. 89. Already in May 1484 the king had caused anger by setting up a fish-garth, to the encouragement of others (pp. 92–3).
[7] p. 117 (6 July 1485). [8] pp. 102–3.

being in these parts, and also I, standing Great Chamberlain to the king's grace), I greatly marvel [that] ye, being head governor and rulers of the said city, have neither certified my Lord nor me. For the which cause I send my right trusty servant this bearer unto you, that I may have clear relation from you by him how the matter is indeed. To the intent that if ye be unable to sustain such honourable liberties and franchises as our said sovereign lord hath granted unto you, to punish and correct the said riot; God helping, I shall endeavour me to assist you to my power, for the fortification of our said sovereign lord's laws and your said franchises, like as my said servant can show unto you.[1]

In other words, 'If you can't fulfil the king's trust by keeping your city in order, by God, I'll come and do it for you.'

The king for his part sent Sir Robert Percy, the controller of his household, to administer a rebuke.[2] The king, like Northumberland, was especially annoyed that his Council of the North had failed in its purpose of preventing insurrection, and that the citizens had taken it upon them to redress their grievances against him without applying to the mayor, 'to whom his said highness hath committed the rule, guidance, and correction of and in every matter concerning the city'. 'Wherefore', concluded Percy, 'his highness is greatly displeased towards you, and how it will please his said highness to deal further in the premisses I am not in certainty.'[3] As soon as Percy had finished on this threatening note, Roger Laton handed him a bill of complaint from the commons against the mayor, the king's faithful supporter Thomas Wrangwish, whom they blamed for the whole affair, and the bill was publicly read.

Whereunto, and unto every article within the same bill comprised, the said mayor immediately, full worshipfully, sadly, and discreetly answered; so that the said controller, ne none other well-advised indifferent man, could find in the mayor no manner of default, but in every point laid his lawful excuse and disproved the said bill in every article and point thereof.[4]

(Or so said the official recorder, evidently no friend of Roger Laton's.)

The commons were not quelled by all this, and the following January there was 'a grete and juperduse scrymisse and affray', with several people injured, when the mayor tried to arrest one of the sheriffs, who answered that he would be his own gaoler, and broke away from the six sergeants of the mace, aided by some of his own retinue armed with glaives, bills, and 'glubbes'.[5] It was this kind of thing that helped persuade smug southerners that northern Englishmen were an unruly lot.

---

[1] pp. 103–4.   [2] p. 104.   [3] p. 105.   [4] Ibid.   [5] p. 110.

A private quarrel which took place in 1490, some five years after Richard's death, has been somewhat misinterpreted, both then and since.[1] John 'Painter' and William 'Plumber', his brother, in whose house various people were drinking shortly after Christmas, were, in May 1491, 'detected' of treason for the things they were supposed to have then said to John Burton, the schoolmaster of St. Leonard's; the mayor having been informed that John Painter had remarked to the schoolmaster that the Earl of Northumberland (who had been killed by dissident Yorkshiremen in 1489) had 'died a traitor to our sovereign lord the king' (i.e. Henry VII). The schoolmaster's own evidence was that Painter had said that Northumberland 'was a traitor and betrayed King Richard, with much other unsitting language concerning the said earl'. John Painter, in evidence, denied this and alleged that the conversation had taken quite another turn; that the schoolmaster 'said that King Richard was an hypocrite, a crouchback, and buried in a dike like a dog', and he himself had objected that on the contrary the king's good grace had given him noble burial. A witness deposed that at this point Painter backed up his argument by aiming a blow at the schoolmaster with a stick which he had in his hand, and the two had to be separated. In other words, as far as it is possible to reconstruct a drunken brawl from the subsequent denials of the parties and their witnesses, the verbal exchanges seem to have been typically confused and illogical.

The matter which concerned the mayor and council was whether or not there had been seditious words about the present king; the late Earl of Northumberland; or any other important lord. There is little to suggest that the company at the house especially resented Burton's opprobrious remarks about King Richard. Their subsequent animosity suggests, rather, that it was he who had made the accusation of treason against the other drinkers. The Prior of Bolton, whose concern was to prevent the matter going any further, gave a discreet summary of the incident by letter. The schoolmaster, he said, came in after the others, and

was busy of language, by the which we supposed he was distempered either with ale or wine, and [we] was irk of his company and desired John Painter to avoid him the house [i.e. turn him out]. But for to say they either rebuked the birth of the Earl of Northumberland,[2] or his truth anent King Richard, I will abide by [it] there was no such language. And where it is reported they should be busy with King Richard, they were not,

---

[1] *Y.C.R.* II (1941), 71–3.
[2] Possibly some of Painter's 'unsitting language' was supposed to imply the illegitimacy of the 4th Earl, and hence of his son, the current holder of the title.

but thus: the said schoolmaster said he loved him never, and [he] was buried in a dike. John Painter said it made little matter neither of his love nor his ['nobody's feelings had anything to do with it'],[1] and as for his burial, it pleased the king's grace to bury him in a worshipful place. And as for any other language, I heard none.[2]

The most interesting of Burton's criticisms of the late king, in view of the period and place, is not the statement that he was a crookback, but the charge of hypocrisy, which parallels both the suspicion voiced in 1482 that Richard would 'grin' at the city, and the stress laid by most of the chroniclers upon his deceit.

---

[1] Raine (*Y.C.R.* II. 73) mistakenly indicates a blank or illegible word in the original at this point.
[2] House Books 7, f. 39a (Raine misnumbers as 39b).

3

Mancini,
the Unsuspected Eye-witness

THE manuscript entitled 'Dominicus Mancinus ad Angelum
Catonem de Occupatione Regni Anglie per Riccardum
Tercium Libellus' is in the Bibliothèque Municipale at Lille.
This unique copy had been noticed in print in 1841 and appeared again in a catalogue of 1897,[1] but remained unknown
to English historians until C. A. J. Armstrong gave a preliminary notice of it in a letter to *The Times* of 26 May 1934.
He published an edition and translation in 1936. The discovery of this authentic description of Richard's usurpation by
a detached observer was a major event. It would be an exag-
geration to say that it revolutionized studies of Richard III
(indeed, it was less influential than it should have been), but
apart from its intrinsic interest Mancini's report was of very
great value in providing historians for the first time with a
reliable yardstick against which to judge the accuracy of other
writers.

Mancini was an Italian friend and protégé of Angelo Cato,
Archbishop of Vienne, who was in London from some time
before the death of Edward IV to shortly after the coronation of
Richard III. When he returned to France his account of the
drama that had been staged during his stay in England proved
so fascinating that Cato made him write it down, with a view
to presenting a copy of the manuscript to one of his own
patrons, Federigo Prince of Taranto. The resulting account is
dated 1 December 1483, so Mancini wrote some four or five
months after leaving London early in July. He had recounted
the story many times in those months, so that his recollections
had already been shaped by repetition and the questions of
his hearers. He says frankly that he was reluctant to commit his
account to paper because he did not know the names of some
of those concerned, or their secret plans and intentions, and
because he was not sure of 'temporum intervallis'—meaning,

---

[1] These details, like the substance of the following account of Mancini, are
taken from Armstrong's introduction.

presumably, how much time had elapsed between the various incidents that he remembered.[1] This last is not so very surprising. Mancini was an elderly man by the standards of the time,[2] some of the events described took place outside London and their exact date would not be generally known, and some of the incidents of the usurpation succeeded each other so rapidly and unexpectedly that time must have become blurred in retrospect.[3] Moreover, Mancini was an outsider and did not feel directly affected by English affairs. He also warns his reader modestly that he cannot pretend that the account is complete in all details.[4]

Mancini's relation thus suffers somewhat, from the point of view of a historian avid for raw facts, from being a polished literary production written in a certain tradition for a specific audience, one of whom at least (Cato) was well informed on the subject already. The end of the story is also, necessarily, implicit in its beginning: the writer's declared aim is 'to describe in writing the machinations by which Richard III, the present king of England, attained the crown'.[5] Nevertheless, in setting his scene he strives to give a just account of Richard's initial reputation:

He very seldom went to court, but remained in his [northern] province, and set himself to win his people by distributing favours and handing out justice, so that by the good fame of his conduct and endeavours he attracted no little regard from outsiders. He was so renowned in war that whenever anything difficult and dangerous had to be done on behalf of the kingdom it would be entrusted to his advice and leadership. In these ways Richard obtained the goodwill of the people.[6]

Even though he was living in London at the time, as a foreigner who probably knew no English Mancini was dependent on informants. He does not specify who these were, apart from one reference to Edward V's physician, Dr. Argentine, and they may themselves have been outsiders. Armstrong points out that Mancini seems, indeed, better informed about

---

[1] p. 56.   [2] p. 1.   [3] Not, however, turned topsyturvy.
[4] 'You should not expect from me . . . that this account should be complete in all details: rather shall it resemble the effigy of a man, which lacks some of the limbs, and yet the beholder delineates for himself a man's form' (p. 57, Armstrong's translation). Happily, Mancini's style becomes less elaborate after his prefatory section.
[5] p. 56.   [6] pp. 62–4.

Edward IV and his court than about Richard,[1] so that his contacts may have been more closely connected with the old regime than the new. Happily they were good gossips. Mancini's short narrative is full of fascinating anecdotes and sidelights— Edward tried to subdue Elizabeth Woodville at the point of a dagger;[2] it was felt by the English that the king should marry a virgin;[3] Cecily Duchess of York was so enraged at Edward's marriage that she threatened to denounce him as a bastard;[4] Clarence was drowned in wine (rather surprising support, this, for a story told later by others);[5] the Archbishop of Canterbury promised the queen that her youngest son would be returned to sanctuary after his brother's coronation,[6] and so on. Mancini makes a few understandable mistakes, like thinking that the Duke of Gloucester had his estates in Gloucestershire,[7] and he has occasioned controversy by his description of multitudinous ceremonies connected with Richard's accession:

[Richard privately sent Buckingham to ask the 'principes' to decide on a king, and from fear they agreed to have Richard.] Next day the chief men met in the house of Richard's mother [i.e. Baynard's Castle], where Richard had purposely gone so that the affair should not be handled in the Tower, where the young king was held. There all the arrangements were made; oaths of allegiance were then given, and everything else necessary was done in due order. On the following two days the same was performed by the people of London and the higher clergy. For these three orders of men, who are called the three estates, debate all matters of difficulty and their decrees have authority.[8]

This suggests a rather confused foreigner who has had the composition of the English parliament explained to him, and perhaps himself witnessed one or more ceremonies whose exact nature he failed to grasp. Armstrong throughout the work translates *principes* as 'peers' or 'lords', but it could equally well have the looser meaning of 'chief men', such as the representatives summoned to attend parliament at London. The account would then square well enough with the traditional one that Buckingham addressed the mayor and aldermen, representatives of the livery companies and important peers at the Guildhall (a matter on which the London chronicles are

[1] p. 16. [2] p. 60. [3] p. 62. [4] p. 60. [5] p. 62. [6] p. 88.
[7] '200 miles from London', p. 70. [8] p. 96.

likely to be right), and that the quasi-parliamentary assembly
that met on 25 June then offered Richard the crown at Baynard's Castle through spokesmen. The reference to subsequent
ceremonies involving 'the people of London and the higher
clergy' may be a misinterpretation of happenings on 26 June
when Richard ascended the King's Bench in Westminster
Hall, was proclaimed, and rode in state to St. Paul's, where
he was met by the clergy in procession and received the
acclamation of the people.

Mancini's general vagueness about dates is tiresome, but
since he is out by two days when he does date the death of
Edward IV,[1] perhaps no dates are better than wrong ones.
At two places his rather loose chronology is a little misleading.
He starts Chapter Six with a description of how Richard,
when he felt secure from 'all those dangers he had first feared',
changed from mourning to royal purple after the execution of
Hastings, 'often' paraded himself through the streets, and
'each day entertained increasingly large numbers to dinner'.[2]
And he publicly showed his hand by suborning preachers
to put forth his claims. Now if Hastings was executed about
noon on Friday 20 June—the date which fits Mancini's chronology—and Sha's sermon was preached on the morning of
Sunday 22 June, Richard had scarcely time to indulge much
increasing ostentation between the two events. This is probably
one of the 'intervals of time' whose length Mancini had forgotten. He may also have found himself faced with a common
problem in fitting a description of background happenings into
a main story that depended on a series of striking events. He
had dealt with the downfall of Hastings, mentioned the
hunt for the Marquis of Dorset, and said that Richard finally
secured himself by executing Rivers and Grey (on 25 June in
point of fact). He then concluded Chapter Five by describing
the seclusion of Edward V and his brother and giving a short
section on Edward's personality and attainments, his fears
for his life, and the suspicion that he was already dead before
the writer left England in July. Taken literally, 'all those dangers Richard had first feared' should refer not only to opposition from Hastings, but also to the risk from Rivers which was

---

[1] 'Septimo Idus Aprilis moritur', p. 58.
[2] p. 94.

not ended until his death on 25 June, and even the continued existence of the rightful heirs to the throne. This literal timing is, of course, absurd: Mancini must mean simply that after 20 June when Hastings and his friends were safely out of the way, Richard first began to live with greater pomp and lavishness.

Mancini is, most unfortunately, equally vague when he says, after describing the sermons promoted to push Richard's claims: 'Interea dux omnes regni principes Londonias convocat. Putabant ii vocari tum ut necis Astinconis [Hastings] causas intelligerent, tum ut de coronando Eduardo iterum ageretur; quia tanta novitate sequta, coronatio in alium diem differenda videretur.'[1] Armstrong, who thought Hastings had died on 13 June, translates: 'In the meantime the duke summoned to London all the peers of the realm: the latter supposed they were called both to hear the reason for Hastings' execution, and to decide again about the coronation of Edward, for it seemed after such an unprecedented alarm that the coronation must be deferred.' But by the time the parliamentary representatives (rather than merely 'peers', surely) knew of the death of Hastings they must also have known that the coronation had been put off. The meaning is rather that the question of the coronation had come up again, because after so much upheaval it had been found necessary to defer the ceremony to a later date.

There is a tantalizing ambiguity in the passage about the proclamation issued after Hastings's execution (the only description of it that we have apart from More's). Mancini says:

But then the Duke [of Gloucester] at once quieted the people by announcing in a proclamation that a plot had been detected at the Tower, and the author of the plot, Hastings, had paid the penalty. All minds might therefore be set at ease. This was believed at first by the man in the street who lacked political expertise. Nevertheless, many spoke the real truth, namely that the plot had been invented by the duke, to escape the blame for so great a crime.[2]

Is Mancini suggesting merely that Richard invented the plot as a pretext to kill Hastings, or is he saying (after the event) that Richard accused Hastings of the very crime—an *insidias*

---

[1] Ibid.   [2] p. 90.

in arce, treason (or an ambush) within the Tower—that he was about to commit himself; that is, the murder of Edward V? In other words, is 'so great a crime' a reference to the murder of Hastings, or to the supposed death of the young king at that time which is adumbrated in the Cely note about the alleged Hastings plot?[1]

Mancini's relation supports the main outlines of the traditional account as given by Tudor historians, though it shows that certain of the later accretions of detail were untrue. There is at first sight a difference of opinion between Mancini and the Crowland chronicler about the disposition of Edward's treasure. The Crowland chronicler says that Richard seized it from Edward's executors at the same time as he determined to take the throne (whenever that was), and with his usual interest in financial affairs stresses that Richard consequently had plenty of money to lavish at the beginning of his reign.[2] According to Armstrong,

Mancini is unique in recording the partition of Edward IV's treasure by the queen, the marquess [of Dorset], and Sir Edward [Woodville]. This is damaging evidence against the Woodvilles. . . . The partition probably resulted in considerable loss to Richard duke of Gloucester and affords further explanation for his rapid impoverishment after his accession which the *Great Chronicle of London* (p. 234) attributes to his reckless purchase of friends.[3]

In fact, however, Mancini does not 'record' this partition; he merely says 'it is commonly believed' to have occurred,[4] and the accusation could have been made by the opposing faction.

The most interesting of Mancini's additions to our knowledge of the period are his story of how the two Genoese captains in Sir Edward Woodville's fleet saved all but two ships for Richard by intoxicating their guards,[5] and his description of Edward V, the doctor's report of his expectation of death, and the complete disappearance of the princes before Richard's coronation on 6 July.[6] Mancini also confirms a number of stories in later chronicles. Notably, he says that the sermons alleged the bastardy of Edward IV, as Polydore

---

[1] Above, p. 41.   [2] p. 567.   [3] pp. 119–20 n. 59.
[4] 'Regie pecunie . . . comparate inter reginam, marchionem et Eduardum creduntur distribute', p. 80.   [5] pp. 84–6.   [6] p. 92.

Vergil insists,[1] though Mancini also knows that the official
basis adduced later for Richard's claim was rather some sort
of pre-contract that invalidated Edward's marriage to Elizabeth Woodville.[2] (He says this was a proxy marriage arranged
by Warwick on the Continent. This was a persistent story, but
he was misinformed if he thought that it was given in official
documents—for the real ground see above, p. 47.) He
agrees with Bernard André and Vergil in saying that Edward
was reported to have appointed Richard protector in his
will,[3] and he states unequivocally that the princes' sequestra-
tion started shortly after the death of Hastings.[4] In other cases,
Mancini and More must at least have heard a similar tale.
More also knew about the captured Woodville armour exhibited to the people[5] (but does not give Mancini's explanation
that it had been collected for use against the Scots);[6] he
apparently knew that Cecily, Duchess of York, was vehemently
opposed to Edward's marriage (but either he did not know, or
preferred not to mention, the story that she claimed at that
point that Edward was illegitimate);[7] he had apparently heard
that the young King Edward made a spirited defence of Rivers
and Grey after their arrest at Stony Stratford,[8] and that he
pined when he found himself secluded in the Tower,[9] and he
complements Mancini's details about the quarrels between
Hastings and Dorset,[10] adding that they had brought Hastings
into royal disgrace and fear of his life at one moment.

Armstrong[11] and R. S. Sylvester[12] were greatly struck by these
similarities in the accounts of Mancini and More, which become less impressive when one considers the divergencies.
More and Vergil could conceivably have seen a copy of Mancini's work, but I think it must be thought unlikely that either
did. It is difficult to imagine that any sixteenth-century
chronicler could have resisted the story of how the Genoese
sailors tricked their guards, and still more improbable that
when the question of the fate of Edward V and his brother was
of burning interest and all kinds of dates and stories were
current, a historian with access to Mancini's work would not

[1] p. 94; Vergil (1844), pp. 184–5.   [2] p. 96.   [3] p. 60 and n. 7.
[4] p. 92.   [5] Yale *Works*, II. 24.   [6] p. 82.   [7] p. 62.
[8] p. 19; Mancini, p. 76.   [9] pp. 84–5.   [10] pp. 51, 225; Mancini, p. 68.
[11] p. xx.   [12] Yale *Works*, II..lxxiii.

have quoted him triumphantly as proof that the boys had
perished at their uncle's hands before his coronation', and
completed the relation with the young king's vision of himself
as a sacrificial victim and with references to the authority of
his doctor and the Italian who had left such a trustworthy
report in writing.

As I have indicated, although Mancini's account explains
much, it contains no shattering revelations. But Gairdner's
Life of Richard would have been very different had he known of
it. As it was, he was forced to rely very largely on 'tradition',
and when 'traditions' differed, there was nothing to say (since
in Gairdner's view a tradition that appeared relatively late
might be as reliable as an earlier one) whether Fabyan, Vergil,
or More might preserve the more authentic story. Since More
usually gave the most plausible and most circumstantial version, Gairdner often followed More, though he admitted on
occasion that not all More's details need be accepted. Sir
Clements Markham's attack on More's reliability was so
intemperate and backed by so little real fact, that it was not
apt to persuade Gairdner or his successors to reconsider this
standpoint.[1] Unfortunately, therefore, Mancini's work came to
light when the lines of battle had been fixed. His evidence
was not altogether welcome to either side. It was distinctly
awkward for the Markhamists, because it did much to destroy
the mystery of the princes' deaths, in so far as it was now plain
that as early as July 1483 Londoners believed them to be dead.
It also demolished the view that Richard's accession was
welcomed by contemporaries as right and just, and that
he was a most popular king until his reputation was destroyed
by the cunning propaganda of his enemies the Tudors and their
paid historians. (The counter-argument seems to be that Mancini was a prejudiced foreigner, almost certainly, since he wrote
in France, further corrupted by minions of the Earl of Richmond.[2]) More sober historians were disturbed for another
reason. Mancini's timing of the execution of Lord Hastings

---

[1] Cf. C. R. Markham, 'Richard III: a Doubtful Verdict Reviewed', *E.H.R.*
VI (1891), with riposte by Gairdner, 'Did Henry VII Murder the Princes?', ibid.;
and *Richard III* (1906).

[2] Cf. 'Richard III: a Correspondence', *History Today*, IV (1954), 707–8.

(discussed above, pp. 24–9) proved to support that of the Tudor chroniclers and to conflict with the sequence of events in the *Crowland Chronicle*. In the next chapter I shall show that the existing text of the *Crowland Chronicle* is not sufficiently reliable to impugn Mancini's accuracy on this point.

4   The 'Second Continuation' of the *Crowland Chronicle*: a Monastic Mystery

I

Some time after April 1486 one of the monks of Croyland, or in modern spelling Crowland, Abbey, near Peterborough in the Diocese of Lincoln, set out to bring up to date the history of the abbey, and of all England, kept by his house in a series of chronicles which had started with the time of King Penda of Mercia. The latest addition to the series (the 'first continuation'), compiled by a former prior, ended with the death of Abbot John Wysbech early in 1469. The new chronicler began the 'second continuation' by observing that his predecessor, a saintly man and somewhat unworldly, had skirted over some of the details of secular events during the period he had covered, so that he proposed to start his own addition by going back to October 1459.[1] The history of the Yorkist period which thus commences abruptly with the flight abroad of Warwick and York contains a number of incongruous passages dealing with matters of domestic concern to the abbey ('meanwhile, back here at Crowland . . .'), but in general bears more resemblance to the memoirs of such historians as Philippe de Commynes than to traditional monastic annals. It repeatedly states that it will end at the death of Richard III, but in fact continues beyond that point by giving brief notice of the coronation and marriage of Henry VII and the rising in the north in the spring of 1486, and by relating at length various quarrels between the abbey and its neighbours. The succeeding 'third continuation', which was incomplete in the version transcribed for William Fulman in the seventeenth century, concludes the series of Crowland chronicles with a little more detail about

---

[1] p. 549: 'praesupponenda sunt aliqua, quae a dicto Chronographo priore, tum sanctae religionis, quae rerum profanarum ignara esse solet, tum brevitatis studio, super expressiore declaratione praemissorum sunt.' Cf. also p. 575: 'Incepimus . . . adjuvantes religiosam laudabilemque ignorantiam Prioris hujus loci qui cetera compilavit, et quemque tanquam peritissimum rerum Divinarum, facta humana rectissime aliquando fallebant.'

events at the beginning of Henry's reign, and rehearses *in extenso* the documents relating to the settlement of the dispute between Crowland and Peterborough which was finally ended in April 1486.

The textual history of the series of Crowland chronicles is discussed at more length in the excursus to this chapter. The fullest text now extant is Fulman's printed version of 1684. This is a reasonably exact copy of a transcript made by an anonymous scribe and edited by Fulman himself, of which portions survive in the Bodleian Library, MS. Corpus Christi College B. 208.[1] The exemplar for the transcript is not identified, but may have been B.M. MS. Cotton Otho B. XIII, which in turn was a fair copy (apparently defective in places) deriving ultimately from lost manuscripts of a series of Crowland chronicles composed at different dates.[2] If Fulman's transcript accurately reflected its source, material at the end of the second continuation (with which we are largely concerned) had been disarranged, or never put into proper order, before it was copied by the scribe of the Cotton manuscript.

II   A COMPOSITE TEXT?

The traditional view about the authorship of this second continuation, as summarized by C. L. Kingsford in *English Historical Literature in the Fifteenth Century*,[3] had three elements:

1. The continuation was believed to have been composed at Crowland by one man, in the form in which we now have it.

2. It was written within a specified ten days in April 1486.

3. It was written by a Doctor of Canon Law, who had been one of King Edward IV's councillors and had been sent in the summer of 1471 on a mission to Charles the Bold, as stated in a marginal note. Kingsford and Gairdner apparently held that proposition (1) meant that the account was the work of the man described in proposition (3), that is, a diplomat who subsequently became a monk at Crowland.[4] Kingsford further

---

[1] C. L. Kingsford, *English Historical Literature in the Fifteenth Century* (Oxford, 1913), p. 179 n. 4; J. G. Edwards, 'The "Second" Continuation of the Crowland Chronicle: Was it Written "In Ten Days" ?', *B.I.H.R.* XXXIX (1966), 117 n. 1.

[2] The first, conceived largely as a relation of events concerning the abbey and a vehicle for charters, was probably forged about 1415: Riley, *Ingulph's Chronicle*, pp. ix–xii.   [3] p. 181.

[4] Gairdner, *Richard III*, p. 12 n. 2, 'the writer, who was one of Edward IV's

stated, rather illogically, that this man seemed to have written his account of the events of June 1483 'from personal experience', but was then 'no doubt in retirement, whether at Croyland or in sanctuary elsewhere'—a somewhat Pickwickian application of 'personal experience'.[1]

Sir Clements Markham retained the traditional idea of monastic provenance, but postulated the existence of two monkish writers; one who 'had probably once mixed in the world' (that is, been a member of the royal council), and a second who 'seems to have known nothing of the outside world'.[2] Markham thus rather casually introduced a new idea: the possibility that the second continuation was a dual composition. He failed, however, to discuss this hypothesis in any detail because he was principally interested in it as support for his theory that one of the monks—the naïve one—had reproduced lies fed to him by 'that unscrupulous intriguer' Bishop Morton. Here, as elsewhere in Markham's work, the intrusion of Morton, his mitred variant of King Charles's head, prevented Markham from pursuing the true significance of his insights, and dissuaded professional historians from giving any serious attention to his ideas.[3] The question of dual authorship was raised again in 1955, in rather similar terms, by Paul M. Kendall; only to be dropped when research appeared to demolish the main arguments for it. In his *Richard the Third* Kendall argued that 'there is considerable evidence to suggest that the materials, if not the actual writing, of most of this narrative, which appears to have been created at Croyland Abbey in the spring of 1486, is the work of John Russell, Bishop of Lincoln',[4] and went on to postulate that one of the monks,

---

Council'; p. 234 n. 1, 'amid the fens of Lincolnshire he knew little of the geography of the Midland district, and had misapprehended the intelligence which came to the monastery at the time'.

[1] *English Hist. Lit.*, pp. 182, 184.

[2] 'Richard III: a Doubtful Verdict Reviewed', pp. 254–5; *Richard III*, pp. 175–6. He thought the first monk's contribution ran from 1471 [*sic*] to the death of Edward IV.

[3] 'There is . . . not the slightest real ground for suspecting a dual authorship; the history presents every appearance of being the work of a single hand', Kingsford, *English Hist. Lit.*, p. 180.

[4] p. 432. At about the same time A. R. Myers ('Richard III: a Correspondence', p. 710) stated that the chronicle 'was clearly written by a councillor of Edward IV (possibly John Russell, Chancellor of Richard III)'.

'perhaps the Prior of the abbey', inserted the matter concerning the abbey, together with some comments of his own and 'an inaccurate and distorted account of Richard's last months which is in startling contrast to the authenticity of the preceding narrative'.[1] Elsewhere he contrasts 'the censorious monk who edited the "second continuation" ' with 'the learned statesman who provided much of the information'.[2]

At this point, while traditional assumptions (2) and (3) were still kept (that is, that the main account had been written by an ex-councillor at Crowland in April 1486), three new questions had been raised:

(a) Is the second continuation a wholly original, or an edited chronicle?

(b) If edited, what was the scope and nature of the editorial work?

(c) Can we identify the author or authors?

Kendall's views on these three aspects of the matter were presumably canvassed in a promised article by J. G. Edwards, George Lam, and P. M. Kendall,[3] but this never reached print, being superseded by an article by Sir Goronwy Edwards alone: 'The "Second" Continuation of the Crowland Chronicle: Was it written "in ten days"?'[4] This contained a masterly proof that the supposed colophon stating that the chronicle had been composed at Crowland in April 1486 is a misplaced sentence intended to refer to the formal process by which Crowland transferred to Peterborough the appropriation of the church of Bringhurst. Sir Goronwy thus convincingly demolished the second, and apparently central, traditional assumption about the composition of the chronicle. He also cast doubt on the validity of the third assumption, that the writer had been a councillor of Edward IV. This question I shall set aside for the moment, to concentrate on the problem of the nature of the extant text and its possible composite authorship. Sir Goronwy touched tangentially on this matter, but did not pursue it, contenting himself with referring to 'the author of the Second Continuation, whoever he was',[5] and to

---

[1] One important inaccuracy—the suggestion that the Duke of Norfolk and other of Richard's supporters fled from Bosworth—is a printer's error (see below, p. 100).   [2] *Richard III*, p. 317.   [3] Ibid., p. 499 n. 9.
[4] Cited in full above, p. 75 n. 1.   [5] p. 118.

an annotator who, at an undetermined date, added certain marginal notes.[1] In fact I would submit that Sir Goronwy's researches greatly strengthen the argument that two hands are involved throughout: one that of an independent chronicler of the rise and fall of the house of York, and the other that of a monk at Crowland who obtained a copy of this work and adapted it to the purposes of a monastic chronicle for the relevant period.

The anonymous Crowland monk who put together the second continuation of the abbey's chronicle, at a time when few monasteries still kept such records, certainly puts forward no claim to be himself the author of the main narrative. Indeed, he makes it tolerably clear that he was not. For a monk to say publicly that the previous chronicler was a most worthy religious but a poor historian of secular matters, so that he must go over part of the same ground again with a vastly superior account of his own, would be contrary to all ideas of monastic humility. The new chronicler surely meant that he had in his possession an authoritative account of the period to be covered, and realized that where it overlapped the existing official chronicle it gave a much better picture of affairs in the world—a *profana regni historia* ('secular history of the realm')[2]— which ought to be preserved. His own interpolations into this account are marked both by their subject-matter—domestic concerns of the abbey—and by differences in style, which are obscured by the standard but very old-fashioned translation by H. T. Riley. Edwards[3] notes the occurrence of what he describes as explanatory comments on the plan of the work, or 'stage directions' offered as guidelines by the author: remarks like the statement that Abbot Forsdyke's death occurred shortly after that of King Richard, 'quo cum reliqua describentes pervenerimus, universae hujus a nobis promissae historiae seriem concludemus' ('When we reach that point in our narrative we shall conclude the whole course of this history that we promised').[4] These seem much better explained as a redactor's attempts to fit his own material into an existing

---

[1] pp. 127–8.

[2] Thus, after one monastic digression, he says 'ad praedictam profanam Regni historiam redeamus' (p. 553).

[3] pp. 118, 120.   [4] p. 570.

coherent account. Where the author of the 'secular history' often writes in the first person singular, the redactor uses an editorial 'we' (for instance 'we are anxious to note first'),[1] or is elaborately impersonal: 'The continuation of these deeds will follow. But before the things to be described are entered upon . . . some matters have to be supplied';[2] 'Writing something of his life and fortunes when the pen reaches the year 1483'.[3]

Thus it is not the author of the 'secular history' but the Crowland redactor who begins abruptly by explaining his reasons for overlapping with the previous chronicle, and who gives near the end a summary of his (borrowed) material:

We began, to summarize, by supplying some gaps in the knowledge of the prior of this house, who had written the rest [i.e. the previous continuation]. He was expert in the things of God, and, in his admirable piety, very properly paid less attention to the deeds of men. We started with the threat of a battle at Ludlow between Henry VI and the Duke of York in 1459, and we have now come to the battle of Mirivale [i.e. Bosworth], which occurred on 22 August 1485. The account thus covers twenty-six years.[4]

It is especially noteworthy that in this last part of the continuation a distinction seems sometimes to be made between an editorial 'we' ('We began, to summarize . . .'), and a writer referred to in the third person: 'The foresaid writer decided';[5] 'Therefore the man who wrote this added to the history previously given a few lines of verse.'[6]

There is a further curious point which is observed but not explained by Edwards. Throughout the narrative the writer keeps stating his intention of ending his history with the death of Richard III. On page 577 of Fulman's text, near the end of the second continuation, it is again said that 'Since it is usual, in writing history, to be reticent about the actions of the living . . . the foresaid writer [not, in fact, identified previously] decided that with the death of King Richard he would end

---

[1] 'Cupimus enim praenotare', p. 549.

[2] 'Sequitur continuatio gestorum . . . Et tamen ante introitum describendarum rerum . . . praesupponenda sunt aliqua' (p. 549).

[3] 'De cujus vita et fortunis aliqua scribens, cum ad annum millesimum quadringentesimum octogesimum tertium calamum divertens' (pp. 560–1).

[4] p. 575.   [5] 'Statuit prefatus scriptor', p. 577 line 22.

[6] 'Addidit ergo praemissae historiae, ille qui haec scripsit, versus pauculos', ibid., lines 38–9.

his work.' The text blandly continues, 'Noting only this, that
. . . Henry married Elizabeth of York on 18 January 1486,
by dispensation of the pope, and that straight after Easter there
was a rising in the north (where all evil comes from) while
the king was there.' The writer has already mentioned local
happenings after Richard's death.[1] Why state so firmly that the
chronicle will not continue beyond 22 August unless that was
the point at which the original material did end, and the
Crowland redactor felt impelled to bring it a little more up to
date? And why, when the account has dealt with the battle of
Bosworth and remarked that Henry VII was hailed as a
saviour, say 'And so concludes the history . . . which we promised to set forth',[2] unless 'the history' was the text which the
redactor had had in front of him hitherto?

If we may judge the redactor on a text whose original is lost,
and which is admittedly corrupt in its present state, he does not
seem to have done his work very skilfully. Edwards showed
conclusively that in the last few pages of Fulman's text matter
concerning the abbey has been displaced, so that it is now
mixed up with the concluding portion of the chronicle of England. But even when the Crowland matter is removed to its
logical place at the end, the text of the rest remains remarkably
confused. The explanation seems to be that the redactor reproduced much of the original conclusion of his exemplar, but
tried to interpolate comments of his own and a poem, or poems,
from yet another source. To summarize very briefly, the conclusion of the account[3] now runs like this:

'. . . After the battle of Bosworth the new king Henry VII was received as an angel
from heaven. And so concludes the history which we promised to set forth up to the death
of the said King Richard, as the truth of things appeared; with no conscious additions
whether of falsehood, hatred or favour.'
We began, to summarize, by adding to the account of the former
prior . . . and came down to the battle of Bosworth. The account thus covers
twenty-six years.
Richard was the first king since the usurper Harold to fall in battle in his
own kingdom. Considering this, the badges of the Yorkists and Lancastrians, the way this battle avenged the sons of Edward IV, and the lives of
the three English kings called Richard, a certain versifier left these verses
written:
Poem I. 'verses of Richard on the three kings of the same name'.

[1] p. 576.   [2] p. 575 lines 18–20.   [3] p. 575 line 14 to p. 578 end.

In Fulman's text, monastic material is intruded at this point,[1] starting incongruously 'Among these events at the beginning of the new reign', and concluding abruptly with '. . . an account of the whole legal process is perhaps written by someone else in its place on a subsequent page, *since it is usual, in writing history, to be reticent about the actions of the living (otherwise, by describing their more reprehensible actions the author will make himself unpopular, and by praising their virtues he will get a reputation as a toady). The writer decided that with the death of King Richard he would end his work.*'[2]

'Noting this only' that after the victory of the said Henry VII he was crowned the next month [*sic*], and the hoped-for marriage with Elizabeth took place, yet he had to put down further trouble in the north.

'Therefore the man who wrote this added to the history previously given a few exhortatory verses on peace and tolerance, for the benefit of posterity, in these words':

11½ lines of Poem II.

'In which the poet alludes to the waste of the great preparations made against the French by King Edward IV, whose like will never be seen again.'[3]

Remaining 9½ lines of Poem II.

Poem III, in praise of Crowland.

Misplaced lines dating the conclusion of the legal process between Crowland and Peterborough, reading 'These things were performed and concluded at Crowland in 1486, in the space of ten days, the last being the last day of April in that year.'[4]

I suggest that the italicized matter probably represents the conclusion of the original or ur-text, and that the rest has been added by the Crowland redactor. There are several puzzles, however. It is not altogether clear whether Poem II was in the ur-text as a conclusion, or whether the redactor made it up himself; that is, whether 'the man who wrote this' ('ille qui haec scripsit') refers to the original author or the redactor, and whether 'the poet alludes' ('alludit metrista') is a gloss by the redactor or a subsequent copyist. Neither is it clear whether Poem I on the three Richards—introduced as the work of 'a certain poet' (apparently called Richard)—was found in the ur-text or not. Possibly not, since the redactor seems to have thought it necessary to preface a lengthy explanation at the cost of disrupting his narrative rather seriously. In this

---

[1] p. 576 line 3 to p. 577 line 20.

[2] The punctuation is Fulman's.

[3] This particular disruption was due to Fulman's printer: below, p. 100.

[4] 'Acta sunt haec et expleta apud Croylandiam, Anno Domini millesimo quadringentesimo octogesimo sexto, per spatium decem dierum quorum postremus fuit ultimus dies mensis Aprilis ejusdem anni.'

connection, it is curious that of the three historical manuscripts which Leland found in the library of Crowland Abbey before 1542, one was a 'History of King Richard written in song'.[1] By 'King Richard' did Leland mean Richard I, Richard II, or the most recent and notorious Richard, and if the last, was this manuscript of the monastery's the source from which the Crowland redactor took Poem I?[2]

The substance of the sentence 'And so concludes the history which we promised . . .' has a ring of the original author's style, and so does 'Since it is usual, in writing history . . . he would end his work'. I have consequently suggested that one may have run on from the other in the original. But the difficulty of disentangling the first author's work from the editor's is illustrated by the passage 'And so concludes the history . . .', which runs in the Latin: 'Et ita finit historia quam usque ad exitum dicti regis Richardi, quoad veritas gestorum se menti offerebat, sine ulla scita intermixtione mendacii odii aut favoris, declarare promisimus.' In a previous passage,[3] after the description of the legal quarrel between Richard and his brother Clarence, the text reads: 'Transeo faciliter rem incurabilem . . . residuum historiae quoad menti occurrit, libera voce, nullo scienter admixto mendacio, prosequi dignum duxi' ('I readily pass over what cannot be mended . . . and have thought it fit to set forth the rest of the history in the way that it strikes me, speaking freely and, as far as I am aware, without falsehood'). This is very similar, which may mean either that the author repeated himself, or that his editor paraphrased his earlier sentence. A firmer deduction is that if the ur-text finished with an explanation of the author's reasons for choosing to stop at the death of Richard III, and perhaps the verses on peace (Poem II), the existing text has been dislocated not only through the accidental misplacing of material that Edwards demonstrated, but also by ill-assimilated insertions of new material by the Crowland redactor.

The 'second continuation' of the Crowland chronicles is thus a composite work in its present state. In 1486 or later the official

---

[1] *J. Lelandi De Rebus Brittanicis Collectanea*, ed. Thomas Hearne, IV (2nd edn., 1774), 30.
[2] Most probably, however, Leland meant some English ballad on Richard I.
[3] p. 557.

chronicler of the monastery obtained a copy of some authoritative memoirs of the Yorkist period, which he adapted to his purpose by adding material of local interest and by editing the original to an undetermined extent. In so far as much of the work preserves these original memoirs virtually unaltered, it is, as earlier historians assumed, an independent and authentic record of events between 1459 and 1485. But in places the surviving text is in a very corrupt condition. This has a particularly important bearing on the distortion which seems to have occurred in the portion describing events between Richard's seizure of Edward V and his accession on 26 June, where the original account may have been condensed and has almost certainly been rearranged in part—a matter discussed in the excursus to chapter 6.

Further, it is by no means clear that the so-called 'third continuation' is in fact distinct from the second continuation. The separation between the two which occurs in Fulman's edition was made by Fulman himself: the transcript from which he worked shows no break at this point. (Neither, admittedly, does it indicate a break between the first and second continuations, which were certainly compiled by different authors. This was probably because in the Cotton manuscript, the putative source, a single copyist was at work throughout.) There are two matters which could have led Fulman to deduce that the third continuation was added later by a different author. In the first place, the compiler of the second continuation says that fuller details of the settlement between Crowland and Peterborough (made in April 1486) may perhaps be given later by someone else: '[The abbot] obtained letters patent from the king directed to the abbot and monastery of Peterborough. Of which, and all the process which ensued, there is perhaps something written by someone else in the proper place on a later page.'[1] The documents are in fact transcribed at the end of the 'third' continuation (pp. 582–93), but this task could well have been delegated to a different scribe.[2]

---

[1] 'De quibus et toto processu inde secuto scribetur fortasse per aliquem alium inferius latius loco suo', p. 577.

[2] The 'third continuator' has the same habit of deferring material: 'But about [Henry's titles to the throne] perhaps something will be said later ['fortasse inferius']', p. 581. In this case the matter is not taken up again, at least in the surviving incomplete text.

Secondly, the 'third' continuation starts with a reference to the previous work of an unknown author who stopped at the death of Richard III:

> Whoever it was who narrated the above chronicle concluded his work at a point beyond which he refused to go, for the reasons he states. Nevertheless, from time to time I find a matter worthy of record, and if it is not immediately put into writing it will be forgotten or inaccurately reported. So I propose, by continuing the preceding chronicle, to set an example to later writers, so that they will follow our custom and record the events of their time as they occur.[1]

I have argued that the writer of the 'secular history' which concluded with Richard's death ('whoever he was'), was not the Crowland monk who edited it for the second continuation, which does go beyond that point. The identity of this editor was surely known to his fellow monks. Moreover, despite his fine protestations about the many noteworthy events that have since happened, the writer of the third continuation gets no further, chronologically, than the compiler of the second continuation, namely 30 April 1486.[2] There is no real reason to suppose that the writer who now takes up the story in the first person singular is other than the previous redactor. The text at the close of the second continuation is, indeed, so confused that it is possible that the redactor's contributions to it, together with the so-called 'third' continuation, were no more than draft additions written variously in margins and on separate pieces of paper, which a later copyist has tried to cast into the form of connected narrative. A similar process has been vividly described by E. Ph. Goldschmidt.[3] If a monk left his work unbound, other monks who later dealt with the sheets would have been unable to distinguish the final redaction of certain chapters from discarded drafts, the notes to be used from the passages into which they had been worked; they might be at a loss about the proper order in

[1] p. 581.

[2] Although the conclusion of the volume was already lacking when Fulman's transcript was made some time before 1684, on p. 53 of the transcript (corresponding to p. 582 of the printed text) there is a marginal note (apparently copied from the original MS.) to the effect that 'From this place to the end of the book nothing more is included beyond the instruments of the concession of the church of Bringhurst or Eston to the Abbey of Peterborough'. The printed text omits the matter preceding 'concession'.

[3] *Medieval Texts and their First Appearance in Print* (Bibliographical Society, 1943), p. 93, quoted by Sylvester, [Yale] *Works of St. Thomas More*, II. xix.

which these written scraps should be placed. If we keep these conditions in mind, we shall quite easily understand why in so many of our medieval books as they have come down to us we find quite uncalled for repetitions, whole inserted pieces recognisably taken from other authors, a chain of argument abruptly ending in the middle of a sentence, taken up again from its first premises thirty pages later, and so on.

There is one other odd thing about the 'third continuation': yet another vaguely identified writer appears in connection with a rather irrelevant account of the death of Cardinal Beaufort, who died in Easter week 1447, just as Cardinal Bourchier, Archbishop of Canterbury, died at Easter 1486. The anecdote of Beaufort's edifying end is introduced with 'While I am writing this, there occurs to me, among other things to be remembered . . .',[1] and concludes 'Indeed, the man who wrote this was present then, and saw and heard all these things, and we know that his testimony is true.'[2] If it were the writer of the third continuation himself who claimed to have been present at the death-bed of Cardinal Beaufort, he would hardly vouch for his own authority with the words 'we know that his testimony is true' (note also the change from singular 'I' to plural 'we'). Once again, therefore, we have a mysterious 'qui haec scripsit' which seems to refer to an independent author to whose work a Crowland chronicler had access. Was the author of the account which is the basis of the second continuation present at the death of Cardinal Beaufort in 1447, and if so, was this anecdote part of his original narrative? Or was the chronicler referring to some monastic source? The problem is tantalizingly similar to the claim in Grafton's earlier editions of More's *Richard III* that 'I myself that wrote this pamphlet truly knew' the details of Edward IV's last illness, and equally insoluble.[3]

---

[1] 'Haec quidem mihi in praesentiarum commemoranti, occurrit inter scribendum', p. 582. Note the use of gerundives, typical of the redactor of the 'second' continuation.

[2] 'Qui enim haec scripsit, affuit, et haec omnia vidit et audivit, et scimus quod verum est testimonium ejus', p. 582. Similar, but more sweeping, claims are made in the Lansdowne MS. of John Hardyng's chronicle (B.M. MS. Lansdowne 200, quoted H. Ellis, ed., *The Chronicle of Iohn Hardyng* (1812), p. xiv), e.g. 'Nota quod totam Cronicam istius Henrici Regis [IV] compilator hujus Libri audivit, vidit et interfuit. Et ut patet clarus in quadam Cronica Magistri Norham doctoris theologie [unidentified].'

[3] Below, Appendix, pp. 203-4.

III   THE ORIGINAL AUTHOR

The 'second continuation' relates that after the return of Edward IV in 1471, Charles Duke of Burgundy sent ambassadors to him to propose a joint expedition against France. After careful consideration it was decided that the king should send someone in his service to talk fully with Charles and report back.

There was therefore sent one of the king's councillors, a Doctor of Canon Law, who had to go by way of Boulogne as Calais had not yet been restored to Edward's rule. He met the Duke at a great and well-fortified town on the Somme called Abbeville . . . By this brief embassy the foundations were laid for the great preparations, to be mentioned later, for restoring the king's rights in France.[1]

In the margin of Fulman's edition, following the transcript in MS. Corpus Christi B. 208 (the parallel passage in the Cotton manuscript is lost), 'unus ex consiliariis regis, Doctor in jure canonice' is glossed 'Ille qui hanc historiam compilavit'. This seems to be a valuable clue to the authorship of the original account, but in the article already cited Sir Goronwy Edwards advanced reasons for thinking that the marginal comment was neither attributable to the author himself nor intended to suggest that the Doctor of Canon Law was responsible for the whole work.[2] On the second point he postulated that *hanc historiam* meant the particular anecdote about a secret embassy to Charles the Bold; a 'story', not 'the history'. I find this argument unconvincing. If 'story' were meant, I agree with Sir Goronwy that the gloss is unlikely to have been added by the author himself, because he nowhere else gives another person as specific authority for one of his statements. Had he wished to do so in this case, he would have said something to the effect that 'this incident was related to me by the man concerned'. The word *compilavit* seems inappropriate, too, in connection with a single incident whose authenticity was being avouched. If the comment is supposed to be due to an annotator who was merely inserting marginal heads, he would have been more likely to write something like 'Embassy to Duke Charles'. Even if one supposes that the words 'Doctor in jure

[1] p. 557.   [2] pp. 126-9.

canonico', now in the text, originally also stood in a marginal annotation, this would be a surprising and pointless comment for an annotator to add to a rather unimportant anecdote. I think it is far more likely that the words 'ille qui hanc historiam compilavit' bear their obvious meaning of 'the person who composed this chronicle', and that in this instance Edwards has not succeeded in disproving the traditional view.[1] The real objection to the original view was that it necessitated supposing that one of Edward's councillors, who showed intimate knowledge not only of the diplomacy and administration of Edward IV but also of events at court under Richard III, had retired to a monastery (before the battle of Bosworth, if not in 1483), where he immediately took a close, pious, and informed interest in local affairs, wrote a continuation of the monastic chronicles, and was quite unknown to the writer of the so-called third continuation, who goes out of his way to mention the previous author, with the characterization 'whoever he may have been'. But if the 'second continuation' is seen as basically the independent work of a statesman contemporary with Edward and Richard which was adopted and altered to fit the scope of a monastic chronicle by a member of the monastic community, the difficulty disappears, and the identification of the author with one of Edward's diplomats becomes entirely plausible. The general tone and preoccupations of his work are by no means incompatible with this identity, and indeed the writer seems especially interested both in foreign relations and in the preparations, especially financial, for the French expedition which, as he says, resulted from the initial overture with which he is associated. He did not, of course, make the clumsy insertions of passages dealing with incidents of purely local interest to Crowland, nor did he add a marginal note to the previous chronicle—the first continuation—drawing attention to his own superior description of the reconciliation between Warwick and Edward IV in 1469.[2] This must have been done by the redactor.

[1] I think, further, that the phrase may originally have been in the text, not the margin, as the author's own self-identification—possibly, therefore, in the form 'ego qui hanc historiam compilavi'.

[2] The first continuation says (p. 543) nothing about Edward IV's imprisonment at Middleham, and relates, absurdly, that after the battle of Edgecote the Archbishops of Canterbury and York, the Duke of Clarence, and the Earl

The most interesting suggestion about authorship so far made has been that by Kendall and A. R. Myers, that John Russell, Bishop of Lincoln and Richard's chancellor, was responsible for the underlying account. The two main grounds for the identification were presumably that Russell was indeed a Doctor of Canon Law and member of Edward's council, and that he was present at Crowland during April 1486 when the chronicle was supposedly compiled. The argument from date was demolished by Edwards, but the argument from Russell's known career deserves further consideration.[1]

Unfortunately we do not know who was entrusted with this particular mission to Charles the Bold. It was an unofficial *pourparler*, and the details were not recorded.[2] The expression 'councillor' did not necessarily mean a permanent member of the king's council,[3] and we have no complete lists of the members of Edward's council or the holders of the degree of Doctor of Canon Law for the relevant period. Russell is not the only possible candidate. But it can be said that he was a likely person for Edward to choose for the embassy: in 1470 he had been a leader of the delegation that conferred the Garter on Charles (the oration which he delivered was printed and is extant). He also took part in the embassy to treat with the Hanse Towns at Utrecht in 1473–4, which is noted in the

---

of Warwick hastened to cheer the king up with protestations of loyalty. Although he at first sulked, he then took them back into favour. A marginal note reads 'Certitudo hujus historiae sub aliis terminis veritati subnixis inferius declarabitur' ('the certainty of this story will be declared below, in other terms which rest on the truth'). The second continuation (pp. 551–2) says Warwick was forced to let Edward escape from custody, because he required his backing to collect troops. Edwards (p. 128 and n.) mistakenly describes this marginal note as referring to the *breach* between Edward and Warwick. It may be noted further that the redactor of the second continuation appears to edit it by omitting a description of Edward's accession with the remark that it has already been noticed by the first continuator: 'modis quibus memoratus Chronographus supra descripserat' (p. 550).

[1] The best outline is given in A. B. Emden, *A Biographical Register of the University of Oxford to A.D. 1500* (Oxford, 1957).

[2] Miss Scofield, however, identified the emissary as Russell on the evidence of the Issue Roll, Easter 11 Edward IV (*Edward IV*, II. 16 n. 2). On this basis she suggested that the author of the second continuation might have been one of Russell's entourage.

[3] J. R. Lander, 'Council, Administration and Councillors, 1461–1485', *B.I.H.R.* XXXII (1959), 151. The term could be applied in connection with diplomatic missions and negotiations.

chronicle;[1] he accompanied Edward on the expedition to
France in 1475, whose outcome is vividly described;[2] and in
1474 he was involved in the negotiations for the betrothal
between the son of James III of Scotland and Edward's
daughter Cecily, which the chronicler also mentions.[3] In fact
quite a distinct picture can be formed of the personality and
interests of the chronicler, and none of it is inconsistent with
what little we know about Russell. Our information about
Russell is that he was a good civil servant—well briefed and
tactful, one supposes, since he handled tricky negotiations—
but probably one with a distaste for politics, since Rous says
that he was reluctant to take office as chancellor,[4] and he was
a highly respected scholar (possibly of a rather old-fashioned
kind).[5] He was much distressed to find Lollard doctrines
current in Oxford in 1491.[6] It is possible to deduce from Stallworth's letter[7] that he was dismayed and alarmed by Richard's
bid for the throne, but frightened by the fate of Richard's
bolder opponents, and from the extant drafts of his parliamentary addresses that he was pious, rather conservative, and
wrote more elegantly in Latin than in English.[8] In the projected conclusion to his speech to the parliament of June 1483
he proposed to introduce the dramatic touch of himself assuming the role of the young king in welcoming the Duke of
Gloucester as protector, so that he was a man of some histrionic sense.

[1] p. 558. For details of the lengthy negotiations see Scofield, *Edward IV*, II.
63 ff.   [2] pp. 558–9.

[3] p. 562. Another instance of special knowledge may be his reference to the
projected escape of the princesses; above, p. 49.

[4] Below, p. 119. S. B. Chrimes says mistakenly that Russell was dismissed from
the chancellorship on 29 July 1485 (*English Constitutional Ideas in the Fifteenth Century*, Cambridge, 1936, p. 167). It is difficult to see why he describes him as a
'trimmer' (ibid.).

[5] More describes him as 'a wise man and a good and of much experience, and
one of the best learned men undoubtedly that England had in his time' (Yale
Works, II. 25).

[6] Cf. his note at the beginning of his excerpts from the works of Thomas Walden:
Bodleian, University Coll. [not, as given by Emden, New College] MS. 156.

[7] Above, p. 42.

[8] *Grants . . . of Edward V*, ed. Nichols, pp. xxxix ff. Interestingly, both chancellor
and chronicler find occasion to cite Roman history with reference to the career
of Marcus Emilius Lepidus: the first to his tutelage of the young Ptolomy (ibid.,
p. xlviii), the second to the proscriptions during the triumvirate of Octavius,
Antony, and Lepidus (*Crowland Chron.*, p. 570).

In the case of the chronicler, the style is genuinely the man himself, since we are dealing with an unknown writer. The account is carefully organized and the language is often terse and even epigrammatic:

Taceo, hoc temporum interstitio, inventum esse corpus Regis Henrici in turri Londoniarum examine: parcat Deus et spatium poenitentiae ei donet, quicunque tam sacrilegas manus in Christum domini ausus est immittere; unde et agens, tyranni, patiensque, gloriosi martyris titulum mereatur.[1]

('I say nothing of the fact that at this moment the lifeless body of King Henry was found in the Tower of London. May God spare the man (whoever he was) who dared lay sacrilegious hands on our ruler in Christ, and grant him time for repentance. The doer of this deed deserves the name of butcher, as the victim deserves that of glorious martyr.')

Throughout (except finally at the battle of Bosworth) the author writes clearly and authoritatively of events, leaving a plain impression that he was himself present on many occasions, and knew what was going on on others. He gives his own opinion about the execution of Clarence: 'But privately (as I judge) the king frequently repented it.'[2] He carefully analyses the cause of the dissension between Edward and the Earl of Warwick, and explains that, whatever the usual opinion, it was really due to Warwick's annoyance when Margaret of York was married to the Duke of Burgundy: 'I consider this a better reason for the dissent between the king and the earl than the one cited above, that is to say the king's marriage to Queen Elizabeth.'[3] (In fact, this marriage is not mentioned earlier in the second continuation. Either, as I think likely, the ur-text started at a much earlier point in Yorkist history than 1459, or the redactor has here altered his source and inserted a reference to one of the errors he has remarked in the first continuation.) In the light of such claims to knowledge, the author's occasional qualifications take on particular significance. Exceptionally, Richard's account of his dream on the eve of Bosworth is not reported at first hand, but qualified by 'ut asseritur' ('as it is claimed').[4] Most tellingly, among the events early in 1484 the author gives a detailed description

---

[1] p. 556.   [2] p. 562.
[3] p. 551. The first continuation (p. 542) says that Edward discarded Warwick in favour of the queen's relations.   [4] p. 574.

of the signing of an oath of allegiance to Richard's son, 'one day in February, in the afternoon, in a lower room near the passage leading to the queen's apartments at Westminster', but he remarks that it was 'a new kind of oath, formulated by some persons unknown to me'.[1] This small confession of ignorance, which no writer at second hand would think of inserting, surely indicates that the author was in fact present, and would ordinarily have expected to be informed on this point.

The whole account in general reflects its writer's interests and expertise. He was well informed about foreign relations, especially with France and Burgundy, interested in Edward's mercantile dealings, and particularly concerned with financial matters, on which his knowledge extended even to the price of the Scottish war of 1482 and the annual defence costs of Berwick: 'This small gain (or should I say loss, since holding Berwick consumes an annual ten thousand marks?) cost the king and country over a hundred thousand pounds at this time.'[2] Probably it was professional interest that caused him to insert a paragraph about Henry VI's style at the readeption (Russell was secondary of the privy seal office 1469–74 and keeper of the privy seal 1474–83): 'Now everything was again issued in the name of King Henry, and letters patent, writs, mandates, deeds and all kinds of documents were published with a reference to the fact that this was the king's second period of government, like this: "The forty-eighth year of the reign of Henry VI and the first year of his readeption".'[3] It may also have been the original author who launched into an explanation of the various methods of dating the year, 'for the instruction of young people, who may not understand the variety of computations',[4] but the passage has a didactic ring more reminiscent of the redactor. The writer sardonically observed details at court, such as the new fashion introduced by Edward in 1482[5] and the fact that Queen Anne and Elizabeth of York were scandalously dressed alike at Christmas 1484;[6] he states bluntly, and interestingly, that Richard was usually afraid to go against the advice of Ratcliff and

---

[1] 'Quodam formatum a quibus nescio, novum sacramentum de adhaerendo Regis filio unico', pp. 570–1.

[2] p. 563.   [3] p. 554.   [4] pp. 552–3.   [5] p. 563.   [6] p. 572.

Catesby,[1] and he accurately reports Richard's meeting with the chief citizens at Clerkenwell to deny the rumours that he would marry his niece, as is shown by the minutes of the Mercers' Company.[2] His accuracy here extends to verbal details: Richard told the citizens that 'it never came in his thought or mind to marry in such manner wise . . . with much more in the premisses spoken', and according to the 'Crowland' chronicler, at a previous council meeting 'the king was constrained to exculpate himself, by denying at great length that the thing had ever entered his head'. He also, alone among fifteenth- and sixteenth-century chroniclers, accurately reports the grounds on which Richard's accession was legitimized by parliament—with a fine scorn for a lay body that presumed to pronounce upon a matter of canon law.[3]

It is clear that the account is a personal one. The author says that he is giving the facts without conscious bias, but 'quoad veritas gestorum se menti offerebat':[4] as he saw things himself. He is usually remarkably definite about their nature, and expresses his views incisively and sometimes with wit:

Great numbers of people openly ascribed the restitution of this most pious king [Henry VI] to a miracle, and this change in affairs to the work of Him who sitteth on the right hand of the Highest. But the judgements of God are incomprehensible, and his ways unknowable. It is well enough attested that scarcely six months later there was no one who dared admit that he had been in Henry's confidence.[5]

I readily pass over this [quarrel between Richard and Clarence], not minding what cannot be mended, and abandoning unruly personages to the rule of their own wills.[6]

Now each began to view the other with something less than brotherly love. Toadies—the sort of men to be found in all princely courts—scurried from one brother to the other, carrying back and forth anything that was said, however privately.[7]

And of Charles the Bold ('le Téméraire'): 'Meanwhile, Charles Duke of Burgundy, with no lack of spirit, not to say rashly ['ne temerarie dicam'], pushed forwards.'[8] Dramatic flourishes are not absent: of the reaction of the Duke of Burgundy and Louis XI to Edward's final victory over the Lancastrians,

---

[1] Ibid.   [2] Ibid.; above, pp. 51–3.
[3] pp. 567, 570.   [4] p. 575.   [5] p. 554.
[6] 'Transeo faciliter rem incurabilem, sine cura, et dimittens homines voluntarios voluntati', p. 557.   [7] p. 561.   [8] Ibid.

'Who was then more gleeful than Charles? . . . Who more downcast than Louis?'[1] Or, 'Sed pauculis post haec verba elapsis diebus, extrema hujus gaudii luctus occupavit' ('But within a very few days of this speech, the end of elation was grief').[2] The author's attitudes are generally urbane and relatively detached, however. He reserves praise for very few of his contemporaries—Bishop Courtenay,[3] Sir Thomas St. Leger.[4] (Morton and Rotherham are no more than 'important prelates'.)[5] His blame, until he comes to the usurpation of Richard, is chiefly for the cunning and untrustworthy Louis XI,[6] to whose subtle faithlessness Bishop Russell ascribed part of the 'pensifous sikenesse' that killed Edward,[7] and his disgust is for uncivilized behaviour on the part of the great, and for breaches of legal decorum:

It is repugnant to describe what happened at the next parliament. The dispute between two brothers of such status[8] was a sorry affair. The king alone accused the duke; the duke alone replied to the king. A number of people were brought forward, but it was quite unclear whether they were supposed to be prosecutors or witnesses. The dual role hardly fits a single person in the same case. The duke turned off all the charges with denials, offering, if allowed, to uphold his cause with his own hand. There is no need to dwell on the matter. The members of parliament thought hearsay accusations[9] were sufficient, and drew up a condemnation.[10]

If the internal evidence so far discussed points to Russell as much as to any of the known candidates for authorship, does the sparseness of the record of events in May and June 1483 rule out a man who had become chancellor early in May? The question is complicated by the fact that the text shows signs of disturbance at this place. But it is unlikely that the redactor has robbed us of highly detailed and frank revelations about the usurpation from a man who was intimately involved. The author may well have been intimately involved, but he appears to have preserved a good deal of reticence on the subject. When they are closely examined, his very reticences, how-

---

[1] p. 556.   [2] p. 566.
[3] 'Venerabilis Pater Petrus Episcopus Exoniensis, flos militiae patriae suae', p. 574.
[4] 'Unus nobilissimus Miles', p. 568. Are the Devon connections significant?
[5] 'Duo praelati majores', p. 566.   [6] p. 563.
[7] *Grants . . . of Edward V*, pp. lii–liii.   [8] 'Tantae humanitatis'.
[9] 'Auditas informationes'.   [10] p. 562.

ever, help connect the account with Russell. In the first place, alone among major chroniclers of Richard III, the author fails to mention the dismissal of Thomas Rotherham, Archbishop of York, as chancellor, and the appointment of John Russell, Bishop of Lincoln. In the second, the *Crowland Chronicle* does say that on the day of Hastings's execution, the protector had cunningly divided the council so that part met, with Hastings, Morton, and Rotherham, at the Tower, and the rest assembled at Westminster.[1] But it is left to Polydore Vergil to tell us that the chairman of the neutral party, sent to Westminster away from the violence, was Russell.[2] And according to Simon Stallworth,[3] one of the 'many others' who in the *Crowland Chronicle* accompany the Archbishop of Canterbury on his mission to persuade Queen Elizabeth to hand over her younger son to Richard was again the chancellor, Russell.

Psychologically, it is quite credible that Russell would deal with the events of June 1483 as briefly as possible. For one thing, what chiefly struck the chronicler in retrospect was the high-handedness shown by Gloucester and Buckingham, and the swiftness with which they acted throughout the whole affair. He remarks of the executions of Rivers, Grey, and Vaughan that this was the second shedding of innocent blood 'in hac subtanea mutatione': in this sudden reversal.[4] Men's satisfaction at the prospect of a peaceful and steady reign by the young Edward V is shattered, just as Hastings's jubilation suddenly becomes horror-stricken grief.[5] He also remembers that people were terrorized by Richard's quick dispatch of the king's loyal supporters—'caeterisque omnibus fidelibus ejus similia formidantibus'—and by the threatened arrival of troops 'in frightening and unheard-of numbers'[6]—both popular reactions that are echoed in Stallworth's letter of 21 June. The brevity of the account serves to reflect the bewildering speed of the events which took people unawares between about 13 June and 26 June.

But also, men who were in the position of serving as advisers to Edward V and as officials in his government felt a personal responsibility for his fate. The council had appointed

---

[1] p. 566.   [2] English trans. (1844), p. 180.
[3] Above, p. 42.   [4] p. 567.   [5] p. 566.
[6] 'Evocatis hominibus armatis in numero terribili et inaudito', ibid.

Richard protector, and then agreed to obtain the person of the young Duke of York so that he might attend his brother's coronation, confidently expected in a few days' time. Almost immediately they found that they had been duped, and had unwittingly betrayed the prince. Richard promptly revealed his intention of dispossessing his nephews, and showed how much he was in earnest by executing the Lord Chamberlain and imprisoning the Archbishop of York and the Bishop of Ely when they opposed his plans. Amid the general shock and horror, Russell, who had taken office reluctantly in the first place, found himself forced to acquiesce in, and indeed lend official countenance to, Richard's coup. If some years later he came to write a personal account of events, he might well feel extreme reluctance to linger over a period which he remembered with such intensity of dismay and shame.

IV   DISSEMINATION OF THE ACCOUNT

I have not discussed the possibility of Russell's authorship at length in an attempt to establish the unprovable. It is too easy to forget how very little we really know about this period, and to fit the few familiar names to any unidentified actor. When the *Crowland Chronicle* says that the petition to Richard to ascend the throne was supposedly conceived in the north, but everyone knew who was behind it in London,[1] Riley observes that this is 'in allusion, no doubt, to the Duke of Buckingham'.[2] He may be right, but how did he know? Why, for instance, Buckingham rather than Catesby? (In fact, I think Richard himself must be meant.) The chronicler's remarks about the murderer of Henry VI are another case in point.[3] He asks God to grant time for repentance to the man responsible for a deed 'for which the doer deserves the name of "tyrannus",[4] the victim, that of triumphant martyr'. This is usually taken to imply that either Edward IV or Richard III

[1] p. 567: 'It was then rumoured that this roll had been conceived in the north, whence such a large force was expected in London. But nobody was ignorant of the identity of the sole originator of the great sedition and on-going infamy in London.'

[2] *Ingulph's Chronicle*, p. 489 n.   [3] p. 556.

[4] The Classical meaning is 'usurper' or 'despot'. The word has always had this primary sense in English, but in Middle and Early Modern English (and so Latin) it could further mean a ruffian or hired bully.

was held responsible (in which case, the time for repentance must have been in purgatory). Without preferring any charge, one might mention as an example of a person upon whom contemporary suspicion could have rested, Robert Radcliffe, who was still alive when the chronicle was probably written, and had been custodian of Henry VI at the time of his death.[1]

But if the author was not Russell, it must have been someone very like him: a man in authority who wrote with corresponding knowledge, and it is improbable that he produced his polished work for such a narrow audience as the monks of Crowland. His reluctance to treat of contemporary history lest he damage his reputation seems less a literary device than desire to avoid offence to highly placed men with whom he was still in contact, and his reluctance to describe the wicked methods of Richard's tax-collectors lest others be seduced[2] also argues for wider circulation. A copy of his manuscript evidently came into the possession of Crowland Abbey (probably, if the author was Russell, through the abbey's connection with some member of their bishop's staff). Other copies may have circulated more widely, and I shall later argue that one was used by Vergil. The mere fact that perishable manuscripts no longer exist is not surprising in the normal course of things.[3] In this case copies might be said to contain the seeds of their own destruction, because the author rehearsed the argument of the Act of Settlement (1484) that defined Richard's title to the throne.[4] This had been repealed by Henry's first parliament of 1485-6, with the decree that all copies of it or rehearsals of its substance were to be destroyed.[5] Under Henry, therefore, the chronicle contained seditious matter, and it might be imprudent to have it in one's possession. This may seem far-fetched, but historians were credited with greater influence in those days, and one should not forget the care

---

[1] A. R. Myers, ed., *English Historical Documents, 1327-1485* (1969), p. 317, quoting Exchequer of Receipt, Issue Rolls (E. 403 no. 844), 1471. Robert Radcliffe, for some time Gentleman Porter of Calais (Cely Letters, *passim*; *C.P.R. 1476-85*, p. 276), was a supporter of the Woodvilles and must be distinguished from Richard's associate, Sir Richard Ratcliff. He was executed by Henry VII for involvement in the Warbeck conspiracy.   [2] p. 571.

[3] Print alone has preserved the whole text of this particular one.

[4] Widely called *Titulus Regis*, which is, properly speaking, the title not of this Act, but of Henry's Act repealing it: *Rot. Parl.* VI. 270b.

[5] *Rot. Parl.* VI. 289.

taken later by George Crofts, chancellor of Chichester cathedral, to check that it would not be dangerous to 'have More's books in keeping'.[1] The 'Crowland' author himself evidently did not consider it injudicious to introduce the matter,[2] but he makes it clear that the petition referring to Edward's alleged marriage with Eleanor Butler was fraudulent.[3] He also emphasizes that parliament had no right to act on such grounds:

[It] confirmed the title by which the king had attained his exalted rank the previous summer. Since matrimonial law was at issue, this body of laymen was not qualified to pronounce on the matter; nevertheless, even the stoutest were so swayed by fear, that parliament took that power upon itself, and did so pronounce.[4]

Vergil, with privileged access for himself, may have considered that the account was politically dangerous in the hands of others, and if he really destroyed any books, might have consigned this one to the flames for heresy. After making use of it, that is. I shall show later that Vergil seems to have taken some of his information and interpretations from this source; that some of his errors derive from misunderstandings of it; and that equally Vergil's account throws light on a section of the *Crowland Chronicle* which is strangely confused in its existing form.[5]

---

[1] Quoted by R. W. Chambers in *The English Works of Sir Thomas More*, I, ed. W. E. Campbell (London and New York, 1931), p. 41.

[2] It is just possible, even, that he wrote before Henry's Act was passed.

[3] pp. 566–7, 'color autem introitus et captae possessionis hujusmodi is erat . . .' *Color* meant 'fraudulent grounds'. The marginal annotation in Fulman's transcript was obliterated before the MS. went to the printer, but the word *falsa* remains legible. This writer, for one, was evidently not inclined to think that Bishop Stillington had whispered his guilty secret about Edward's marriage to a startled Richard early in June, as vividly described by Kendall, *Richard III*, pp. 203–5, 215–20, following Markham, *Richard III*, p. 97.

[4] p. 570.   [5] Below, excursus to chapter six.

A. FULMAN'S TEXT

The earliest manuscript of the Crowland chronicles that is now extant formed part of Sir Robert Cotton's collection and is now British Museum MS. Cotton Otho B. XIII.[1] The volume suffered severely in the Cotton library fire of 1731: at the beginning and end much has been lost altogether, and some parts are represented only by small fragments, often almost illegible because the vellum has been shrunk and distorted by heat, and in some places rendered transparent. Originally the volume contained the so-called 'chronicles of Ingulf and Peter of Blois', together with the three continuations. It is written throughout in the same fifteenth- or early sixteenth-century hand, the earlier portion to f. 72^v (i.e. the beginning of the second continuation) being ornamented with red initial letters. The manuscript is therefore a fair copy of the text of what were originally a series of chronicles by different compilers. The reputed holograph of the first in the series—the pseudo-Ingulf— was kept under lock and key in the church at Crowland after the Dissolution, according to Spelman. Selden failed in his strenuous efforts to obtain it, and when Fulman inquired he was told that it had disappeared.[2] When Fulman printed the text of the Crowland chronicles in 1684 he therefore took the 'Ingulf's chronicle' from an old manuscript owned by John Marsham.[3] Where a leaf had been cut out, he supplied matter furnished by Gale from the Cotton manuscript. Fulman's text of the chronicle attributed to Peter of Blois was similarly taken from the Marsham and Cotton manuscripts, both of which apparently lacked the conclusion.

It does not seem, however, that the Marsham manuscript contained the three continuations to the 'Ingulf' and 'Peter of Blois' chronicles. Fulman prints the continuations at the end of his volume (separated, that is, from the Crowland 'Ingulf' and 'Peter of Blois' chronicles by the Melrose Chronicle and the Annals of Burton),

---

[1] Since there is nothing to indicate that it belonged to the abbey, it is not mentioned in *Medieval Libraries of Great Britain*, ed. N. R. Ker (R. Hist. Soc. Guides and Handbooks No. 3, 2nd edn., 1964).

[2] These details are taken from Fulman's introduction to his volume. B.M. MS. Arundel 178 is a sixteenth-century transcript which differs from the copy printed by Henry Savile in *Rerum Anglicarum Scriptores post Bedam* (1596); May McKisack, *Medieval History in the Tudor Age* (Oxford, 1971), p. 65 n. 6.

[3] Son of Sir John Marsham (1602–85). According to H. T. Riley (*Ingulph's Chronicle*, p. ix and n. 10), this in turn was subsequently lost. It was allegedly stolen by Obadiah Walker (1616–99), a Delegate of the Oxford University Press and Master of University College.

and he does not state his source for them, mentioning merely that it was 'alicubi mancam, quod fortasse non satis advertit exscriptor'.[1] He indicates in fact that there were considerable lacunae, especially at the beginning of the first continuation and the end of the third, which suggests not a careless scribe but physical damage to an exemplar at some stage of transmission. Sir Goronwy Edwards has said[2] that as far as can now be ascertained the Cotton manuscript appears to be the source of Fulman's transcript.[3]

As Edwards also pointed out, the intermediary between Cotton Otho B. XIII and Fulman's edition of the continuations was a seventeenth-century transcript which now survives in part in the Bodleian Library (Corpus Christi College MS. B. 208). The volume comprises transcripts in various hands of chronicles printed in Fulman's *Rerum Anglicarum Scriptorum Veterum*. These, edited by Fulman, were evidently used as printers' copy. Fulman may not have commissioned them all himself. The transcript of the Melrose Chronicle concludes with a dorsal note[4] dated January 1650/1: 'Received of Mr Bee for the writing this History of Melros out of an old Copy borrowed out of Sir Thomas Cottons Library the summe of— £3 00 00. By mee Raph Jennyngs. Which I promise to compare, when desired, with the originall. Raph Jennyngs. Witnesse John Fosbroke.'

The continuations of the *Crowland Chronicle* have been copied in a rather loose and unformed hand, very different from the elegant writing of Mr. Jennings in the Melrose transcript. Fulman's editorial hand is evident throughout, clarifying readings, underlining proper names, and dividing matter into paragraphs. More important, he has shortened some marginal annotations (copied by the transcriber from the original and set off in 'boxes'), so that, for example, on p. 11 'Reconciliatio Ducis Clarentiae cum fratre ejus Rege Edwardi' becomes 'Reconciliatio Ducis Clarentiae cum fratre Rege', and on p. 53 'Ab hoc loco usque ad finem libri nihil aliud conettus prae instrum[en]talia de concessione ecclesiae' [etc.] loses the first twelve words. A missing annotation in the transcript (or rather its exemplar) has been filled in as 'Tres Cancellarii, 1473'. Fulman also emended readings in the transcript (whether

---

[1] Unfortunately, sixteenth- and seventeenth-century historians were more interested in 'early' productions like the Ingulf chronicle (now known to be forged) than in comparatively recent documents like these later—and much more informative—continuations, so that Fulman apparently thought it unnecessary to identify his original.

[2] 'The "Second" Continuation of the Crowland Chronicle', p. 117 n. 1.

[3] In this case, did Gale perhaps supply Fulman with the transcript of the continuations, as he had apparently supplied missing matter from 'Ingulf'?

[4] f. 274^v ('66').

or not by checking it against the original is unfortunately not clear). Thus in 'quasi multitudine daemonum trucidatus' the last word has been altered to 'circumdatus'; 'parvo' becomes 'puero', and 'Fflandijs' becomes 'Fflandrijs'. Finally, Fulman has supplied 'Continuations Two and Three' with titles, where the transcript runs straight on without a break. It was thus Fulman who divided the 'third continuation' from the 'second', by instructing the printer to begin a new page and inserting in the transcript the words 'Alia ejusdem Historiae Continuatio'. In the printed volume the divisions between the three continuations are further marked by the provision of title-pages.

Other alterations appear in the printed copy but are not marked in the transcript. Changes in spelling, especially of proper names, may be due to the compositor or a proof-reader: the transcript spellings *elimosinarij, Wideville, confidebat, hostia*, for example, become in the printed text *Eleemosynarii, Widevyll, confitebat, ostia*. *Subiti* on p. 49[1] of the Corpus transcript has been changed by Fulman to *subici*, but is printed *subigi*.[2] Similarly, the transcriber had *Denereux* among Richard's supporters, which Fulman corrected to *Devereux*. The printer in turn has changed this to *Deveereux*.[3] On p. 577 of the printed text a double error has occurred. The transcriber had disrupted a line of the verses on 'peace and toleration' with a note beginning 'ubi alludit metrista defectionem tanti apparatus'. Fulman, intending that this comment should be transferred to the margin, wrote in the left margin 'Ubi alludit Metrista . . .' The printer evidently misunderstood this direction and left the comment in the text, bisecting a line of verse, but inserted Fulman's marks of omission between *Metrista* and *defectionem*, as though to indicate a lacuna in the manuscript.

One serious blunder that is commonly attributed to the author of the second continuation, the statement that the Duke of Norfolk and others of Richard's chief supporters deserted him at Bosworth, is entirely due to the printer. The Corpus transcript (p. 44) reads: 'Deinde praefato Duce Norfolchiae, Ricardo Ratclyff [etc.], et multis alijs, in eo furore bellico interfectis, ac multis maxime Borialibus in quibus Rex Richardus adeo confidebat, ante ullas confertas manus fugam ineuntibus, nullae partes dignae siue habiles remanserunt.' The compositor's eye jumped from the first *multis* to the second, so that the printed version (p. 574) omits the important words 'alijs, in eo furore bellico interfectis, ac'.

---

[1] These figures refer to the numbered pages of the fragmentary transcript of the Crowland continuations, not to the folios of the volume as a whole.

[2] p. 577.   [3] p. 574.

B. SIR GEORGE BUCK'S QUOTATIONS FROM THE 'CROWLAND CHRONICLE'

The quotations from the *Crowland Chronicle* in George Buck's *History of the Life and Reigne of Richard the Third* (1646), based on the manuscript of his great-uncle Sir George Buck (?1562–1622), sometimes differ so significantly from their equivalents in Fulman's edition as to arouse the suspicion that Sir George might have used a different version of the *Chronicle* in his researches. Unfortunately, the second Buck produced a travesty of his source (now B.M. MS. Cotton Tiberius E. x) which was badly damaged in the same fire that destroyed most of the Cotton manuscript of the *Crowland Chronicle*, so that little comparison is possible. The best-preserved of Sir George's quotations from the 'Crowland' chronicler concerns Richard's accession. It is printed here from MS. Cotton Tiber. E. x ff. 36^v–37 with missing words supplied from B.M. MS. Egerton 2216, one of the great-nephew's copies, in parallel with the equivalent passage from Fulman's direct source, Corpus Christi College MS. B. 208, p. 32. Important differences are italicized.

Ricardus protector eodem die quo re[igmen sub] titulo regii nominis sibi vendic[avit, viz. 26°] die Iunii, anno dom. [1483, se apud magnam aulam Westmonasterii in cathedram marmoreum] *imisit*	dictus Richardus protector, vice-simo sexto die praefati mensis Iunii regimine regni sub titulo regii nominis sibi vendicavit; seque eodem die apud magnam aulam Westmonasterii in cathedram mar-moriam ibi *intrusit. Color autem introitus et captae possessionis huiusmodi is erant :*
et tunc mox omnibus proceribus tam laicis quam ecclesiasticis et caeteris astantibus, etc. ostendebatur rotulis quidam in quo per modum suppli-citionis *in nomine procerum et populi Borealis exhibitae sunt Primum,* quod filii Regis Edwardi erant bastardi, supponendo illum praecontraxisse *matrimonium* cum quadam Domina Alienora Boteler [etc.]	ostendebatur per modum suppli-cationis in quodam rotulo pergameni, quod filii Regis Edwardi erant bastardi, supponendo illum prae-contraxisse cum quadam Domina Alienora Boteler [etc.]

It is possible that these two versions derive from different manu-script exempla, but both Buck and Fulman are known to have had access to the Cotton collection, and the balance of probability is that both relied on Cotton Otho B. XIII, and that Buck's altera-tions (in so far as they do not merely confuse summary with quota-tion) were designed to support his thesis in support of Richard.

There are still more striking differences in the concluding poem on the three Richards as printed by Fulman and George Buck junior (without attribution to the *Crowland Chronicle*), but the last part of Sir George's manuscript is totally burnt, and no conclusions about his version can safely be drawn.

5   Miscellaneous Native Chroniclers: Facts and Fictions

So far this study has concerned two early narratives that can be regarded as generally reliable accounts of the periods they cover. The works which remain to be discussed in these succeeding chapters ought all to bear the caveat 'Historians proceed with utmost caution', because none of their testimony can be accepted unreservedly unless it is supported by documentary or more nearly contemporary evidence. Mutual support from this group of histories is useless. It is quite common to find reputable scholars commenting that an anecdote in Vergil's *Anglica Historia* must be true because it is also found in More's *History of King Richard the Third,* or that a certain statement of More's is supported by the *Great Chronicle of London.* It is one aim of this book to show that such comparisons are as illogical as suggestions that a tradition reported by Vergil is authenticated by its appearance in the work of Edward Hall, in a case where Hall's text is little more than a translation of Vergil's.

Having said that, it must immediately be added that the more important chronicles to be discussed in this chapter derive much of their value from the possibility that they may preserve a certain amount of genuine tradition, which is the more welcome because Mancini and the 'Crowland' chronicler are often very selective. Much of the fascination of the history of Richard III derives from the need to make an individual decision about the relative weight to be allotted to one somewhat untrustworthy chronicler rather than another, and some of those thought most unreliable by modern scholars were the authorities who played the greatest part in shaping the views of Richard held by their immediate successors. 'Traditions' may therefore be valuable for any of three reasons: as genuine historical evidence, as an interesting indication of opinion current at the time they are recorded, and as subsequently influential. An especially entertaining rehearsal of current stories occurs in John Rastell's *The Pastime of People* [1529].[1] More cautious authors like the

---

[1] *The Pastime of People, or, the Chronicles of Divers Realms,* ed. T. F. Dibden (1811), pp. 292–3.

'Crowland' chronicler, Vergil, and even Rous, had said the details of the princes' murder were unknown. Rastell, making little claim to be a historian in his own right, gives the avid reader plenty of choice:

But of the manner of the death of this young king, and of his brother, there were divers opinions; but the most common opinion was that they were smothered between two feather beds,[1] and that in the doing the younger brother escaped from under the feather beds, and crept under the bedstead, and there lay naked a while, till that they had smothered the young king so that he was surely dead. And after that one of them took his brother from under the bedstead, and held his face down to the ground with his one hand, and with the other hand cut his throat-bole with a dagger.

Rastell then rather spoils this magnificently circumstantial accodnt by going on:

And after that, the bodies of these two children, as the opinion ran, were both closed in a great heavy chest, and by the means of one that was secret with the protector, they were put in a ship going to Flanders, and when the ship was in the Black Deeps, this man threw both those dead bodies, so closed in the chest, over the hatches into the sea. And yet none of the mariners, nor none in the ship, save only the said man, wist what things it was that was there so enclosed. Which saying divers men conjectured to be true, because that the bones of the said children could never be found buried, neither in the Tower nor in none other place.

Alternatively, the children were persuaded by a cry of 'Treason!' to hide in a chest, and were buried alive in it in a great pit under a stair, and subsequently disinterred and thrown into the sea in 'the Black Deeps'. These conflicting stories probably were current at Rastell's time, and may even reflect gossip going back to Richard's reign. They become a subject for appropriate fun in the Grafton/Hall version of More's *Richard III*.[2]

Of the earlier Tudor accounts of the reign, by far the oddest is that by John Rous, which forms part of a longer history evidently compiled by the author towards the end of his life (he died before 19 January 1492).[3] Since no English translation of this work exists, and even the Latin is not widely available, and since it has some claim to be the most thoroughgoing of attacks

---

[1] The two beds are mentioned in *The Great Chronicle of London,* ed. A. H. Thomas and I. D. Thornley (1938), p. 236.
[2] Below, pp. 211–12.   [3] *C.P.R., 1485–94,* p. 371.

on Richard, a translation of the relevant portion is appended as an excursus to this chapter. Rous has earned the obloquy of historians by writing fulsomely of Richard while that king was still alive, and rivalling Bernard André in vilifying him after his death. His tales of Richard's monstrous birth and deformity were much to the taste of the age, but in themselves deter a later time from taking him seriously, and his extremely jumbled account of events makes it seem more likely that he concocted his history from other sources than that it is in any sense an eye-witness's testimony. Rous has acquired such credit as he has from the fact that he was a contemporary of Richard's. The idea that any person who lived at the time of the events he reports is necessarily a reliable witness to them would not be entertained by any historian who gave the matter due thought, and a journalist, lawyer, or policeman would assure him that even actual eye-witnesses seldom agree about the details of what they saw. But all the same it is often taken for granted that Rous and Fabyan knew what they were talking about because they lived at the period concerned. Rous was, as it happens, a chantry priest in Warwickshire, so has not even Fabyan's claim to have been a citizen of London at the time of Richard's usurpation. He reports in detail on Richard's entourage at Warwick on his progress in the summer of 1483, but his sole specific claim to personal observation concerns an elephant which he viewed in London during the reign of Edward IV.

The title given to Rous's work by Thomas Hearne when he published it in 1716 (*Joannis Rossi Antiquarii Warwicensis Historia Regum Angliae*) is very apposite. Rous was an old-fashioned antiquary rather than a historian—a busy-minded man who loved gossip. His *History* in general is discursive and quite undiscriminating, as witness his description of King Bladud's foundation of a university at Stamford with four professors imported from Athens, which he supports with a quotation from John Hardyng's rhymed chronicle.[1] The book recalls Polydore Vergil's dismissive characterization of early monastic chronicles as 'sparse, haphazard, artless and untrue'.[2]

---

[1] Ed. Hearne, p. 23.
[2] 'Nudi, rudes, indigesti ac mendosi'; quoted Hay, *Anglica Historia* (1950), p. xxviii.

Rous writes much more fully when he reaches 1483, but his previous showing inspires little confidence in his accuracy, and he has so little to say about Henry VI or Edward IV that his more detailed account of Richard's career suggests the fullness of malice. The work concludes with a direct address to Henry VII, Seventh of England but Sixth of Ireland, where many prophecies are current about his glorious future.

Rous's narrative of Richard's reign is a rag-bag of gleanings, in which are all mixed up the appointment of a new chancellor, the poem written by Rivers before execution, a physical description of Richard, the creation of new lords, and a story that Richard bestowed the wealth of Edward V upon the Duke of Buckingham, who then boasted that he had as many men bearing his badge of Staffordshire knots as the Earl of Warwick had formerly had with ragged staves. Among this mishmash occur interesting items. Rous mentions that money was coined in the name of Edward V (another antiquarian's touch), that the Marquis of Dorset and Edward Grey, Lord Lisle, fled London and were accused of conspiring to kill the protector, that Rivers and his companions were tried by the Earl of Northumberland, and that Richard poisoned his wife. The story that Richard perished at Bosworth shouting 'Treason! Treason! Treason!' also seems to have originated with Rous. Predictably he has the popular story about the prophecy that G would follow E. He also has a relatively complete account of the arrests at the Tower (out of order, since it appears after the execution of Rivers and Richard's ascension of the throne): 'He beheaded Lord Hastings, the chamberlain of King Edward IV, without trial, and imprisoned the Archbishop of York and the Bishop of Ely in separate places, Henry Duke of Buckingham urgently persuading him to this. Also Lord Stanley was wounded, arrested, and imprisoned, but he shortly regained the favour of the king together with his freedom.'[1] There are two noteworthy things about this. First, Rous, like some of the chronicles of London, but unlike earlier authorities, says that Stanley was wounded and imprisoned briefly. Secondly, he stresses Buckingham's influence, which may be the origin of More's statement, in the Latin versions of his work, that Buckingham personally had

[1] Ed. Hearne, p. 216.

Hastings executed with the minimum of delay and despite his
pleas for mercy.[1] Rous's omissions are even more interesting.
He has nothing about sermons, or speeches by Buckingham.
Of the grounds for Richard's accession he says merely 'With
the arrival in London of the Earl of Northumberland, the
Duke of Gloucester, protector of the kingdom, immediately
found a title by which to disinherit his lord the king, Edward V,
and promote himself. Or rather, not "found" but fabricated.'[2]
The reference to Northumberland is curious, but untrue if
Northumberland was at Pontefract for the execution of Rivers
and the others on 25 June.[3] The northern troops under his
command did not reach the capital until early in June. Possibly
Rous knew that the petition presented to Richard on 26 June
was supposed to have come from the north, and assumed that
it was brought by the Earl. Surprisingly, by failing to mention
Sha's sermon he passes by an opportunity to cite Richard's
slur on his mother's chastity as another example of Richard's
deplorable behaviour. And while he gives the date of the
death of Edward IV and says that Edward V was killed within
about three months of his accession, he does not, unlike most
chroniclers, give a date for the execution of Hastings, or for
Richard's coronation.

Another short Latin account of the usurpation occurs in
Bodleian MS. Ashmole 1448, f. 287.[4] This volume, which bears
the signature of Humphrey Lluyd (whose Welsh patriotism
was so affronted by Vergil), is a miscellany of fifteenth-century
manuscripts, chiefly scientific, and the material on Richard
seems to have been added to some genealogical notes on the
royal families of England compiled mainly in the reign of
Edward IV, but completed early in that of Henry VII. On
f. 275 Edmund Earl of Richmond has been added to a genealogical tree, and there is an entry that Margaret, daughter and
heir of the Duke of Somerset, married the Earl of Richmond,
uterine brother of King Henry VI, and had a son called
Henry who overcame Richard III at 'Brownheath' and took

[1] Yale *Works*, II. 49, 222.   [2] p. 214.
[3] Rous says he was the chief judge at their condemnation, but he may here have
been echoing some Neville gossip against a Percy.
[4] Printed in William Henry Black, *A Descriptive Catalogue of the Manuscripts . . .
Bequeathed unto the University of Oxford by Elias Ashmole* (Oxford, 1845), p. 1231.

the kingdom and married Elizabeth, eldest daughter of King Edward IV. The account of Richard runs, in translation:

Through the envy of the devil and through an insatiable ambition to succeed to the kingdom, after his brother King Edward IV had gone the way of all flesh, Richard Duke of Gloucester cunningly took into his charge the two sons of that unconquered king: Edward, Prince of Wales, and his brother Richard, Duke of York; until with the instigation, advice, and aid of Henry Duke of Buckingham he had had himself crowned on fraudulent grounds. Shortly afterwards, Anthony Earl Rivers and Richard [Grey], his brother [*sic*], together with a certain lord Thomas Vaghan, were beheaded together at Pontefract without any process of law. And also he maliciously had a council meeting called at the Tower of London, and there William, Lord Hastings (because he would not freely agree to have this man crowned) was slain by sword on the stock of a tree [*super truncum arboris gladio peremptus est*], no respite given. And Richard had himself crowned at Westminster on the Sunday after the martyrdom of St. Peter the Apostle [i.e. 6 July]. Being afraid that his nephews might prevent him from reigning with the approbation of the kingdom, Richard (first taking counsel with the Duke of Buckingham, as said) removed them from the light of this world, by some means or other, vilely and murderously. Alas, that such noble princes, heirs to so rich a kingdom, should thus end their lives, innocent of any offence which merited such violence!

King Edward V exercised rule from 7 April [*sic*] to the feast of the martyrdom of St. Peter the Apostle [i.e. 29 June, but the writer may mean Richard's coronation within the octave of that feast].

King Richard III, brother of Edward IV. In the first year of his reign his son died. In the second his queen was buried at Westminster. In the third, according to his deserts, by the providence of God he was miserably slain in battle near Leicester by Henry Earl of Richmond and other exiles. *Tu autem* [*Domine, miserere nobis*].

Although *gladius* could be used for an axe as well as a sword, this account seems to parallel Mancini's description of Hastings's death: 'Then the soldiers, who had been placed by their lord, and the Duke of Buckingham came running, and beheaded Hastings with a sword, on the false accusation of treason.'[1] The 'truncum arboris' recalls the log of timber in other accounts, such as Fabyan's.[2] Curiously, this manuscript makes the same mistake as Mancini in saying that Edward

---

[1] p. 90. A sword certainly seems a more likely instrument than the official headsman's axe for such a hurried execution, but Armstrong comments (n. 81): 'Mancini is mistaken in supposing that Hastings was murdered immediately the armed men intruded. Such procedure was un-English and reminiscent of Italian practice' [!]

[2] Robert Fabyan, *New Chronicles of England and France*, ed. H. Ellis (1811), p. 668.

IV died on 7 April. He died in fact during the night of 8–9 April.[1]

Some private copyists were content with still less information, and that often inaccurate. The commonplace books of the London merchants Richard Arnold and Richard Hill contain brief city annals. Arnold's entry for 1482–3 (the first account of Richard's usurpation to appear in print, since Arnold's compilation was published in 1502 or 1503) reads:

> Edmond Shaa, mayor. William Whyte, John Mathew, sheriffs. The 22 year. This year deceased the king, in April, entering into the twenty-third year of his reign, and the two sons of King Edward were put to silence. And the Duke of Gloucester took upon him the crown in July [*sic*], which was the first year of his reign, and he and his queen crowned on one day, in the same month of July.[2]

Hill's entry is a little fuller:

King Edward the 4th. ⎫ ⎬ 1483 Edmond Shawe King Richard the 3rd. ⎭		⎧William Whit ⎨ anno 22. ⎩John Mathew
King Edward dead. King Richard the Third	This year, the 22 day of April [*sic*] died King Edward, and then Richard Duke of Gloucester took upon him the crown in July by the counsel, help, and aid of the Duke of Buckingham. And after that the said Duke of Buckingham raised a great people again the said Richard Duke of Gloucester at Breknok in Wales, and would have subdued him, and he was taken by King Richard and his head smit off at Salisbury. And Prince Edward and his brother taken at Stony Stratford by the said King Richard.[3]	

Already in these chance survivals similarities of phrasing can be seen (Hill oddly echoes the Ashmole manuscript's 'instigatione et concilio et auxilio Henrici Ducis de Bokyngham'), and there are various mistakes: Richard was not crowned in the same month that he ascended the throne (though William Rastell also says this in an apparent interpolation into More's text),[4] and the young Duke of York was not present at Stony Stratford, though many chroniclers confuse him with his

---

[1] *Acts of Court*, ed. Lyell, p. 146.

[2] *The Names of the Baylifs Custos Mairs and Sherefs of the Cite of London . . . wyth odur dyvers maters* (Antwerp, ?1502), sig. A.7.

[3] Balliol MS. 354, F. ij C xix[v].   [4] See Appendix, p. 201.

half-brother, Richard Grey, who was. Arnold and Hill illustrate two truisms. First, the ordinary man prefers to take his history ready-made from books, rather than draw on his own resources of knowledge. Arnold, a London merchant and contemporary of Fabyan, must have known something of events in London in 1483, either at first or second hand, but he did not bother to record any details. Secondly, manuscript histories circulated widely, and it is a fair deduction that one initial exemplar might very soon produce derivatives which diverged considerably both from the original and from each other.

Writers can impose an infinite variety on the same basic material. Modern techniques of photographic copying have greatly facilitated the production of books that consist largely of chunks from the writings of others. In the days of hand writing, sheer boredom must often have forced some degree of originality on anybody with aspirations beyond those of a mere scribe. This makes it difficult to disentangle the relationships between the extant London chronicles for this period. Happily, it is unnecessary for the purposes of this study to go into the arguments about dates, scribes, and interconnections.[1] It is sufficient to say that the three 'civic' chronicles to be examined—B.M. MS. Cotton Vitellius A. XVI,[2] Robert Fabyan's chronicle, finished in 1504 and published posthumously in ?1517 (new style) as *The New Chronicles of France and England*,[3] and *The Great Chronicle of London*, finished in 1512[4]

---

[1] For these see Kingsford, *English Hist. Lit.*, chap. iv, and the editors' introduction to the *Great Chronicle of London*.

[2] Ed. C. L. Kingsford, *Chronicles of London* (Oxford, 1905).

[3] Fabyan died 28 February 1512/13.

[4] The date at which the MS. was written has not been certainly established, but it seems to be early sixteenth century. It, or its lost source, was well known in the sixteenth century—it must have been familiar to More, and Grafton apparently drew on it for his account of the years 1509-12 in the continuation to his *Chronicle of John Hardyng* (1543). Hall, Foxe, and Stow also used it, and someone who had the MS. before Stow annotated it and added dates, probably from the printed edition of Fabyan's chronicles. After Stow it was lost to scholarly view, to reappear when Quaritches bought it from the Bromley family early in the present century. Kingsford was allowed to look at it when he was writing his *English Historical Literature*, but did not make the full examination which might have changed some of his conclusions about the relations of various city chronicles. When he wrote, he expected that Mr. Ernest Dring of Quaritches would shortly be bringing out an edition of the whole work. Nothing in fact came of this project, and in 1933 the MS. was purchased by Viscount Wakefield, the philanthropist

—all have unmistakable connections, along with some interesting differences.[1] John Rastell's history, *The Pastime of People* [1529], is another relation of this group. Fabyan, like Rastell, seems to have been a compiler and correlater rather than a composer of original work, so that the fact that he was a prominent Londoner, sheriff in 1493, need have little to do with the authenticity of the work ascribed to him. The statement in the *Dictionary of National Biography* (Epitome) that the *Chronicles* were an expansion of his diary can be safely disregarded. Further, the publication date of his work may well be irrelevant in any consideration of its influence on other writers, because it is very likely that it circulated in manuscript before reaching print.

As an example of some of the problems of textual criticism raised by the London chronicles, and also of the kind of material that was probably available to Polydore Vergil, Grafton, Hall, and More, compare the accounts of Buckingham's speech at the Guildhall (? on 24 June 1483), from Rastell's *Pastime of People*, MS. Cotton Vitellius A. XVI, Fabyan's *Chronicles*, and the *Great Chronicle*.

Rastell:[2]

And after that, at the Guildhall, the Duke of Buckingham, in a long oration there by him made, and exhortation with elegant words preferred the title of the said protector of the realm.

Cotton Vit. A. XVI:[3]

And upon the Tuesday following came the Duke of Buckingham unto Guildhall, and there showed unto the mayor and his brethren, and to a great multitude of the citizens, the title of the Duke of Gloucester that he had unto the crown, exciting the people to take him for their king.

Fabyan:[4]

Then upon the Tuesday following, an assembly of the commons of the city was appointed at the Guildhall, where being present the Duke of Buckingham with other lords sent down from the said lord protector, and there,

---

and former Lord Mayor, who not only presented it to a fitting home in the Guildhall library, but also defrayed the costs of the elaborate and scholarly limited edition which appeared in 1938.

[1] Grafton's reproduction of two passages, about ecclesiastical ceremonies at Richard's accession and the northern troops mustering in London, which are paralleled respectively in the *Great Chronicle* (p. 232) and Fabyan (ed. Ellis, p. 669) strongly suggests that all three used the same lost source at that point.

[2] Ed. Dibden, p. 292.   [3] Ed. Kingsford, pp. 190–1.   [4] Ed. Ellis, p. 669.

in the presence of the mayor and commonalty, rehearsed the right and title that the lord protector had to be preferred before his [nephews the sons] of his brother King Edward to the right of the crown of England. The which process was in so eloquent wise showed and uttered, without any impediment of spitting or other countenance, and that of a long while, with so good sugared words of exhortation and according sentence, that many a wise man that day marvelled and commended him for the good ordering of these words; but not for the intent and purpose the which that thereupon ensued.

Great Chronicle: [1]

Then upon the Tuesday next ensuing the foresaid Sunday the Duke of Buckingham came unto the Guildhall, where against his coming the mayor with his brether and a fair multitude of citizens in their liveries were assembled. To the which assembly the said duke then made an oration, in rehearsing the great excellency of the lord protector and the manifold virtues which God had endowed him with, and of the rightful title which he had unto the crown. That it lasted a good half hour, and that was so well and eloquently uttered and with so angelic a countenance, and every pause and time so well ordered, that such as heard him marvelled and said that never tofore that day had they heard any man, learned or unlearned, make such a rehearsal or oration as that was. The which when he had finished and goodly exhorted the said assembly to admit the said lord protector for their liege lord and king, and they to satisfy his mind, more for fear than for love, cried in small number 'Yea! Yea!', he so departed.

These extracts are in order of length, not supposed date. Kingsford suggested that the relevant part of MS. Cotton Vitellius A. XVI must antedate Fabyan's chronicle because the latter was so much more interesting.[2] This is a reasonable argument, but it is not sure that chroniclers always preferred detail to brevity. Rastell's short account, for example, was printed after Fabyan's and is almost certainly derived from it.

An early sixteenth-century historian who used several of these local chronicles had not only the problem of choosing between versions of the same incident that differed slightly in details and emphasis. He would find bewildering differences in sequential arrangement: different suggestions, for instance, about the point in the story at which Rivers was executed, at which Dorset escaped, and at which the princes were murdered or rumour first reported the crime. He would also find differences that probably arose directly from the varying interpretations which had been placed on slightly ambiguous state-

---

[1] p. 232.   [2] *Chronicles of London*, p. xvii.

ments in some original source. For instance, there is some verbal uncertainty in this group of chronicles about the claim made in Sha's sermon. Fabyan (followed closely by Rastell) says that the sermon 'showed openly that the children of King Edward IV were not legitimate nor rightful inheritors of the crown, with many disslanderous words'.[1] Kendall took this to mean that Sha, according to Fabyan, told only the story of Edward's precontract.[2] MS. Cotton Vitellius A. XVI has 'that King Edward's children were not rightful inheritors unto the crown',[3] and the *Great Chronicle* 'that the childer of King Edward were not rightful inheritors unto the crown, and that King Edward was not the legitimate son of the Duke of York, as the lord protector was'.[4] It is possible that all four versions really mean that because Edward IV was a bastard, his sons' title was neither legal nor just, 'they were not legitimate inheritors, nor rightful'. As Mancini puts it, 'Neither had [Edward IV] been a legitimate king, nor could his issue be so.'[5]

Secondly, none of the London chronicles mentions that Bishops Rotherham and Morton were present at the Tower when Hastings was arrested, and they all contrive to suggest by their wording that these two were arrested quite separately from Hastings.[6] Fabyan will not even vouch for the arrests of the bishops at all: '[after the execution of Hastings, Richard] shortly after set in sure keeping such persons as he suspected to be again him, whereof the Bishops of York and Ely were two, as it was said.'[7]

Thirdly, MS. Cotton Vitellius A. XVI, like Mancini and the other early writers, makes no reference to Lord Stanley's presence at the Tower. The *Great Chronicle* and Fabyan, like Rous, say that he was wounded and arrested. In the *Great Chronicle* he 'was immediately set at his liberty' (apparently without imprisonment) for fear of his son, but according to Fabyan he was 'kept a while under hold'. Grafton, followed by Gairdner,[8] extends his period of imprisonment until 4 July,[9] which is certainly wrong because he witnessed the delivery of the great seal to Russell on 27 June.[10]

---

[1] p. 669.   [2] *Richard III*, p. 477 n. 17.   [3] p. 190.   [4] pp. 231–2.   [5] p. 95.
[6] Rous could also be read in this sense.   [7] p. 669.   [8] *Richard III*, p. 100.
[9] *The Chronicle of John Hardyng* (S.T.C. 12767), f. lxxviii. Grafton may not have intended the date to be taken exactly, however.   [10] Rymer, *Foedera*, XII. 189.

If such uncertainties are understandable, it is surprising that the civic chroniclers fail to record one incident on which they should have had information—Richard's public denial, to the mayor, aldermen, and members of the livery companies, that he intended to marry his niece. The *Great Chronicle* says merely: 'much whispering was among the people that the king . . . had poisoned the queen his wife, and intended with a licence purchased to have married the eldest daughter of King Edward.'[1] On the other hand, they seem to be unique in recording riots in the north shortly after Richard's coronation. According to the *Great Chronicle*:

> Immediately after the time of the coronation was overpassed, the king with large rewards given unto the northern men which he had sent for against his coronation, that were numbered at four or five thousand men, he sent them home again. Of the which, some bearing them bold of the king's favour, after that they had rested them there awhile, began to make such masteries that the king was fain to ride thither himself, where at his coming he put some in execution and so pacified that country and returned again to London. And shortly after he created his son legitimate Prince of Wales . . .[2]

Is this in reality a reflection of Lovel's rebellion which faced Henry VII on his visit to the north after Easter 1486, a few months after his own coronation, or were there such otherwise unrecorded disturbances in the summer of 1483?

When the *Great Chronicle* adds to the information given by Fabyan for the period of Richard's reign, its details are often interesting, but not, it turns out, always reliable. For instance, it records various opinions about the death of the princes:[3] 'Some said they were murdered atween two feather beds, some said they were drowned in malvesy,[4] and some said they were sticked with a venomous potion.'[5] Its allegation that Richard himself persuaded the queen to deliver her son from sanctuary[6] does not appear to tally with Stallworth's letter;[7]

---

[1] p. 234.   [2] p. 233.   [3] pp. 236–7.

[4] This form of death had seized the chronicler's fancy. He also reports a story that Humphrey Duke of Gloucester had been drowned in wine, and then carefully dried again (p. 179).

[5] The scribe seems to have omitted something: the meaning was surely 'sticked with a dagger or poisoned with a venomous potion', unless the MS. reading *pocion* is a mistake for *poncion* 'dagger'.

[6] pp. 230–1.   [7] Above, p. 42.

the suggestion that on the morning of his execution Hastings had dined with Richard, and went to the Tower riding behind either Richard or Buckingham, does not square with Mancini's account that Hastings and his friends went to the Tower on a courtesy visit to the protector;[1] the statement that the first widespread rumour of the princes' death appeared after Easter 1485[2] is contradicted by the 'Crowland' chronicler and Mancini; no other source says precisely that most of Richard's close supporters fell away the night before Bosworth, telling 'Master Brawghyngury' (i.e. Brackenbury) of their intention;[3] and no other source says that Sir William Stanley crowned Henry after Bosworth.[4] This anecdote is not in Fabyan or MS. Cotton Vitellius A. XVI (or, for that matter, in the *Crowland Chronicle*). It is possible, however, that in this instance the *Great Chronicle* is correct.[5]

On two matters the *Great Chronicle* is infuriatingly vague. There is little point in telling us that the princes were seen shooting and playing in the garden of the Tower on various occasions during the mayoralty of Edmund Sha, i.e. between 29 October 1482 and 28 October 1483,[6] or that the murderer of the children was thought to be either Sir James Tyrrell or 'an old servant of King Richard's named [no name given]'.[7] In the second case either a blank was left in the exemplar which the scribe of the existing copy has omitted, or the name was perhaps a word similar to the following word, which is *Whan*, and this coincidence caused the scribe to skip it by accident.[8]

The historical evidence presented by the city chronicles is thus, for our period, often vague, sometimes conflicting, and usually difficult to assess for validity. There is little to suggest that they derive from sound first-hand information, and as they stand they present a baffling mixture of borrowed material and innovations. The *Great Chronicle* is much the

[1] p. 231; Mancini, p. 90.
[2] p. 234, but the chronology is wildly astray in this part.
[3] p. 237.   [4] p. 238.   [5] Below, pp. 133-4.   [6] p. 234.   [7] p. 237.
[8] For example, it could be supposed that the original had 'an old servant of King Richard's named Wharff. Whan . . .' The name is chosen to illustrate this type of scribal error. It would seem that one John Wharff was in fact keeper of the beds at the Tower in 1483 (*C.P.R., 1476-85*, p. 386), but it would be very unsafe to draw any deductions from this.

most interesting of the group, but when one is dealing with historical sources, it is not always true that biggest or most interesting is best. A wealth of detail may be due to authentic tradition, or to a craftsman's desire to embellish his own work and improve on that of others, and the author of the *Great Chronicle* was a capable, though often unpolished, writer. It is very dubious whether many chroniclers, or their readers, made the modern distinction between surviving tradition, legend, and private embroidery. But as far as concerns 'tradition', even modern historians sometimes romanticize a little.[1] Gairdner could place a touching faith in its value: 'It is possible that the circumstances of the case [Richard's complicity in the murder of Prince Edward after Tewkesbury] were preserved only by tradition, till the days of Polydore Vergil and of Hall the Chronicler; but they are not on that account unworthy of credit.'[2] This view is in some ways the precursor of the more recent interest in 'oral history', which employs a tape-recorder (and preferably a trained interviewer) for the study of contemporary or near-contemporary events, and emphasizes the importance of 'the amount of history surviving in oral form'[3] in discussing Vergil, More, and Shakespeare. This fashion has produced important new ideas and evidence, but must not be followed to the point of ignoring the influence of *ex post facto* deductions, or even of written records. The need for a historian to balance 'living tradition' and 'written authority' is demonstrated by a conversation in 1535 between Chapuys and Thomas Cromwell. Chapuys said it was notorious that King Richard had proclaimed his brother Edward IV a bastard, and had called his own mother to witness the fact, besides getting preachers to proclaim it. Cromwell agreed that this was true.[4] This, said Gairdner, strikingly bears out Vergil's report of the matter. But had Cromwell and Chapuys, or their informants,

---

[1] And it is sometimes forgotten how far sheer carelessness can operate. It is unlikely that Mrs. Penrose, writing the famous *Mrs. Markham's History of England* in 1821, was echoing a living tradition when she graphically described the arrest of Hastings at Westminster Hall [*sic*] on 13 May [*sic*]. Dickens's *A Child's History of England* is equally unreliable, even when it is just plagiarizing More.

[2] *Richard III*, p. 14.

[3] Denys Hay, *Polydore Vergil: Renaissance Historian and Man of Letters* (Oxford, 1952), p. 95.

[4] *Richard III*, p. 81 n. 2, quoting *Cal. Letters and Papers Henry VIII*, VIII. 281.

read Vergil's work, published the previous year, or even a manuscript of Sir Thomas More's on the subject? That is, how far had oral tradition been shaped by the historians?

The London chronicles did one notable disservice in muddling the chronology of Richard's reign. Not only did mayoral years become confused with regnal or calendar years, so that the *Great Chronicle* places the Buckingham rebellion apparently in 1485 and Bosworth in 1486, but Fabyan—or perhaps, to be fair, the editor who prepared his manuscript for press, since publishers seem to have liked dates better than historians did —helped further the confusion by saying that Richard ascended the throne on Thursday 20 June and was proclaimed king on Friday 21 June ('corrected' in later editions to an equally impossible 22 June).[1] These dates were added to the *Great Chronicle* by the anonymous annotator who had the manuscript at some time before it came into the possession of Stow. They were repeated, in the more logical guise of Friday 20 June, by John Rastell, Vergil, and Grafton. Their validity was accepted so long that in 1854 Riley, translating the *Crowland Chronicle*, silently substituted 'Friday 20 June' for the correct 'vicesimo sexto' (26 June) of his source.[2]

[1] 20 June was a Friday in 1483.
[2] *Ingulph's Chronicle*, p. 489.

Excursus John Rous's account of the reign of Richard III[1]

King Edward IV died at Westminster on the ninth of April in the twenty-third year of his reign, and was buried royally at Windsor in the sumptuous new building erected by him, opposite the tomb of King Henry VI, who was translated thither from the abbey of Chertsey after the death of the said King Edward. . . . In the days of this king an elephant was brought to England, which I saw at London, but it soon declined.

To King Edward IV succeeded, but for a lamentably short time, his son King Edward V, who resided at Ludlow at the time of his father's death, when the boy was about thirteen and a half, or thereabouts. He was brought up virtuously by virtuous men, remarkably gifted, and very well advanced in learning for his years. On the death of his father his father's friends flocked to him. On the morrow of St. George's day,[2] after the accustomed service of the Knights of the Garter had been solemnly celebrated at Ludlow after the English habit, concluding with a splendid banquet, the young king removed towards London. Richard Duke of Gloucester, brother of the deceased king and by his ordinance protector of England, came upon him with a strong force at Stony Stratford and took the new king his nephew into his governance by right of his protectorship. The rest, namely Anthony Earl Rivers, elder brother of the queen and the new king's uncle, Richard Grey, brother of the king on his mother's side, and Sir Thomas Vaughan were removed from their office, forthwith arrested, and sent to be imprisoned in the north at Pontefract,[3] and there shortly after they were unjustly put to death. And so the new king was removed from his loyal servants and received with kisses and embraces, like an innocent lamb falling into the hands of wolves. His special tutor and diligent mentor in godly ways, Master John Alcock Bishop of Worcester, was removed like the rest, but not, however, subjected to the rigour of imprisonment. What more? The new king was taken to London and received with fitting honour by the mayor and citizens. In his name the laws of the kingdom were enforced at Westminster and throughout the realm in the accustomed way. Coins were struck in his name, and all royal honours were paid to him as usual. The king was at that time staying in the palace of the

---

[1] Translated from B.M. MS. Cotton Vesp. A. XII ('Historia Johannis Rossi Warwicensis de Regibus Anglie'), ff. 131ᵛ–136ʳ. Hearne's printed text differs very little from this version.   [2] i.e. 24 April.

[3] Initially, in fact, Rivers was imprisoned at Sheriff Hutton and Grey at Middleham (Armstrong, n. 85).

Bishop of London where he had been from his first arrival in London. The king's mother, Queen Elizabeth, hearing of the arrest of her brother and sons, fled with her possessions from the royal palace of Westminster to the abbey, to take shelter in the security of that privileged place. She kept with her her son the boy Richard, Duke of York, and her daughters. There also fled to other places the queen's son by her other marriage, Thomas Grey, Marquis of Dorset, his uncle Edward Grey, Lord of the Isle, otherwise de Lyle, and many more. A charge was concocted against them that they had themselves plotted the death of the Protector.

Then the Protector appointed new officers. He removed the Archbishop of York from the office of chancellor, and Master John Russell, Bishop of Lincoln, formerly keeper of the privy seal, replaced him, though much against his will. Master John Gunthorp, Dean of Wells, was then promoted to the office vacated by Russell. About this time the King of France died,[1] and the Queen of France presided over the kingdom, it is said, for eleven months. Shortly after, the lords previously named were cruelly killed at Pontefract, lamented by almost all and innocent of the deed charged against them, and the Earl of Northumberland, their chief judge, proceeded to London. Anthony Lord Woodville, Earl Rivers, was found to be wearing, at the time of his death, the hair-shirt which he had long been in the habit of wearing against his bare flesh. At the time of his imprisonment at Pontefract he wrote a ballad in English, as it was told me, whose words follow:

> Sumwhat musyng
> And more mornyng
> In remembryng
> The unstydfastnes
>
> Thys world beyng
> Of such whelyng
> Me contrarieng
> What may I gesse?
>
> I fere dowtles
> Remediles
> Is now to sese
> My wofull chaunce.[2]
>
> Lo in thys traunce
> Now in substaunce
> Such is my dawnce.
> Wyllyng to dye

---

[1] 30 August in point of fact.

[2] Eight further lines are given at this point in the version quoted by Gairdner, *Richard III*, pp. 74–5, from Ritson, *Ancient Songs*, II. 3.

Me thynkys truly
Bowndyn am I
And that gretly
To be content.

Seyng playnly
That fortune doth wry
All contrary
From myn entent.

My lyff was lent
Me to on intent;
Hytt is ny spent.
Welcum Fortune!

But I ne went
Thus to be shent
But sho hit ment.
Such is hur won.

And so the said lords were condemned to death as though they
had in fact plotted the death of Richard Duke of Gloucester, at that
time Protector of the Kingdom of England; and, for a thing they
had never contemplated, the innocent humbly and peaceably
submitted to a cruel fate from their enemies' butchers. The consecrated hair-shirt of Earl Anthony was long after hung before the
image of the Blessed Mary the Virgin at the Carmelite Friars at
Doncaster.

The Earl of Northumberland coming, as mentioned, to London,
at once the Duke of Gloucester, the Protector, found a title to the
crown to disinherit his lord the king, Edward V; that is, not found
but feigned it for his own advancement. And shortly he imprisoned
his lord King Edward V, king in deed but not crowned, together
with his brother Richard who had been taken from Westminster on
the promise of safety. In this way it was afterwards known to very
few by what manner of death they had suffered. The usurper King
Richard III then ascended the throne of the slaughtered children
whose protector he was himself. Richard was born at Fotheringhay
in Northamptonshire, retained within his mother's womb for two
years and emerging with teeth and hair to his shoulders. He was
born on the Feast of the Eleven Thousand Virgins [21 October].[1]
At his nativity Scorpio was in the ascendant, which is the sign of a
house of Mars.[2] And like a scorpion he combined a smooth front
with a stinging tail. He received his lord King Edward V blandly,

[1] In fact 2 October.
[2] Unfortunately for this sinister horoscope, presaging death by steel, Richard
was born under Libra, not Scorpio.

PLATE II

John Rous's description of Richard (lines 21-3)

To face p. 12

with embraces and kisses, and within about three months or a little more he killed him together with his brother. And Lady Anne, his queen, daughter of the Earl of Warwick, he poisoned. Anne, his mother-in-law, the venerable Countess, widow and right heir of this noble lord, fled to him as her chief refuge and he locked her up for the duration of his life.[1] And, what was the most detestable to God and all Englishmen, and indeed to all nations to whom it became known, he caused others to kill the holy man King Henry VI, or, as many think, did so by his own hands. And because there was a certain prophecy that after E. (that is, after Edward IV), G. should reign, for this ambiguity George Duke of Clarence, who was the middle brother between Edward and Richard, was killed on account of his name George. And the other G., that is Gloucester, lived to fulfil the prophecy. For a similar prophecy Humphrey, Duke of Gloucester, was said to have been destroyed, but undoubtedly that Duke of Gloucester killed himself, and everything came true in the despicable person of this Richard III, formerly Duke of Gloucester.[2]

This King Richard was praiseworthy for his building, as at Westminster, Nottingham, Warwick, York, and Middleham, and many other places, which can be viewed. He founded a noble chantry for a hundred priests in the Cathedral of York, and another college at Middleham. He founded another in the church of St. Mary of Barking, by the Tower of London, and endowed the Queen's College at Cambridge with 500 marks annual rent. The money which was offered him by the peoples of London, Gloucester, and Worcester he declined with thanks, affirming that he would rather have their love than their treasure.[3] He was small of stature, with a short face and unequal shoulders, the right higher and the left lower.[4]

He beheaded Lord Hastings, the chamberlain of King Edward IV, without trial, and imprisoned the Archbishop of York and the Bishop of Ely in separate places, strongly encouraged in these things by Henry Duke of Buckingham. Lord Stanley was also wounded,

[1] It is impossible to check this story.

[2] Cf. 'Sir Thomas Vaughan, going to his death, said "Ah! Woe worth them that took the prophecy that G. should destroy King Edward's children, meaning that by the Duke of Clarence, Lord George, which for that suspicion is now dead. But now remaineth Richard G. Duke of Gloucester, which now I see is he that shall and will accomplish the prophecy and destroy King Edward's children and all their allies and friends, as it appeareth by us this day" ': More, Yale *Works*, II. 58, collation; Grafton–Hall text.

[3] Cf. Bishop Langton's comment (above, p. 50) 'And in many great cities and towns were great sums of money give him, which all he hath refused.'

[4] In the MS. the words 'right' and 'and the left' (*dexter* and *sinisterque*) have been written in later, possibly in a second hand (Plate II).

seized, and imprisoned, but he shortly regained the king's favour and his liberty. Finally, when he was crowned with his queen he made new lords: Henry Duke of Buckingham was made great chamberlain and steward of England; John Howard, Duke of Norfolk; Thomas, his son and heir, Earl of Surrey; William Lord Berkeley, Earl of Nottingham and marshal of England, and Lord Lovel, the king's chamberlain. When King Edward V had been imprisoned, King Richard III gave all his treasure to Henry Duke of Buckingham, who then distributed his livery[1] of Stafford knots and boasted that he had as many of them as Richard Neville Earl of Warwick had formerly had of the branched rods called 'ragged staves'. But they were greatly inferior in numbers, and it was not long before the underlying hatred between the king and the duke began to grow. The king then removed to[2] Oxford, and to Wood-stock, where by popular request he disafforested a great area of the country which King Edward IV his brother had annexed and incorporated in the forest of Wychwood under forest law, against conscience and to the public damage. Thence he went to Gloucester, and for the ancient title of his dukedom, instituted a mayor and aldermen there.[3] And then he went to Worcester, and finally War-wick, where the queen joined him from Windsor. There ambassa-dors from the King of Spain came to the king for a marriage be-tween the king's only son and the daughter of the King of Spain. There were then with the king at Warwick the bishops of Worcester, Coventry, Lichfield, Durham, and St. Asaph's; the Duke of Albany, brother of the King of Scotland; Edward, Earl of Warwick; Thomas, Earl of Surrey, the steward of the King's household; the Earl of Huntingdon; John, Earl of Lincoln; and the Lords Stanley, Dudley, Morley, and Scrope; Francis, Lord Lovel, the king's cham-berlain, and William Hussy, chief justice of England, and many other lords. And ladies of similar rank with the queen. From here, after a stay of a week, the king moved to Coventry, Leicester, Nottingham, and Pontefract, where he instituted a mayor. Then he came to York, where on the Feast of the Nativity of the Glorious Virgin Mary [8 September], his little son and heir, aged a little over seven, was knighted and made Prince of Wales, with many other great honours. And shortly after such rejoicing a great con-spiracy was made against the king and a great insurrection. The king rode south with his followers in a great army, and the Duke of Buckingham was taken and led to the king at Salisbury and there beheaded. Then many lords fled from the country, and shortly

---

[1] *liberatum dans* inserted later in a blank space, or over an erasure.
[2] 'Bristol' cancelled.   [3] *vicecomites*. Above this is written *dubito* ('I doubt this').

after the prince died a tragic death at Easter-tide. And in August next following the body of King Henry VI was disinterred and translated to the new college church at Windsor Castle, and honourably received there, and with utmost solemnity reinterred on the south side of the high altar. That holy body was very pleasantly scented, and certainly not from spices, since he was buried by his enemies and butchers. And for the most part it was uncorrupted, the hair in place, and the face as it had been except it was a little sunken, with a more emaciated appearance than usual. And at once miracles abundantly attested the king's sanctity, as appears sufficiently in writings there. Not long after the death of the prince, to which I have referred, the young Earl of Warwick, Edward, eldest son of George Duke of Clarence, was proclaimed heir apparent in the royal court, and in ceremonies at table and chamber he was served first after the king and queen. Later he was placed in custody and the Earl of Lincoln was preferred to him, who was called John Pole, son and heir of John Pole, Duke of Suffolk.

At last, as the life of King Richard approached its evening, many secretly deserted him and joined the exiles from the south who were with Henry, Earl of Richmond, nephew (by his uterine brother) of Henry VI. On the Feast of the Transfiguration [6 August] Henry landed in Wales at Milford Haven with a few followers and was joined by many recruits. When at length he met King Richard and his great army on the eighth day of the Feast of the Assumption [22 August] A.D. 1485,[1] King Richard was killed on the field of battle on the border of the counties of Warwick and Leicester.

This King Richard, who was excessively cruel in his days, reigned for three years [*sic*] and a little more, in the way that Antichrist is to reign. And like the Antichrist to come, he was confounded at his moment of greatest pride. For having with him the crown itself, together with great quantities of treasure, he was unexpectedly destroyed in the midst of his army by an invading army small by comparison but furious in impetus, like a wretched creature.[2] For all that, let me say the truth to his credit: that he bore himself like a noble soldier and despite his little body and feeble strength, honourably defended himself to his last breath, shouting again and again that he was betrayed, and crying 'Treason! Treason! Treason!' So, tasting what he had often administered to others, he concluded his life most miserably, and at last was buried in the choir of the

[1] The last digit of the date has been added later.

[2] *ut miser extinctus est*. It is tempting to suppose, from the stress laid on the treasure, that Rous may here have intended something of the later English sense of 'miser', a person who lives wretchedly from avarice.

Friars Minor at Leicester. Although his days were short, they were ended with no lamentation from his groaning subjects. And thus the Earl of Richmond became king under the name of Henry VII. Who immediately married the noble lady Elizabeth, daughter and heir of Edward IV.[1]

[1] Rous was clearly anxious to curry favour with Henry Tudor, and it is possible to see this account as straightforward political propaganda. But Rous had also been an ardent admirer of the Neville family. His animus against Richard may therefore derive in part from the belief that Richard had murdered his wife, Anne Neville.

6   Polydore Vergil, the Second Italian

I

POLYDORE VERGIL was already a scholar of international standing when he came to England in 1502. With the encouragement of Henry VII he undertook to write a history of England, and after some twelve years of research he produced a first complete draft which went up as far as September 1513.[1] He subsequently added and altered material, and the work seems to have circulated in manuscript, as one would expect, before the first edition was published at Basle in 1534.[2] The beauty and elegance of this volume, a remarkable contrast to the homely black-letter prints produced in England at the time, appropriately symbolize the difference in quality between Vergil and the English chroniclers discussed in the last chapter.

There is no need to detail Vergil's considerable merits as a historian in general: the ground has been ably covered by Professor Denys Hay.[3] Vergil produced a sophisticated work by applying modern humanist principles to native material, and the English, although indignant at his debunking of some of their cherished national myths,[4] were charmed to find their history so elegantly set forth. For the purposes of this book it is chiefly Vergil's history of Richard III that must be discussed. There are three pertinent matters. Was his treatment of Richard's reign deliberately designed as Tudor propaganda, or

---

[1] It is not clear whether, when Vergil went back to Italy on a visit in the spring of 1514, he had with him a completed MS. of the whole work, or only a draft and notes which he then wrote up at Urbino. Nor is it certain that he had completed his account of Richard III before embarking on the reign of Henry VII. For the dating, see Denys Hay, 'The Manuscript of Polydore Vergil's *Anglica Historia*', *E.H.R.* LIV (1939), 241–3, and *Anglica Historia 1485–1537* (1950), pp. xiii–xvi, and Cecil H. Clough, 'Federigo Veterani, Polydore Vergil's "Anglica Historia", and Baldassare Castiglione's "Epistola . . . ad Henricum Angliae Regem" ', *E.H.R.* LXXXII (1967), 772–8.

[2] *Polydori Vergili Urbinatis Anglicae Historiae Libri XXVI* (Basle, 1534). 'As one would expect' because historians seldom keep a finished work private for twenty years. There is a reference in the *Dialogi de Prodigiis* which suggests that Vergil's History was well known by at least 1526: Hay, *Polydore Vergil* (1952), p. 82.

[3] Cf. especially *Polydore Vergil* and the introduction to *Anglica Historia 1485–1537* (1950).   [4] The Welsh were furious.

notably slanted to agree with contemporary views? What were his sources, oral and written, and how did he treat their evidence? And how was Vergil's work used by subsequent historians?

II VERGIL AS TUDOR PROPAGANDIST

Vergil is sometimes written off as a party hack; as far as regards his account of Richard III, the author of an official history that is mere propaganda for Richard's enemies. This approach can be extremely useful: where Vergil's statements are inconvenient to one's pet theory they can be labelled lies, and where they happen to fit in, truth told by the devil must be especially potent. But the view that Vergil was a propagandist contains some more general misapprehensions. There is no real reason to suppose that he wrote history to order in any crass way. The rejection of Geoffrey of Monmouth that made him so unpopular with the Welsh suggests on the contrary that he was a man of independent mind and an honest scholar who followed his own judgement.[1] Had Henry been interested in obtaining a totally fictitious report on his predecessor's character and reign he could have hired a less distinguished writer (somebody like Rous or a second André) more cheaply and with better results. The value of propaganda was, of course, perfectly well known,[2] but in this case Henry had no need to blacken the name of the man he had defeated, because that name was dark enough already. The idea that Richard was an excellent king and a beloved man in his lifetime and the malevolence of Tudor historians utterly falsified his reputation has its own perverse attraction. But even when it was first fully developed by Sir Clements Markham it had to be supported by the thesis that the *Crowland Chronicle* was reliable only in selected parts, and the discovery of Mancini's work has since made it clear that many of the major items of so-called Tudor propaganda against Richard were charges that had already been levelled against him in England in the first weeks of his reign.

---

[1] Nor was he uncritical of Henry VII: he states (after Henry's death) that Bray and Morton exerted a restraining influence on Henry (*Ang. Hist.* (1950), pp. 128*–9*).

[2] To the Plantagenets as much as the Tudors.

In these circumstances, neither Henry VII nor his son was likely to feel himself particularly flattered by any further aspersions upon the character and appearance of Richard. Vergil's flattery of Henry and his kingdom was much more subtle: it lay in his production of a national status symbol of sixteenth-century Europe—a narrative in emulation of classical writings, which raised English history to a level that accorded with aspirations to become an important political power. In this history as a whole the reign of Richard III had been just an unfortunate incident that preceded, and paved the way for, the triumphant establishment of a new dynasty. Denigration of Richard was not, therefore, Vergil's chief aim. But he was not altogether guiltless of suppressing truth and suggesting falsities. If a Tudor king was not to be flattered by lies about Richard, he could be upset by injudicious statements on certain subjects. Vergil was in much the same position as a modern historian of repute who undertakes to write the history of a large business firm. No doubt he accepted the work from genuine professional interest, recognizing the scope it gave his talents, grateful for the access to records it allowed him, and with the understanding that he did not intend to concoct wholesale falsehoods. None the less, he would recognize that some tact was called for when he came to cover recent events and deal with the personalities of those still living, or recently dead but succeeded by important descendants. The 'Crowland' chronicler was shrewd in refusing to bring his history too far up to date. The three earliest editions of the *Anglica Historia*, like other sixteenth-century publications, show small alterations as the climate of official opinion changed; for instance the discreet omission of the characterization of Thomas Boleyn as 'adolescen[s] corpore pariter atque animo floren[s]'.[1] Vergil's coverage of Richard's reign can therefore be expected to show such minor omissions and distortions as might be found in a modern business history or 'official' biography, where people familiar with the subject may see between the lines things tactfully veiled from the general reader.

In this way, Vergil avoided giving the impression that Richard's accession met with any sort of general acceptance.

---

[1] Hay, *Polydore Vergil*, pp. 82–4 and Appendix II; *Ang. Hist.* (1950), p. 94 and n.

Not only does he say 'Thus Richard, without assent of the commonalty, by might and will of certain noblemen of his faction enjoined the realm, contrary to the law of God and man',[1] but he seems even to slur over the fact that the council appointed him Protector, with the words 'then did Duke Richard assume the government wholly'.[2] Similarly, it is possible that more explicit details about the opposition of Hastings, Morton, and Rotherham were current than it was expedient to put in print, just because (although the legal position was rather tricky) Richard as Protector had undoubtedly been entitled to allegiance. Although a Tudor historian might be expected to extol the participants in a courageous act of rebellion against an enemy of the Tudors, it was really safe to praise sedition only when the rebel was the successful Earl of Richmond. In June 1483 Hastings and his friends were not acting on Henry's behalf, and it would not have been wise for Vergil or other Tudor writers, remembering Perkin Warbeck, Lambert Simnel, and the de la Pole family, to praise such conspiracy against lawfully constituted authority. Hence, perhaps, some ambiguity about Hastings in Vergil's account: he was an innocent victim of Richard who perished for his inconvenient loyalty to Edward V, but his death was also divine retribution for his part in murdering the heir of Henry VI[3] (an aspect of the matter that does not seem to have occurred to Mancini's contemporaries).

Where Vergil does seem deliberately to lie (or at any rate prevaricate) is in his vehement attempt to refute persistent stories that the bastardy of Edward's children was alleged as grounds for Richard's accession. His rebuttal is distinctly disingenuous. He says that 'there is a common report that in Sha's sermon Edward's children were called bastards, and not King Edward himself, which is devoid of any truth' because there are men still alive who remember the Duchess of York's indignation at being labelled an adulteress.[4] Mancini agrees that the sermon cast aspersions on the chastity of the duchess.[5] But Vergil then fails to mention what Mancini[6] and the Crowland chronicler[7] (backed by the Rolls of Parliament) say respectively—that Buckingham's speech at the Guildhall and

[1] Ed. Ellis (Camden, 1844), p. 187.   [2] Ibid., p. 176.   [3] p. 181.
[4] pp. 184–5.   [5] Ed. Armstrong, p. 94.   [6] Ibid., p. 96.   [7] p. 567.

the petition from the quasi-parliamentary assembly of 25 June alleged a precontract of some kind that illegitimized Edward's children. As I have pointed out previously,[1] discussion of this alleged precontract was not encouraged by Henry VII, since it affected the title of his wife. Vergil could not suppress all reference to the matter, but he played it down as much as he could with a refutation that neatly sidestepped the real point at issue.

III   THE SOURCES

Vergil's treatment of evidence

While Fabyan and his fellow writers might sometimes indicate some doubts about a story, Vergil's stature as a historian is clearly shown by his handling of conflicting interpretations. In discussing the events of the reigns of Edward IV and Richard III he will characteristically rehearse a variety of opinions; some ascribed to 'men worthy of credit' or to current belief (whether written or otherwise is not always clear), others to rumour. He usually tries to evaluate these views, castigating some as popular nonsense, and offering corroborative evidence for others. For instance, a tale that Edward abused Warwick's hospitality by molesting a woman of his house is plausible, he concludes, in view of Edward's reputation.[2] He also makes his own deductions: Edward's reproach that no man begged mercy for Clarence both corroborates his repentance and suggests that Edward himself must have blamed the Duke's death on the envy of the nobility.[3]

Vergil's methods can be seen in his treatment of the relations between Buckingham and Gloucester. After the death of Edward IV, Richard met Henry Duke of Buckingham at Northampton 'with whom the Duke of Gloucester had long conference, in so much that, as is commonly believed, he even then discovered to Henry his intent of usurping the kingdom [the ground for which belief was especially] for because the Duke following afterwards his humour, whether it were for fear or for obedience, held ever with him'.[4] After Richard's coronation the first cause of discord between Buckingham and Richard was Buckingham's demand for the Earl of Here-

---

[1] Above, p. 96.   [2] (1844), p. 117.   [3] p. 168.   [4] p. 174.

ford's patrimony, which Richard rejected in angry and in-
sulting terms. Buckingham went to Wales and partly smarting
from this rebuff, partly repenting his hand in Richard's wicked
enterprises, conspired with Bishop Morton, and explained to
him his scheme for uniting the houses of York and Lancaster
in the persons of Elizabeth of York and Henry Earl of
Richmond.

> This truly was the matter for the which dissension sprang betwixt the King
> and the Duke, and whereupon conspiracy was made against him.[1] But the
> common report was otherwise, for the multitude said that the Duke did the
> less dissuade King Richard from usurping the kingdom by mean of so many
> mischievous deeds, upon that intent that he afterward, being hated both of
> God and man, might be expelled from the same, and so himself [i.e.
> Buckingham] be called by the commons to that dignity, whereunto he
> aspired by all means possible, and that therefore he had at the last stirred
> up war against King Richard.[2]

The last, 'common report', Vergil apparently adds as an
example of the far-fetched explanations of which popular
opinion is fond. It is common practice among sixteenth-
century historians to attribute stories current in their own day
to people contemporary with the event described (compare,
for example, Rastell as quoted above, p. 104).[3]

As Professor Hay has pointed out,[4] it is sometimes difficult
to judge whether Vergil's source is oral tradition or written
evidence, and one might add that, with Vergil as with More,
it is possible that fiction has sometimes been disguised as historical relation. Thus, was Vergil told that after Ralph Sha's
sermon Richard hung back, although his friends 'urged him
to utter himself plainly and to dispatch at once that which
remained',[5] and did he really know that after the murder of the
princes Richard was popularly blamed for any storm that
arose?[6] Either is the sort of thing an author might add for
artistic reasons, and equally such rather vague or irrelevant
but vivid details are just what occur in the reminiscences of
the elderly. There is no difficulty in believing that Vergil's

---

[1] In Vergil's MS. (Hay, *Polydore Vergil*, p. 197), he says he learnt this true story
of the quarrel 'a fide dignis viris' ('men worthy of credit').

[2] (1844), p. 195.

[3] But in the other direction, cf. Vergil's description of a story apparently taken
from the *Crowland Chron.* as 'even now current' (below, p. 139).

[4] *Polydore Vergil*, p. 92.   [5] (1844), p. 185.   [6] p. 191.

concluding description of Richard[1] came, in its essentials, from people who had known him; and the anecdote, for example, that Edward IV would advert to Clarence's fate when anyone pleaded for his intercession,[2] sounds authentic. So may be Vergil's information that Richard was himself lodged in the Tower when both princes were there after 16 June,[3] since this is implied by Mancini.[4] (Vergil was wrong, however, in saying that Edward V was not moved there until 16 June.[5]) Vergil's assertion that Gloucester, Clarence, and Hastings killed Prince Edward after Tewkesbury[6] may, on the other hand, be either general gossip or artistic enlargement on a deduction from earlier written sources.

Much has been said about the people who could have given Thomas More information for his *Richard III*. Partly, perhaps, because it was earlier thought that Vergil's work was composed after More's, less has been written on Vergil's possible contacts with men who had played a part at Richard's court, though this is a question of still greater moment. Bernard André, writing about 1502, explained that he could obtain no certain details about the Battle of Bosworth.[7] Evidently Vergil was more successful in gathering information, at least about the affairs of Henry and his supporters. It is generally agreed that he obtained first-hand accounts about these from witnesses to whom he would have ready access like Bishop Fox, Reginald Bray, and Christopher Urswick. It should not be forgotten either that papal servants like Vergil's patron Adriano Castelli wrote diplomatic reports on happenings in England.[8] Vergil himself states that when he approached contemporary events and could obtain no written annals, 'I betook myself to every man of age who was pointed out to me as having been formerly occupied in important and public affairs, and from all such I obtained information about events up to the year 1500.'[9] On the question of the final breach between the Duke of Clarence and Edward IV he claims specifically to have consulted surviving prominent members of Edward's circle: 'As touching the cause of his death, though I have inquired

[1] pp. 126–7.   [2] p. 168.   [3] p. 179.   [4] p. 90.   [5]Above, p. 35.
[6] (1844), p. 152.   [7] Above, p. 53.   [8] Cf. Hay, *Polydore Vergil*, p. 6.
[9] May McKisack, *Medieval History in the Tudor Age*, p. 100, quoting F. A. Gasquet, 'Polydore Vergil', *Trans. Royal Hist. Soc.*, N.S. XVI (1902), 11.

of many who were not of least authority amongst the king's council [read, rather, 'court'] at that time, yet have I no certainty thereof to leave in memory.'[1] One would like very much to have the names of the persons he consulted. Of Edward's known council in 1477, very few, at least of the senior members, were still alive when Vergil came to England in 1502.[2] Curiously enough, the account of Clarence's downfall which Vergil does adopt is indeed that furnished by a man alleged to have been one of Edward's councillors—the author of the 'second continuation' of the *Crowland Chronicle*—but Vergil has taken it from a written, not an oral, source.

Specific informants can be suggested for one or two of Vergil's statements about the usurpation. Vergil, alone among chroniclers, mentions that after his arrest Rotherham was committed to the care of Sir James Tyrrell (whom he later blames for the murder of the princes),[3] and he also says that after his release, Rotherham, 'a grave and good man',[4] received Richard's confidences about his distress at being childless, whereupon Rotherham spread it about ('foreshadowed . . . to divers his friends') that Richard's queen was unlikely to live much longer.[5] These two matters suggest that although Rotherham had died in 1500, Vergil might have obtained information from one of his intimates, since these are not details that anyone would bother to make up. Archbishop Rotherham was also in a good position to furnish a description of the scene at the Tower when he was arrested along with Bishop Morton and Lord Hastings. Vergil's report is very detailed, introducing for the first time Richard's accusation of witchcraft and giving (in the manuscript but not the printed editions) the names of his concealed supporters.[6] The possibility that this account derived from first-hand information must therefore be carefully considered, but unhappily the issue is very difficult to decide on the available evidence. Vergil was not writing 'scientific' history, and a dramatic

[1] (1844), p. 167. 'Causam autem necis licet ipse de multis qui id temporis inter aulicos, non mediocris autoritatis erant, quaesierim, nullam tamen certam habeo tradere', Basle, 1534, p. 530. *Aulicos* suggests 'household' rather than 'council'.

[2] Cf. the lists in J. R. Lander, 'Council and Administration'. Among them were Thomas Lord Stanley (cr. Earl of Derby in 1485, d. 1504), and Sir Thomas Tyrrell, councillor in 1474, d. 1510.

[3] (1844), p. 182.   [4] p. 211.   [5] p. 226.   [6] See below, pp. 167-8.

scene required dialogue, which he could have supplied from his own imagination. Mancini had heard only that Hastings was accused of 'plotting within the Tower'.[1] It is quite possible, however, that a detailed account of the affair was not made public until long after Mancini had left England, for there must have been numerous people present who later felt free to talk. It has been widely assumed (without substantive proof) that John Morton did so, and I have suggested another possible informant in Rotherham. Unlike these two, Thomas Lord Stanley was still alive when Vergil first came to England. He had also been a councillor of Edward IV in 1477 and was therefore an obvious person for Vergil to have consulted about Clarence. Did he give Vergil information about the arrests at the Tower? And if so, was it reliable? Such hypothetical questions are worth raising because it is clear from 'The Song of the Lady Bessy' that the Stanley family later created for themselves a kind of private historical apotheosis which bears little resemblance to fact,[2] and because at three points in the story Vergil assigns to Lord Stanley a role which is not confirmed by evidence. The first occasion is the arrest of councillors at the Tower on 20 June 1483. As I have mentioned, Vergil's statement that Lord Stanley was one of those seized occurs first in Rous and some of the group of 'city' chronicles: there is nothing to support it in Mancini, the *Crowland Chronicle*, or the contemporary Stonor and Cely letters.[3] But it is true that Vergil refers to Stanley rather as an afterthought, and (unlike More) does not include the *Great Chronicle*'s detail that he was wounded in the scuffle. It is perhaps unlikely, therefore, that his new details about Richard's accusations came from a Stanleyite source.

Vergil's descriptions of Lord Stanley's actions before and just after Bosworth are open to still more doubt. His anecdote that after the battle Lord Stanley placed Richard's crown on the head of the new king[4] may reflect the story in the *Great Chronicle* which ascribes the action to Thomas's brother Sir William. Sir William Stanley had been executed for treason

[1] p. 90.
[2] For versions of this see Gairdner, *Richard III*, pp. 345–62, and Kingsford, *English Hist. Lit.*, pp. 250–2.
[3] Above, pp. 41, 42.   [4] p. 226.

against Henry in 1495, and it could have seemed politic to Vergil or his source to transfer the role. Vergil also states unequivocally that before his army met Richard's Henry paid a secret visit to both Stanleys at their camp at Atherstone and discussed strategy.[1] In 1963 K. B. McFarlane drew attention to testimony from Lord Stanley himself which directly contradicts both these stories.[2] It appears from papal records that on 16 January 1486 Stanley (by then Earl of Derby) testified before the Bishops of Worcester and London that he had known Henry since 24 August 1485: that is, that he first met him two days after Bosworth. Professor Chrimes has recently discounted this sworn evidence for the reasons that 'it is inconceivable that Henry did not meet Lord Stanley until the second day after the battle'[3] and that everyone concerned must have known that Stanley's statement was untrue.[4] Sir John Weston, Prior of the Hospitallers, similarly deposed that he had known Henry for the same period: 'a vicesimo quarto die Augusti ultimo preterito'. This evidence Chrimes tries to discredit on the odd ground that there is no way of controverting it.[5] I suggest that it is perverse to prefer a chronicler's account, written from hearsay twenty-nine years later, to evidence given on oath before a papal commission only five months after the event, when the deponents had no discernible reason to lie; and that in three cases Vergil was misled about Lord Stanley's part in events. It seems possible that after Henry's accession the Stanleys took pains to write themselves into the record of opposition to Richard from an early stage, and that their claims were accepted by some English chroniclers. It is not clear, however, whether Vergil's information came directly from the Earl of Derby (or one of his household), or reached him from some popular source.

Written sources

For the reigns of Edward IV, Edward V, and Richard III, two of Vergil's written sources seem to have been some version of the city chronicles that are now represented most elaborately

---

[1] p. 221.

[2] Reviewing *Cal. of Entries in the Papal Registers*, XIV (1960), in *E.H.R.* LXXVIII (1963), 771–2.

[3] S. B. Chrimes, *Henry VII*, pp. 44–5 and note.

[4] Ibid., p. 331.   [5] Ibid.

by the *Great Chronicle,* and a version of what we know as the
'second continuation' of the *Crowland Chronicle.* From the city
tradition he could most notably have taken the general outlines of such incidents as Sha's sermon, Sha's death shortly
after, and Buckingham's speech at the Guildhall. It is probable
that he took his chronology from such a source: he dates
Buckingham's speech 'about the thirteenth kalends of June',[1]
i.e. 20 May, no doubt a slip for 19 June, which is in line with
the tradition that dated the events of 20–26 June a week too
early. From a city chronicle he would take, with mis-spellings,
the names of the mayor and sheriffs whom Richard summoned
to the Guildhall to approve his accession[2] (but he got those of
the wrong year), and from similar confusion of mayoral and
calendar years he probably derived the error by which he
dates Edward IV's death correctly in 1483, but Richard's
coronation in 1484 and the battle of Bosworth in 1486.

The *Crowland Chronicle* has never been suggested as a possible
analogue, presumably because it has not previously been
hypothesized that it is based on an account which circulated
beyond the abbey.[3] The parallels are sometimes extremely
close, both for extended passages and in shorter echoes. Compare, for example, the description in the *Crowland Chronicle*
of how Buckingham (having repented) and Morton sent for
Henry: 'To this end a message was sent by the said Duke of
Buckingham, on the advice of the Bishop of Ely . . . that
[Henry] should hasten into England with all the speed he
could muster and take in marriage Elizabeth, eldest daughter
of the dead king, and along with her possession of the whole
kingdom';[4] with Vergil's '[Henry was to be] sent for in all haste
possible, and assisted with all that they might do, so that he
would promise before by solemn oath that after he had once
obtained the kingdom he would take to wife Elizabeth, King
Edward's eldest daughter.'[5] (Tactfully, Vergil does not give
Crowland's explanation that Buckingham and the other
English conspirators only bethought themselves of Henry

[1] p. 185.   [2] Ibid.
[3] It is, of course, possible that Vergil consulted the abbey's own version, but I
have noted no correspondences between his work and the 'first continuation',
which was apparently written in the same volume as the second.
[4] p. 568.   [5] p. 194.

when they were persuaded that Edward V and his brother were dead.) Particular incidents in Vergil, like the alliance between Hastings, Richard, and Buckingham before the coup at Stony Stratford.[1] Richard's soothing letters to Queen Elizabeth,[2] his division of the council before the arrest of Hastings,[3] and his dream on the eve of Bosworth,[4] may also derive from the same source as the *Crowland Chronicle*, that is the ur-account possibly written by Russell.

Vergil's attitude towards this authority is, however, curiously ambivalent. In the matter of the final quarrel between Edward IV and Clarence, his summary of the view which he approves follows the *Crowland Chronicle* with fidelity, though Vergil relates the story in a rather cursory, or oblique, fashion. The Crowland chronicler fills in the details:

After the death of Charles the Bold it was commonly said that his widow, the Duchess Margaret, who always favoured her brother the Duke of Clarence above all the rest of her family, was working strenuously for a marriage between Charles's only daughter and heiress, Mary, and Clarence, whose wife had recently died. The king did not care to contemplate such grand prospects for his disaffected brother, and he did his best to raise impediments, so that nothing should come of the proposal. Instead he supported the marriage between Mary and Maximilian, son of the emperor, which in fact took place.

No doubt this increased Clarence's displeasure still further, and each began to regard the other with unbrotherly eyes. . . . But the arrest of the duke to force him to answer charges against him happened like this. A certain Master John Stacy, called astronomer but also known to be a great necromancer, in league with a certain gentleman of the duke's household called [Thomas] Burdet, was accused of many charges, including the moulding of leaden images and so forth to destroy Richard, Lord Beauchamp, at the behest of his adulterous wife. Being examined under torture about his practice of the accursed art, he confessed a great deal which implicated both himself and the said Thomas. Both were arrested, and eventually, in the King's Bench at Westminster, before the judges and nearly all the temporal peers, sentence of death was passed upon each. They were

---

[1] pp. 173, 174.   [2] p. 173.   [3] p. 180.
[4] *Crowland Chron.*, p. 574: 'As it was reported, that night he experienced a terrifying dream, as though he had been surrounded by a host of demons, and this he testified in the morning. As a result, his face, always wasted, looked still more deathly pale.' Compare Vergil (Basle, 1534, p. 555): 'It is related that the same night a terrible dream came to Richard. In his sleep he seemed to see shapes, as it were of horrifying demons, watching about him, and they would not let him rest. Lest, when he appeared before the host so downcast, they should say he was overcome by fear, he related his dream to many people in the morning.'

drawn to the gallows at Tyburn and being allowed to make a short state-
ment before death, they declared their innocence; Stacy feebly enough, but
Burdet with spirit and at great length, so that he concluded like Susanna:
'Behold, I die, but I did none of these things.'[1]

The next day the Duke of Clarence came to the council chamber at
Westminster, bringing with him Master William Godard,[2] a famous doctor of the order of Friars Minor, in order to read this declaration of innocence
before the lords in council, which he did and retired again. The king was at
Windsor at this time. When he subsequently heard about the affair he was
very angry and recalled to mind the evidence of his brother's activities
against him which he had long stored up in his breast. The duke was summoned to appear on a certain day in the king's palace of Westminster, in the
presence of the mayor and aldermen of London, and the king proceeded
with his own lips to enlarge upon this action of the duke's, among others,
as contempt of court and an insufferable menace to the king's judges and
jury. What can one add? The duke was placed under arrest and never
regained his freedom from that day till his death. [In parliament the king
then secured his condemnation on dubious grounds, but execution was
delayed until the speaker came to the upper house with his fellows and
requested that the matter should be concluded. Consequently, a few days
later, whatever the means employed, the duke was privately put to death in
the Tower.][3]

To this account Vergil adds only a story of Edward's heart-
broken reproaches, and gives the date '1480: 19 Edward IV',
where present texts of the *Crowland Chronicle* have correctly
'1478:18 Edward IV'.[4] Vergil starts by rehearsing the popular
story that Edward was alarmed by a prophecy that G. should
follow E., but then goes on:

But others give a different cause for his death, after this style. At that time,
when old hatreds were swelling between the two brothers (and nothing is
more intense), the duke, who had lost his wife, sought by means of his
sister Margaret to marry Mary, only daughter of Charles, Duke of Burgundy. Edward prevented that connection through jealousy of his brother's
prosperity. Then, when the quarrel had been thus renewed, an official of
the duke's was convicted of sorcery and executed. In the face of this, the
duke could not contain himself, but burst out angrily, and the king, greatly
annoyed, sent him to prison. Not long after he was condemned of treason,
legally or illegally, and put to death. But it can be proved that Edward soon
repented this deed, for they say that whenever anyone interceded for the

---

[1] They were convicted of conspiring, not the death of Lord Beauchamp, but
those of Edward IV and his heir, by highly devious means: *Third Report of the
Deputy Keeper of the Public Records*, App. II, pp. 213–14.

[2] Read, probably, John Godard.   [3] p. 561.

[4] In another place he does, unlike the Crowland chronicler, mention the butt of
malmsey.

life of a condemned man, he used to exclaim 'O unhappy brother, for whose reprieve there was no man at all to plead', so that clearly he ascribed his death to the envy of the nobles. . . . This happened in 1480, that is in the nineteenth year of Edward's reign.

And so, secure from the wars and domestic seditions which had been a danger before, the king began to take unusually severe notice of offences among the nobility, and to pay keener attention to amassing money.[1] For this reason, many were persuaded that he was turning into a hard ruler, for after the death of his brother he realized that he was feared by all, and he himself was now in fear of no man [*propter quod multi persuasum sibi habebant, illum deinceps evasurum durum principem, cum post mortem fratris, se a cunctis timeri animadverteret, et ipse iam timeret neminem*].[2]

In the *Crowland Chronicle* the parallel to the last paragraph runs:

After this action many acquiesced in Edward's persuasion that he could rule the whole kingdom at his will [*ab hoc actu multi Regem Edwardum persuasum relinquebant, quod ad libitum dominari posset super totum regnum*], now that he had removed those general idols on whom the people, ever anxious for change, had fixed their gaze in time past. They regarded as idols of this sort the Earl of Warwick, the Duke of Clarence, and any other magnate who might withdraw from the royal circle. Although, as I judge, the king often inwardly repented the deed, for the rest he performed his office so grandly that he seemed feared by all his subjects, while he himself was afraid of no one [*ita magnifice tamen de cetero fecit officium suum, ut ab omnibus incolis formidari, neminem ille metuere videretur*]. For he distributed his more trustworthy servants through all the realm, as keepers of castles, manors, forests, and parks, so that no man, however high-ranking and treacherous, could have made any attempt in any part of the kingdom without facing immediate resistance.[3]

On other occasions, Vergil appears to quote the Crowland source (again without attribution), only to dismiss its conclusions in scornful terms. The *Crowland Chronicle* says that Warwick allowed Edward to escape from Middleham 'in an almost miraculous manner'[4] (a similar story is told in greater detail by Hall[5]). Vergil says a rumour was spread to this effect, but argues that it is not credible.[6] Earlier

---

[1] Edward's increasing wealth is mentioned earlier in the *Crowland Chron.*

[2] Basle, 1534, p. 530. For the Latin of the rest, see below, pp. 144–5.

[3] p. 562.   [4] p. 551.   [5] *Hall's Chronicle* (1809), p. 275.

[6] (1844), p. 124. The whole affair was puzzling to contemporaries themselves. In October 1469 John Paston II wrote that the king had come to London accompanied by the Archbishop, who had escorted him from York, and 'the king himself hath good language [i.e. speaks well] of the Lords of Clarence, of Warwick, and of my Lords of York [and] of Oxford, saying they be his best friends. But his house-

he had asserted that Edward's marriage to Elizabeth Woodville in place of Bona of Savoy (incongruously called 'Lady Bone' in the English translation) was either the ground of the quarrel between Edward and Warwick, or inflamed an existing enmity.[1]

On the other hand:

A story even now circulates among the populace, which alleges that the reason for their quarrel was that the earl tried to dissuade the king from marrying his sister Margaret to Charles, son of Philip Duke of Burgundy, whom he hated worse than any other mortal [*quem ipse peius quam mortalem quempiam odisset*]. And because Edward would not listen to his advice, this great hostility arose between them. As though to say that such a small thing could, or should, estrange the earl from his prince. But this is a mere fairy-tale of the common people.[2]

This 'mere fairy-tale' is argued by the Crowland author with a scrupulosity worthy of Vergil himself:

I now come to the sixth year of the reign, when Elizabeth, the king's eldest daughter by this marriage, was born in February [1466]. At this period, ambassadors came from Flanders to England to seek the Lady Margaret, sister of King Edward, in marriage to Charles, eldest son of Philip Duke of Burgundy (for his father was then alive). The marriage was solemnized in July of the next year, that is 1467. Richard Nevyl, Earl of Warwick, who had tried for some years to promote French interests at the expense of the Burgundians, was extremely annoyed about this.[3] He would have preferred to arrange a different marriage for Margaret, in the kingdom of France, to encourage a friendly understanding between the kings of these countries, rather than allow Charles, now Duke of Burgundy, to enjoy any influence with England. For he regarded that man with deadly hatred [*odio enim capitali prosecutus est hominem illum*].[4]

I consider this a better reason for the dissension between the king and the Earl of Warwick than the one adduced above, that is the king's marriage to Queen Elizabeth. The earl had certainly inveighed against that union, since he had been working for a marriage between the king and the widowed

---

hold men have other language, so what shall hastily fall I cannot say' (ed. Davis, no. 245). Professor Davis has kindly informed me that the reading 'paue other langage' in this edition was a printer's error which occurred after proof was finally passed.

[1] pp. 116–17.   [2] Basle, 1534, p. 507; cf. (1844), p. 118.

[3] He was, nevertheless, charged with the negotiations: Rymer, *Foedera*, XI. 564.

[4] It is noteworthy that here and in the passage on Clarence, Vergil's apparent borrowings will change the context and connotations of words. Crowland's 'mortal hatred' becomes 'mortal man', and where in the *Crowland Chron.* 'many people left Edward undisturbed in his persuasion', in Vergil 'many persuaded themselves that he would prove a hard ruler.' This is a recognized phenomenon in literary borrowings.

queen of Scotland; but he, and all the bishops and chief noblemen of the realm, had long since formally sanctioned and approved it, at Reading. And the earl continued to countenance the queen's relations until they promoted this other marriage. . . .[1]

Vergil's *furor scholasticus* in this case matches the vehemence with which he dismisses allegations about the bastardy of Edward's children as 'a rumour of the people . . . which is totally devoid of any truth'. (The Crowland chronicler re-hearses the latter, not in connection with Sha's sermon, but (quite truthfully) as occurring in the petition to Richard to take the throne.[2]) The Crowland reason for Warwick's disgust—that Edward had spurned Warwick's advice—is really not so silly as Vergil makes out. The author's real crime may have been that he failed to mention the celebrated Bona, who was (al-though Vergil does not say so) a convenient straw figure to explain stories about Edward's precontract.[3] In this case Vergil's evaluation of his source was not free from prejudice.

A more complicated problem is raised by the parallels between Vergil and the Crowland chronicler's account of events between the death of Edward IV and the coronation of Richard III. For much of the period they are very close. They both have Richard's oath of fealty to Edward V at York, his letters to Elizabeth Woodville, Hastings's letters to Richard and Buckingham, the meeting of Buckingham and Richard at Northampton and their arrest of Rivers at or near Stony Stratford, the queen and her party taking sanctuary on receipt of the news, and another party forming under Hastings (though there is here the striking difference that while the *Crowland Chronicle* refers generally to 'great doubts' about the imprison-ment of the Woodvilles, Vergil has an implausible story that Hastings was immediately conscience-stricken about it). There is then the story about the division of the council, with oddities in both texts. Vergil was plainly not dependent ex-clusively on the Crowland account. In particular his descrip-tion of the arrests and execution at the Tower introduces entirely new elements: Richard's claim to have been

---

[1] p. 551.   [2] p. 567.

[3] Vergil muddles his own story on the subject by dating Edward's marriage, and Warwick's discomfiture, 1467 instead of 1464; i.e. he attaches Crowland's date for the quarrel to a different incident that occurred three years before.

bewitched by the queen, his pretended proof of ill health, and then his sudden turning on Hastings, the names of other people present, the fact that Rotherham was committed to Tyrrell's custody, the arrest of Stanley and his release through fear of his son, Lord Strange, and the fact that Hastings was barely given time for confession. The two last additions are also in the city chronicles, as are Sha's sermon and Buckingham's Guildhall speech, which are not in the *Crowland Chronicle*. Apart from these, however, the general outlines are very similar. The correspondence could have arisen because Vergil and the *Crowland Chronicle* in its present form used the same source, or because basically both give an authentic account. Two independent accounts of the same series of events, both equally 'authentic', are seldom so close, however. Mancini's 'authentic' relation of these affairs is very different in arrangement and emphasis from that in the *Crowland Chronicle* and Vergil.

We come here again to the difficulty of reconstructing the ur-text behind the *Crowland Chronicle* from the (possibly abbreviated) version produced by a redactor, and have the added problem that if Vergil used a related version of the ur-text, it may not have been identical with the text adapted for Crowland. The relations between Vergil and the *Crowland Chronicle* at this point are therefore discussed in greater detail in the excursus to this chapter.

There is, however, one clear example of an error in Vergil which seems to stem from a version of the *Crowland Chronicle* account. Immediately after his description of the murder of the princes and their mother's anguished reaction, Vergil says[1] that Richard and his queen went crowned in a general procession at York, and that shortly afterwards a parliament was called, which created Richard's son Prince of Wales, Sir John Howard Duke of Norfolk, and Thomas Howard Earl of Surrey. Richard also then appointed northerners to his council. But Prince Edward died 'the third month after he had been made Prince of Wales', and after that Buckingham rose in rebellion. This is all grossly confused. The Buckingham rebellion occurred in October 1483; Parliament met in January 1484; and Howard had been created

[1] (1844) pp. 187–8, 190–2.

Duke of Norfolk before the coronation, on 28 June 1483, an elevation that had nothing to do with parliament. The *Crowland Chronicle* gives an accurate account of these various events, but it does it in a way that could have led to Vergil's misunderstandings, especially since there is evidence that Vergil sometimes relied on jotted notes from his sources.[1] According to the *Crowland Chronicle*, Richard went to York immediately after his coronation at Westminster, and at York he re-enacted his coronation and created his son Prince of Wales.[2] Next year, after the Buckingham rebellion had been put down, the chronicle relates that parliament met (at London) in January, and Richard obtained much property from attainted rebels, which he bestowed on the northern supporters whom he established in offices throughout the kingdom.[3] In February there was administered an unusual oath of allegiance to the Prince of Wales, at which ceremony John Howard, 'who had lately been created by the king Duke of Norfolk', played a prominent part.[4] Next April the prince died suddenly.

Vergil has evidently telescoped these two separate accounts of Richard's creation of the Prince of Wales at York and the oath of loyalty taken to him the following year at Westminster, and therefore put the parliamentary session, the creation of the Duke of Norfolk, and the death of the Prince of Wales all together in the summer of 1483 (or 1484, by his erroneous chronology; but in any case before the Buckingham rebellion). It is difficult to account for this series of blunders except on the assumption that he used a version of the *Crowland Chronicle*— no other source would be likely to have the precise wording which could occasion Vergil's impression that parliament had, in 1484, conferred on Howard the title of Duke of Norfolk.

IV VERGIL'S INFLUENCE

The main disadvantages of Vergil's account of Richard III for a modern historian are the fact that he so seldom indicates any source for his information, and his frequent vagueness about the course of events. The second may sometimes be

[1] Hay, *Polydore Vergil*, Appendix III, E.
[2] p. 567.   [3] p. 570.   [4] pp. 570–1.

due to policy, sometimes to a multiplicity of sources and the need to reconcile conflicting statements, sometimes to sheer lack of information rather than too much, and sometimes to a humanistic sense that it was more artistic not to be highly specific. Like Mancini, Vergil has bridge passages between the main events of his narrative where the chronology becomes rather uncertain. But Vergil is particularly unhelpful in discussing Richard's actions after obtaining the young Duke of York, and then after the execution of Hastings. In the first case he seems to suggest that Richard desired to usurp the throne but was deterred by his conscience, so that he tried to bribe both the people and his enemies with rewards and promises, and inveigled most of the noblemen by crafty and subtle discussion, 'so many matters did he so often propound, and so few explain, according as a guilty conscience is wont to be of many minds'.[1] It may be true that Richard was not at all clear about his future course at this point, and certainly it is one of the attractive things about Vergil that he conveys the sense that human choices are involved in history, whereas the older chronicles are so often 'the record of inevitable events'. But all this padding and references to the working of a guilty conscience do not amount to much in the way of evidence or convincing argument. Rather than a statement that Richard tantalized the people by 'staying and tarrying' over announcing a date for the coronation,[2] we would like, for instance, some concrete information. But Vergil was not a modern journalist trained to ask 'Who, what, why, when, where, and how',[3] and if he had been, it is unlikely that he could have obtained many answers to these questions. On many points of fact, Vergil probably knew less than we do. It is possible, for example, that he did not know the exact date of Rivers's execution, since it occurred in the north and is not dated by the chronicles. At the same time, Vergil was engaged on an extensive work, and could not afford to expatiate on minor incidents within his total framework. Comparison of his account of Clarence's downfall with that of the *Crowland Chronicle* shows how much he may abridge.

[1] pp. 178–9.   [2] p. 179.
[3] This formula had already been devised, but it was used to instruct businessmen, not historians.

For Vergil's contemporaries, the great merit—and novelty—of the *Anglica Historia* was that it treated history as literature. (It is quite absurd to confer on More the title of 'father of modern English history', unless Vergil is to be disqualified as an Italian who wrote in Latin.) In the classical manner, Vergil related his story with all the refinements of the stylist, from elevated rhetoric to the homely proverb; introduced imaginary orations and arguments (e.g. Richard's arguments to the council for taking York from sanctuary); dramatized established incidents (Sha's sermon and the audience's reaction; the battle of Bosworth); graphically described new ones (Queen Elizabeth's grief on hearing of the death of her sons, and the symptoms of Richard's guilty conscience); and attempted to deduce and explain motivations. Very soon after it appeared in print, English chroniclers paid Vergil the compliment of plagiarizing his book on a large scale. Richard Grafton used a close translation of Vergil's books on Edward IV and Henry VII, and the concluding part of his book on Richard III, for his continuation of John Hardyng's rhymed chronicle, first published in 1543,[1] and Edward Hall based himself rather more loosely on the same source for his *Union of the Two Noble Families*, which Grafton published in 1548. Both writers fall strictly outside the period selected for this study, but it happens that some brief consideration of their treatment of Vergil's work is relevant to the later discussion of More's *History* in the Appendix. A comparison of Vergil's passage about Clarence (quoted in translation above, pp. 137–8) with the equivalent in Grafton (from his first edition, S.T.C. 12768, with additions from the second edition, S.T.C. 12767, in square brackets)[2] and Hall (second edition) shows the differences.

Vergil:

Inde redintegrata simultate, quidam ducis administer eodem tempore veneficii damnatus afficitur supplicio. Contra id factum, cum dux non potuisset se tenere, quin vehementer reclamaret, rex ob eam querimoniam valde commotus, ducem in carcerem detrusit, ac non multo post iure sive iniuria perduellionem iudicatum morte affecit. . . .

[1] The work is dated January 1543, and it seems that Grafton started the year on 1 Jan., not 25 Mar.
[2] For the order, see App., p. 202 n. 3.

Ita posita bellorum et domesticarum seditionum quae accidere antea potuissent, omni[a] cura, rex severius solito nobilitatis crimina notare, et avidius pecuniae conciliandae studium habere coepit, propter quod multi persuasum sibi habebant, illum deinceps evasurum durum principem, cum post mortem fratris, se a cunctis timeri animadverteret, et ipse iam timeret neminem. Sed per brevitatem vitae nam biennio [*sic*] post mortem obiit, id fieri non licuit.[1]

Grafton:

After that, they both bearing in their minds mortal hatred, one of the said duke his servants was accused of witchcraft and charming, for which offence he was put to death. The duke, seeing that, could not but speak and resist against the king his commandment [variant reading: against that doing, as he thought, injurious], and therefore was committed to prison, and there being was killed, and proclaimed after as a traitor to the king [and attainted by parliament]. . . .

And two years then after following the king died; before the which years he began to be very hard and covetous in getting money, and also very diligent in marking and attaching his lords that did offend. [But now he left that and fell to gentleness.][2]

Hall:

This privy displeasure was openly appeased, but not inwardly forgotten nor outwardly forgiven, for that notwithstanding, a servant of the duke's was suddenly accused (I cannot say of truth, or untruly suspected by the duke's enemies) of poisoning,[3] sorcery or enchantment, and thereof condemned, and put to taste the pains of death. The duke, which might not suffer the wrongful condemnation of his man (as he in his conscience adjudged) nor yet forbear nor patiently suffer the unjust handling of his trusty servant, daily did oppugne and with ill words murmur at the doing thereof. The king, much grieved and troubled with his brother's daily querimony and continual exclamation, caused him to be apprehended and cast into the Tower, where he being was adjudged for a traitor, and was privily drowned in a butt of Malvesey. . . .

King Edward in the 19 year of his reign, forgetting as well all exterior invasions as civil war and intestine trouble, which before that time he had abundantly tasted, and more than he was willing, had both felt and had in continual experience, began first more than he was before accustomed, to search out the penal offences, as well of the chief of his nobility as of other gentlemen being proprietories of great possessions, or abundantly furnished in goods, beside merchants and other inferior persons. By the reason whereof, it was of all men adjudged, more than doubted, considering his new fame of riches and his greedy appetite of money and treasure, that he would prove hereafter a sore and an extreme prince amongst his subjects, and

---

[1] Basle, 1534, p. 530.   [2] f. xxviii[v].
[3] Poisoning seems to be Hall's alternative translation of *veneficii*.

this imagination in especial wandered through the heads of all men, that after his brother the Duke of Clarence was put to death, he should say that all men should stand and live in fear of him, and he to be unbridled and in doubt of no man.[1]

Grafton gives rather a bare rendering of his source, with occasional omissions and alterations (and some editorial corrections and additions in the second of his two editions). Hall (whose excessive length is due to his determination never to use one word where two will do) reproduces Vergil's phrasing very closely at times, but at others freely interpolates his own comments: Vergil says nothing about Burdet's guilt or innocence, or Clarence's conscience, or 'daily' complaints. Nor does he say that the king prosecuted his wealthy subjects in order to reap fines, and clearly this was not the meaning of the source that lay behind Vergil (above, p. 138). Hall also contrives to twist the final remarks about Edward's supremacy. Since it is quite certain that Vergil was the source for both Grafton and Hall at this point (and since the translations of Grafton and Hall seem to have been made independently), the passage furnishes a useful object lesson in the way in which a record can be distorted by an over-zealous redactor.[2]

Both Grafton and Hall deserted Vergil in favour of Sir Thomas More when they came to the history of Richard's usurpation. No doubt, like Gairdner, they found More's much fuller account more satisfying, both aesthetically and as history. In making their choice, Grafton and Hall were probably no more aware than their successors have been that such historical validity as More's narrative possesses is due very largely to Polydore Vergil. I have also to suggest in the next chapter that Vergil's new historical methods were at once the inspiration and the butt of More's *History*. The arguments about More's use of Vergil have not been systematically pursued; partly because it was thought until comparatively recently that More's work antedated Vergil's, or that each wrote

---

[1] Sig. I. ii (Edward IV, ff. l[v], lij[v]).

[2] Hall also conceals Vergil's unwontedly specific statement about consulting the intimates of Edward IV with the phrase 'to men that have thereof made large inquisition of such as were of no small authority in those days, the certainty thereof was hid.'

independently at about the same period.[1] Vergil's completion of his first draft has now been dated to 1513 or 1514, and More's work has been put back to somewhere about 1516–18 (though there is little firm evidence on the point). R. S. Sylvester[2] suggests that Vergil could 'have had More as one of his oral informants', but admits that 'we cannot completely preclude the possibility that More himself had either seen Polydore's manuscript or had talked with him about the details of various events that are common to both narratives'. He objects, however, that there is very little verbal correspondence between the Latin of the two writers. This, I think, rests on a misapprehension about More's methods, and an erroneous view that More initially composed part of his work in Latin. The question is not susceptible of proof either way, but in my opinion More used Vergil in much the same fashion as Vergil used a version of the *Crowland Chronicle* (and not at all in the way in which Hall used Vergil).[3] That is, More and Vergil adopted material selectively as it suited their individual purposes; they treated the works of others less as 'authorities' than as sources to be used or rejected at will, and above all as furnishing a useful framework. Sir Thomas, especially, transmuted what he chose to borrow beyond the range of mere verbal similarity.

[1] e.g. Kendall, *Richard III*, p. 404 (disregarding Professor Hay's researches), 'Both men were seeking information at about the same time. More wrote his account in 1513; Vergil was completing his story of Richard's reign about 1517–18.'

[2] Yale *Works*, II. lxxvi.

[3] Note for instance how More (ibid., p. 7) could be summarizing Vergil's summary of the Crowland account of Clarence's death: 'At the leastwise heinous treason was there laid to his charge, and finally, were he fauty were he faultless, attainted was he by parliament and judged to the death, and thereupon hastily drowned in a butt of Malmsey. Whose death King Edward (albeit he commanded it) when he wist it was done, piteously bewailed and sorrowfully repented.'

Excursus The Usurpation in Vergil and the *Crowland Chronicle*

Although Vergil was no slavish copyist, there are considerable similarities between the framework of his description of events between 30 April and 6 July 1483, and the account in the *Crowland Chronicle*. The following outline summarizes the two versions in parallel.

Crowland	Vergil
1 At news of Rivers's arrest the queen took sanctuary. Her partisans and Hastings's met separately.	The queen took sanctuary. Hastings, who hated the Woodvilles, repented of encouraging Richard when he saw the fate of her relatives, and at a meeting with his friends discussed seizing Edward from Richard by force. But it was decided to await events.
2 After the royal party returned to London, a council was formed and met for several days. This (a) removed the king to the Tower; (b) made Richard protector; (c) fixed a definite date when Edward would certainly be crowned. Everything seemed to be going well, but there was uneasiness about the position of the queen and the imprisonment of her relatives.	Richard assumed the government. [See above.]
3 But Lord Hastings, who had acted for the dukes in everything, was jubilant that the government was in their hands without bloodshed. Shortly his joy turned to woe. For the day before [*Nam pridie*] Richard cunningly divided the council into two parts, and on 13 June seized Hastings and two bishops. The dukes then did whatever they desired.	Richard urged the council to remove York and the queen from sanctuary. The council agreed to send a delegation which obtained York. Richard had almost obtained all his heart's desire. Edward and York were taken to the Tower.
4 'The next Monday' they went to Westminster with armed men and persuaded the queen to give up York.	Richard put off declaring the coronation date while he plotted. About 12 June he summoned members of the council to two separate meet-

	ings next day, one to announce the coronation date. At the Tower he seized Hastings [detailed description of the scene].
The dukes then acted quite openly.	Richard no longer had to dissemble his purpose,
	but gave orders for Rivers's execution.
5 They summoned huge numbers of armed men from the north and Wales	
	[Intervening matter about Sha's sermon and Buckingham's speech.]
and Richard took the throne on 26 June on the grounds of a false petition [details given] brought by these people from the north.	Richard usurped the throne on 21 May [read 20 June].
6 Accordingly, these armed multitudes, on their way, executed Rivers, etc.	Richard summoned armed men from the north, whose commander executed Rivers, as already mentioned.
7 Richard was crowned and from that day was called Richard III.	Richard was crowned, and was called Richard III.

There are several matters here for comment. First, Vergil's double reference to the execution of Rivers may derive from Crowland's rather confused double reference to the troops from the north. Second, both texts seem to misplace matter about Lord Hastings. Vergil's story about his inexplicable remorse as soon as Richard had carried out his instructions seems most unlikely. It is far more probable that if it has any basis of truth, it refers to a coup contemplated at a much later date, when it was obvious that Richard intended to revoke his promise to crown Edward. (Curiously enough, there is some slight evidence—in the Cely note[1]—that rumour after Hastings's death did suggest that an attempt had been made to rescue Edward and his brother, and even that the young king had been killed in the course of the enterprise.) The Crowland redactor's description of Hastings's triumph, on the other hand, would seem to belong more relevantly after the passage about Rivers's arrest. Mancini says at this point that 'some nobles said openly that it was much better for the young king to be with his paternal uncle than with his mother's relatives.'[2] The *Crowland Chronicle* had earlier said that in April the more prudent members of

[1] Above, p. 41.   [2] Ed. Armstrong, p. 78.

the council wished to exclude the Woodvilles from guardianship.[1]

Vergil does not repeat the *Crowland Chronicle*'s mistake of putting the execution of Hastings before the seizure of York: either he had better information, or the error was not in his copy of the manuscript. I have suggested that in fact the Crowland redactor changed the order which he found in his exemplar. It will be noted that paragraph 4 in the above summary could follow paragraph 2 as smoothly as it follows paragraph 3, and that 3 and 4 end similarly.

Finally, both texts have a common story about Richard dividing the council so as to trap Hastings among enemies, and Vergil makes the surprising statement that the neutral portion of the council was to announce the date of the coronation on that day. As a matter of historical fact, this cannot be right. Hastings was executed on 20 June, two days before the coronation if it had been set for 22 June, and it was more likely deferred than announced on 20 June. Coronations are not arranged in two days. The date had not been officially proclaimed by 9 June, when Stallworth wrote to Stonor (above, p. 35), though the proclamation then expected must have been a formality.[2] It is possible that the council approved the arranged date at the same time as it decided to extract York from sanctuary so that he might attend the ceremony, and that this meeting was held on Friday 13 June. (York was removed on Monday 16 June.)[3] Vergil and the Crowland redactor both thought, however that Friday 13 June was the date of Hastings's execution.

I suggest that Vergil and the Crowland redactor may have had copies of an ur-text which contained, among other things, the following statements:

Hastings was the leader of the anti-Woodville faction in London, and rejoiced when Edward was removed from their power. But many people had misgivings about the treatment of the queen and her relations. Hastings himself later repented his devotion to Richard. The coronation date was announced by the council, as a certain thing, on 13 June. Next Monday

[1] 'Regimen . . . avunculis et fratribus ex sanguine matris, prudentiores de Consilio censebant penitus interdicendum', p. 564.

[2] Summonses had been sent to those eligible for knighthood at the beginning of June (Rymer, *Foedera*, XII. 185), and the civic authorities of York voted on 13 June to give their parliamentary representatives two days' extra wages to enable them to attend the coronation and lobby useful peers (*Y.C.R.* I. 72). Nevertheless, both the Crowland chronicler and Stallworth on 9 June write as though there had been considerable uncertainty.

[3] Armstrong, p. 124 n. 74. More's suggestion that a delegation went to the sanctuary of Westminster immediately after the council had agreed to remove York is probably artistic licence. Mancini, the *Crowland Chronicle*, and Stallworth (*Stonor Letters*, No. 331) say that troops were deployed, and these would have to be obtained.

York was handed over. Hastings fell into a trap prepared a day before-hand when Richard arranged for the council to meet in two separate parts. [Note that in the existing Crowland text this sentence starts vaguely *Nam pridie*; 'For the day before . . .']

I would hypothesize further that Vergil and the Crowland redactor were variously led to misinterpret this by their conviction that Hastings had died on 13 June. Vergil (probably working from notes) naturally assumed that the two council meetings—the 'coronation' meeting and the 'Hastings trap' meeting—had taken place on the same day. The monk, realizing that the Monday after 13 June was 16 June, transferred the events of that Monday to a (to him) logical place *after* the execution which he thought had occurred on 13 June. He then tidied up any remaining confusion to his own satisfaction by deleting 13 June from the account of the council meeting and adding it to the account of Hastings's execution.

I

DEBATES about Thomas More's *History of King Richard the Third* have chiefly concerned the questions of which came first, the English or the Latin version; whether More or Morton wrote it; who supplied More's information if not Morton; why the text survives in five different versions of differing length; and why the first published version (1543) is so different from the 'authentic' text printed fourteen years later by More's nephew.[1] A far more central problem—More's intentions in the work—has received rather less attention.

More's *History* presents us with a full account of Richard's usurpation, written in finished, if sometimes cumbrous, prose; and, with a slight change of style, the beginning of an account of his subsequent reign. Basically this history covers much the same ground as Polydore Vergil's treatment of the same period, but far more detail is given, and certain incidents are so graphically described that they have often been supposed to depend on the relation of an eye-witness: as Sir Sidney Lee commented, 'the tone often implies that the writer was a contemporary witness of some of the events described'.[2] Recent research[3] and the publication of Mancini's narration have shown that the author had an extremely accurate knowledge of certain events and personalities of the period. But hostile critics from Sir George Buck onwards have also maintained that the work is so intemperate as to be a travesty of historical method: 'the gross inaccuracies of this work, its apparently wilful distortions

---

[1] The last two problems are considered in the Appendix. It should be noted here that two assumptions are made in this chapter. The first is that More originally took the work only to Richard's accession (the point at which it ends in the Latin version printed in 1565). The second is that the versions of More's *History* in Grafton's continuation to the *Chronicle of John Hardyng* and Hall's *Union of the Two Noble Families* derive from a manuscript which contained revisions made by More himself, the text eventually published by William Rastell in 1557 being merely an interim draft.

[2] *Dictionary of National Biography*, s.v. Thomas More.

[3] Summarized in the notes to the edition by R. S. Sylvester. This is the edition here cited (as Yale *Works*), unless another is specified.

of fact and urgent bias, are not nearly so surprising as the positive virulence which informs it';[1] and even scholars who have largely accepted More's integrity as a historian have had to concede that some of his slurs on Richard were unworthy of so great a man.

The book acquires literary status from More's style and the vigorous asperity of his personal comments; from his vivid portrayal of character through action; and from the long passages of oration or dialogue in the classical mode. Roger Ascham praised it enthusiastically as a model of historical writing,[2] but more recent commentators have found its quality harder to assess, and (as with *Utopia*) have usually been reduced to emphasizing one aspect of a complex work at the expense of others.[3] The difficulty is partly that, viewed as a piece of straightforward historical writing, the *History* is curiously uneven, and the author's purpose seems unsure. The long debate about the privilege of sanctuary overbalances the narrative (as the unfinished report of the conversations between Buckingham and Morton bids fair to do later on); the widely praised description of Mistress Shore has so little to do with the matter in hand that it looks like self-indulgence on the part of the writer; and the superstitious elements in the work are strange indeed from a man like More, who elsewhere attacks superstition in the strongest terms. Modern estimates of More's achievement in the *History* vary widely. J. D. Mackie saw the work as More's 'attack upon the *Realpolitik* practised by the princes of his day',[4] while Kendall described it as a kind of 'Education of an Unchristian Prince'.[5] Where A. F. Pollard pointed out that More's 'history is literary art, and not historical science' and quoted with approval Sir James Ramsay's dictum that More's narrative 'is really a mere historical romance',[6] A. L. Rowse has pictured More as a journalist:

---

[1] Kendall, *Richard III*, p. 422.

[2] 'Letter to John Astley', *The Whole Works of Roger Ascham*, ed. J. A. Giles (1864), III. 6.

[3] Cf. *Twentieth Century Interpretations of 'Utopia' : A Collection of Critical Essays*, ed. William Nelson (Englewood Cliffs, N.J., 1968).

[4] *The Earlier Tudors* (Oxford, 2nd. edn. 1957), p. 258.

[5] *Richard III*, pp. 422–3.

[6] A. F. Pollard, 'Sir Thomas More's "Richard III" ', *History*, XVII (1933), 320, 318 (quoting Ramsay, *Lancaster and York*, II. 486 n.).

It must be remembered . . . that [More's *History*] was an experiment, or an exercise, and that it is only a first draft, uncorrected, full of gaps of names or dates or things that escaped More's memory at the time to be filled in later, and also with some errors of detail that are perfectly understandable in these circumstances. . . .

On the other hand, herein lies the work's value: it is a historical exercise, written down *pari passu* in English and Latin, in writing down instalments as More remembered them of the dramatic events of Edward's death and Richard's seizure of power. A number of the speeches are written up in dramatic form; the work is in every sense unfinished, it ends abruptly with Morton persuading Buckingham to revolt against Richard. We can only deplore that it is an unfinished fragment, More has so much to tell us that comes from people concerned in those happenings. . . . There was no lack of people who knew what had happened; but it was too appalling and too dangerous to write it down.

More was appalled by the story, but got most of it down. . . . A closer study of More has revealed in how many respects he has subsequently been corroborated in details, where his memory or that of his informant was not at fault, from the documents.[1]

C. S. Lewis, on the other hand, revealed an elevated (and characteristically elitist) vision: 'The *Historia* in its entirety will succeed only with readers who can enjoy the classical sort of history—history as a grave and lofty Kind, the prose sister of epic, rhetorical in expression and moral in purpose. . . . If read in the right spirit, More's performance will seem remarkable.'[2] The reader may wish to be assured here that Rowse and Lewis were really talking about the same book. Rowse's description contains scarcely a hint that More's *History* may be a work of lovingly elaborated craftsmanship (extant not in one 'first draft' but in at least three versions), and Lewis, surprisingly for one who wrote so perceptively about *Utopia*, considers the *History* with small reference to More's comic gifts. No commentator, whether literary critic or historian, conveys a sense that the author of the *History*, though an unsystematic thinker, had one of the subtlest intellects of his age. I suggest that if, to adapt Lewis's phrase, we try reading the work in the spirit in which its author actually conceived it, More's performance will appear still more remarkable. We may also understand it better as a coherent whole.[3]

[1] A. L. Rowse, *Bosworth Field* (New York, 1966), pp. 257–8.
[2] *English Literature in the Sixteenth Century, Excluding Drama* (Oxford, 1954), p. 167.
[3] Coherent, that is, with the proviso that, as *Utopia* demonstrates, More's sense of humour tended to operate at the expense of consistency.

II MORE'S INTENTIONS

Two propositions are essential to a right understanding of More's achievement in the *History*. First, he allowed his satiric instincts full play in the work, so that in some important respects it forms a Lucianic, and so irreverent, comment on the whole craft of history.[1] Secondly, the *History* belongs in Thomas Wilson's class of 'feigned narrations and witty invented matters [told] as though they were true indeed'.[2] That is, it is more profitable to regard it as literature than as a work of scholarship embodying the results of historical research. The authenticity of More's material was of minor importance to him, and Horace Walpole was not far wrong in describing him as 'an historian who is capable of employing truth only as cement in a fabric of fiction'.[3] For instance, More can say at one place that a story is rejected by the best judges, and at another present it as certain truth.[4] Like Shakespeare's history plays, his work stands at one pole of the definition of history offered by Sir Thomas Elyot:[5] it is an expounding or interpretation—an imaginative reconstruction—where Vergil's at the other is an inquiry. In this sense, the *History* has a place in a study of historiography only in so far as all history is no more than an attempt to impose some *ad hoc* form upon the inchoate past. Misunderstanding of these two points has been helped by the natural desire of earlier historians like Gairdner, to whom the *Great Chronicle of London* and Mancini's account were unknown, to make the most of any evidence available and so to treat More as a first-hand 'source' in the technical

[1] Leonard F. Dean, 'Literary Problems in More's *Richard III*', *P.M.L.A.*, LIII (1943), 22–41, examines the elements of Lucianic irony in More's *History*, but Dean concentrates on 'irony' in the formal rhetorical sense, and does not suggest that More might have been influenced as well by the more fundamental satire and parody in some of Lucian's works. William Nelson, *Interpretations of 'Utopia'*, p. 8, remarks that, like Lucian with the *Odyssey*, More in *Utopia* 'makes fun of the tradition at the same time as he makes use of it'.

[2] *Wilson's Arte of Rhetorique, 1560*, ed. G. H. Mair (Oxford, 1909), p. 199.

[3] *Historic Doubts on the Life and Reign of King Richard the Third* (1768), p. 116.

[4] See Appendix, pp. 207–8. A. R. Myers has rightly said that 'it is questionable whether More regarded himself as writing history; his story is much more like a drama, unfolded in magnificent prose, for which fidelity to historical fact is scarcely relevant'; 'The Character of Richard III', *History Today*, IV (1954), 515.

[5] Quoted by F. Smith Fussner, *Tudor History and the Historians* (New York and London, 1970), p. 259.

sense of the term. Further, it was part of More's purpose to be misleading. He describes himself in *Utopia* as clowning so hard that people took him for a fool,[1] ironically twisting his biographers' observation that he joked with such a serious face that even his family were often in doubt about his intentions. Our own efforts to interpret them are further hampered by distance of time. Clearly, the comic and the serious coexisted for More more happily than they do for us, although we have the advantage over the Victorians, whose legacy of a solemn interpretation of More still lingers, that we have become familiar with the critical concept that a work of art may have validity at various levels of meaning. *The Four Last Things* (1522) is an admirable example of More's complex attitude. Here a grim sermon on death is studded with entertaining *exempla* from domestic life, and such light-hearted foolery as the citation, as scholarly authority for the effect of drink on women, of a graffito whose precise bawdy significance More pretends he cannot fathom.[2]

Critics are now returning at last to the view of More's friends that *Utopia* was conceived as a joke (operative on various levels), and it is time that we stopped reading the *History* with a deadly literalness. More's English prose style has perhaps been a final stumbling-block. His long Latinate sentences are of a kind regarded in the nineteenth century as the perfection of good prose. Stunned by these mighty lines, in which 'the subordinate clauses beat on the ear in monotonous succession, each demanding the same degree of attention',[3] the modern reader too readily assumes that such weighty prose enshrines matter of equal gravity.

Perhaps More's methods and purposes can be elucidated if we examine a crucial early passage from Rastell's text with the same care that went into its composition:

[1] *Utopia*, trans. and ed. P. D. L. Turner (1965), p. 54: 'Among those present was a professional diner-out, who wanted you to think that he was merely acting the fool [*qui videri volebat imitari morionem*], but played the part almost too convincingly.'

[2] 'Men are wont to write a short riddle on the wall that "D. C. hath no P." Read ye this riddle, I cannot. But I have heard say that it toucheth the readiness the woman hath to fleshly filth if she fall in drunkenness'; *English Works* (1931), p. 97.

[3] I. A. Gordon, *The Movement of English Prose* (Bloomington, Ind., and London, 1966), p. 78.

[Richard] slew with his own hands King Henry the Sixth, being prisoner in the Tower (as men constantly say); and that without commandment or knowledge of the king, which would undoubtedly, if he had intended that thing, have appointed that butcherly office to some other than his own born brother.

Some wise men also ween, that this drift, covertly conveyed, lacked not in helping forth his brother of Clarence to his death; which he resisted openly, howbeit somewhat (as men deemed) more faintly than he that were heartily minded to his wealth. And they that thus deem, think that he long time in King Edward's life forethought to be king in case that the king his brother (whose life he looked that evil diet should shorten) should happen to decease—as indeed he did—while his children were young. And they deem, that for this intent he was glad of his brother's death, the Duke of Clarence, whose life must needs have hindered him so intending, whether the same Duke of Clarence had kept him true to his nephew the young king, or enterprised to be king himself. [*The Grafton text adds:* Every one of these casts had been a trump in the Duke of Gloucester's way. But when he was sure that his brother of Clarence was dead, then he knew that he might work without jeopardy.] But of all this point, is there no certainty, and whoso divineth upon conjectures, may as well shoot too far as too short.[1]

This is usually taken to be a singularly unscrupulous piece of propaganda; a disingenuous slur on Richard's reputation, cunningly contrived to leave the worst possible impression on the mind of the reader while avoiding any outright lie. So in a sense it is, but the propaganda is not More's. The passage is parody of the kind of argument put forward by contemporary 'Richard experts'; the 'wise men' or 'credible informants', frequently cited by Vergil, to whom More consistently attributes his more outrageous bits of gossip. The first paragraph is cleverly twisted, so that by a completely illogical *non sequitur*[2] the unwary reader is left with the idea that Richard's guilt in the death of Henry VI has somehow been proved by Edward's innocence and an emotive phrase about 'butcherly office'.[3] In the second paragraph More uses one of his favourite techniques: to rehearse, in all apparent seriousness, a real or imagined opinion, and then point out that

[1] pp. 8–9. Additions from Grafton's text are from the second edition (usually miscalled the first), S.T.C. 12767.

[2] A Gogolesque 'pseudo-explanation', for which see Geoffrey Clive, *The Broken Icon: Intuitive Existentialism in Classical Russian Fiction* (New York, 1972), pp. 24–9. More had as keen a sense of the Absurd, at all levels, as any Existentialist.

[3] Bernard André had said 'Lo, Richard Duke of Gloucester, that thirster after human blood, was sent by his brother Edward IV to butcher Henry': *Historia Regis Henrici Septimi*, ed. Gairdner, p. 23.

it is ludicrous. If Richard had, 'as they deem', been aiming at the throne even before the death of Clarence, he was remarkably optimistic and unbelievably foresighted. As the Grafton text adds, the cards were heavily stacked against him. After this, More has the effrontery to espouse the assertion which he has just called improbable and unprovable: the idea that Richard had aimed at the throne for over five years when four people had a better claim.[1] In proof of this, he offers one of the 'conjectures' whose validity he has just denied, a casual prophecy by one of Gloucester's men:

... Whoso divineth upon conjectures, may as well shoot too far as too short. Howbeit, this have I by credible information learned, that the self night in which King Edward died, one Mystlebrooke, long ere morning, came in great haste to the house of one Pottyer, dwelling in Red Cross Street without Cripplegate. And when he was with hasty rapping quickly letten in, he showed unto Pottyer that King Edward was departed. 'By my troth, man', quoth Pottier, 'then will my master the Duke of Gloucester be king!' What cause he had so to think, hard it is to say—whether he, being toward him, anything knew that he such thing purposed, or otherwise had any inkling thereof—for he was not likely to speak it of nought.[2]

The story is most convincing and narrated with all More's dramatic effect. Names and places are given, and it is true that Edward died in the night and the news spread in such a way.[3] For better measure, in the '1565' Latin version, More tells us that he himself (aged five) heard the thing reported to his father by someone who was present. The point at issue, however, is not in fact the veracity of the story, but what possible relevance it can have—how a member of Richard's household could have 'any inkling' of his secret intentions. With mock solemnity, More concludes by explaining, lest we have missed this point, that indeed it is 'hard to say'. But of course as serious historians we must hold that there is no smoke without fire: 'he was not likely to speak it of nought.'[4] That this section is a very important key to More's intentions is borne out by the

[1] The Latin text (Yale *Works*, II, p. 9, ll. 6–8) says 'But on this I can say nothing for sure, being dependent on the suspicions and guesses of others, and although one may sometimes reach the truth by such paths, *so also one often goes astray*' (my italics).
[2] p. 9, ll. 6–17.   [3] *Acts of Court*, ed. Lyell, p. 146.
[4] The syntactical confusion in the concluding sentence is, I suggest, intended to reflect the illogicality of the argument.

fact that in the Grafton/Hall text, where the equivalents of the two passages just quoted are separated, the significant word *conjecture* is carefully stressed (see Appendix, p. 211).

I have already suggested that More used Polydore Vergil's account as the basis of his *History*. It is extremely likely that in a broader way the *Anglica Historia* was the begetter of More's work. The new methods of historiography which Vergil had introduced to England must have been the subject of passionate interest and debate among English humanists, and More's work is best seen as arising out of such discussion.[1] At such a time More might well have echoed Lucian, in his essay in historiographical criticism 'How to Write History': 'Everyone's writing history now, and I don't want to be left out of the furore.'[2] According to Stapleton,[3] More read all the histories he could find. These must have included not only the Greeks and Romans, but also Polydore Vergil and such native writers as city chroniclers and Rous. But Hall's comment on More's mordancy is also a description of his procedure as a historian: 'He thought nothing to be well spoken except he had ministered some mock in the communication.'[4] More thus introduces stylistic parodies of other historians into his own *History*, and mocks scholarly credulity in a Lucianic fashion, using phrases like 'it is for truth reported', 'as men constantly say', 'as I am credibly informed' as danger (or joke) signals to the alert reader.[5] More generally, he comments, either directly or by exemplification, on the main problems that face any historian. He was thus well aware of the political uses of history. Besides parodying contemporary slanders on Richard, More gives two ironically opposed accounts of the reign of Edward IV: one, ostensibly his own, a most unrealistic view of the supposedly ideal condition in which Edward left

[1] For a summary of the evidence of personal connections between More and Vergil, see Sylvester, Yale *Works*, II. lxxv.

[2] Retranslated from *The Works of Lucian of Samosata, Complete with Exceptions Specified in the Preface*, ed. H. W. Fowler and F. G. Fowler (Oxford, 1905), II. 110.

[3] Thomas Stapleton, *Tres Thomae* (1588), trans. P. E. Hallett (1928), p. 15

[4] Quoted by G. R. Elton, 'Thomas More, Councillor', *St. Thomas More: Action and Contemplation*, ed. R. S. Sylvester (New Haven, Conn., and London, 1972), p. 122 n. 89.

[5] Nevertheless, historians are regularly taken in: e.g. F. Smith Fussner, p. 256, 'More was considerably less critical of his sources than Polydore Vergil.' Also, on More's credulity, Sylvester, pp. lxx–lxvi (but for parallel with Tacitus, p. xcvi).

the country at his death,[1] and the second, put into Buckingham's mouth, an attack on Edward which is equally exaggerated. Official propaganda is further parodied in the report of Richard's proclamation about Hastings.

More also knew, as Vergil stressed, that there were factual discrepancies in the various accounts of what had happened a generation earlier, and many different interpretations. Vergil was scrupulous—sometimes too scrupulous—to present all views on any dubious matter. As he says of the origin of the British:

> of long season authors have not agreed thereof; as touching which thing, lest I should over-rashly plight my troth in affirming, or on the other side get envy by refuting or falsifying, I thought good in this place to repeat their sentences in order, and to lay them before the eyes of the reader, to the intent that all things may stand to the arbitrament of other men.[2]

This was all very well (not that Vergil always kept to his principles), but More saw that there was gentle fun to be derived from his dubieties, and that fair scrutiny of all opinions meant countenancing some wild legends. There was also the question of conjecturing men's motives and secret thoughts. The humanist could not exclude the human reasons which lay behind historical actions, but how far was it possible to know them? The answer of a hard-headed lawyer was that it must be chiefly a matter of conjecture—sheer guesswork—and that therefore one might as well 'shoot too far as too short'. For himself, therefore, he would not be bound by facts (which were, in any case, often unrecorded), but would aim at poetic truth as he deduced it—a life of the tyrant on the lines perhaps of Tacitus or Suetonius, with a liberal admixture of his own sardonic wit. What he in fact produced, however, was a new and highly individual genre, from which we can now see the Shakespearian history play struggling to break out. More's interest in drama needs no stressing. He was remembered as a boy for his ability to step up on the stage and play an impromptu part, and if we required the reminder, his works,

---

[1] pp. 4–5: 'no fear of outward enemies, no war in hand, nor none toward . . . He had left all gathering of money . . . for his tribute out of France he had before obtained' [!].

[2] *Anglica Historia*, Book I. English translation ed. Henry Ellis (Camden, 1846), p. 36.

including the *History*, are full of explicit references to stage plays.[1] It was partly also that More's imagination was peculiarly suited to a dramatic form. He loved to translate an abstract into concrete terms, and he could scarcely help visualizing a scene. Vergil (who could be dramatic enough when he wished) tells us flatly that Queen Elizabeth was dismayed by the imprisonment of her relations and took sanctuary at Westminster with her younger children.[2] More sees all the details, including the helpers who helped themselves to the queen's goods (and how excellently the style suits the matter):

[The Archbishop of York] came yet before day unto the queen. About whom he found much heaviness, rumble, haste and busy-ness; carriage and conveyance of her stuff into sanctuary—chests, coffers, packs, fardels, trusses all on men's backs; no man unoccupied; some lading, some going, some discharging, some coming for more, some breaking down the walls to bring in the next way, and some yet drew to them that holp to carry a wrong way. The queen herself sat alone a-low on the rushes, all desolate and dismayed.[3]

III MORE'S SOURCES

Although More often treated them with scant respect, it is necessary to give some consideration to the question of his sources of information. For a long time critics were so impressed by the immediacy of his 'eye-witness accounts' that they supposed the real originator of the *History* to be not Thomas More but John Morton. This idea, patently absurd as it is, is not without its historical and psychological interest. It arose from Sir John Haryngton's chance remark that although most people supposed More to be the author, he had heard that it was really Morton,[4] an opinion probably based on no more than the long-continuing illusion that if private conversations were reported, one of the participants must have given information about them. It would be quite as logical to suppose that *Macbeth* was based on family traditions communicated to Shakespeare by James I and VI. No doubt Haryngton further

---

[1] Richard makes his first appearance as an actor early in the 1565 Latin text: 'He could assume any role, and sustain it with consummate ability. Thus he would be cheerful, severe, grave, or relaxed as convenience dictated, and drop these parts as easily' (p. 8).

[2] Ed. Ellis (Camden, 1844), p. 175.   [3] p. 21.

[4] In *The Metamorphosis of Ajax* (1596). The whole question is discussed at great length by R. W. Chambers, 'The Authorship of the "History of Richard III" ', in *English Works* (1931), pp. 24–41.

enjoyed the sensation of being privy to special knowledge unsuspected by the common run. The story that Morton was responsible for More's book was enthusiastically taken up by Sir George Buck. But if there is any truth at all in his second-hand report of a book in Latin written by Morton against Richard,[1] there is no reason to suppose that any such polemical work formed a basis for More's *History*.

The absurdities in this attribution of More's work to Morton have always been recognized by people of common sense. But as sometimes happens with scholars, a phenomenon occurred which might best be described as potent fall-out from an exploded fallacy. The historians saw that the story of Morton's authorship was merely silly, and the evidence non-existent, but they were reluctant to rid themselves of the conviction that More had derived his information from Morton, and pointed in triumphant proof to the fact that More had been brought up in Morton's household as a boy. This is undeniable, though the length of time he spent there and the likelihood of a great official reminiscing, in the presence of a sharp thirteen-year-old page, about events in which he had played an inglorious role, have been much exaggerated.[2] But it became an article of faith that Morton's influence lay behind More:

It is unquestionably from [Morton's] relation in after times that Sir Thomas More obtained a large part of the information contained in his *History of Richard III* . . . to Morton is alike due the minuteness and the partiality of More's picturesque and most interesting narrative.[3]

It must be accepted that, whosesoever was the hand which put it into shape, much of the material can have come, whether directly or indirectly, from Morton alone.[4]

No one, of course, doubts that much of the information contained in the *Life* was derived from Cardinal Morton: conversations are recorded which can have no authority but his . . . The passage which most clearly must derive from Morton [is] the account of his secret conversation with Buckingham.[5]

[1] See W. Gordon Zeeveld, 'A Tudor Defense of Richard III', *P.M.L.A.* LV (1940), 946–57.
[2] Buck himself (if correctly reported) seems to have imagined that More served Morton as an adult: 'when he was young, and servant to Dr. Morton, and before that a clerk to one of the sheriffs of London, of small reputation' (B.M. MS. Egerton 2216, quoted Zeeveld, p. 955).
[3] Gairdner, *Richard III*, p. 68.   [4] C. L. Kingsford, *English Hist. Lit.*, pp. 186–7.
[5] R. W. Chambers in *English Works*, p. 26. Hall, nevertheless, managed to complete this scene without benefit of Morton.

One would scarcely dare voice a dissenting opinion, had not A. F. Pollard somewhat mitigated this dogmatism by listing other associates and relations of More who could have been in a position to give him information about events in 1483.[1] The matter rests there. It can only be added that if More systematically canvassed surviving witnesses, there is much that they failed to reveal. What were the real motives, and intended actions, of Hastings, Rotherham, and Morton himself before their arrest? What were Buckingham's motives in first supporting, then opposing Richard? (Plainly More did not know and would have liked to.) When did Bishop Stillington reveal the secret story of Edward's prior betrothal (if he really did)?[2] Why did Richard send for troops from the north as early as 10 June? When was Edward V's coronation postponed for the last time? Neither More nor Vergil discovered the answers to these questions.

Whether or not Cardinal Morton or members of his household liked to gossip about his conspiracies against the late king —a subject calling for some discretion—there need be no doubt that people in general did talk about the events of Richard's reign, and More must have listened. He knew details about the quarrels between Hastings and Rivers and Dorset which are not in other chronicles; he knew Mistress Shore was arrested about the same time as Hastings (as we know from Stallworth); he knew that the deposed boy king fell into despair (as Mancini tells us: Dr. Argentine no doubt mentioned the matter to others besides the Italian); and he knew about the relations between Hastings and Catesby, for instance. But is the *History* 'a work derived almost exclusively from oral tradition', as Pollard asserted?[3] I think not. It has long been accepted that More used Fabyan (or one of his sources), and the publication of the *Great Chronicle* makes it clear that that work too must have been known to him. A further source of information could well be legal documents of Richard's reign: as a lawyer and under-sheriff, More would have ready access to such records. Buckingham's Guildhall speech in More closely

[1] 'The Making of Sir Thomas More's *Richard III*', in *Historical Essays in Honour of James Tait*, ed. J. G. Edwards *et al.* (Manchester, 1933), pp. 223–38.
[2] Cf. Kendall, *Richard III*, pp. 215–19.
[3] 'The Making of . . . Richard III', p. 233.

parallels the argument, and even at times the wording, of the petition rehearsed in the Act of Settlement of 1484.[1]

More apparently read these sources and remembered what he read (though it is unlikely that he worked with any other chronicle in front of him, and his memory was sometimes at fault in matters like the Christian names of Hastings and Buckingham, which are corrected only in the Grafton/Hall texts). But the main body of his work is almost certainly derived from Vergil. Vergil's history is known to have circulated before its publication in 1534, and it seems very likely that More, a member of the same circle, saw it soon after its first completion, if he did not see drafts in progress. The similarities in structure and treatment between Vergil's account of the usurpation and More's are striking, and it can hardly be accidental that most of the orations inserted by More are paralleled or adumbrated by Vergil. With Vergil's work in existence, there was no need for More to do his own research. For his own very different purposes, it was enough to accept Vergil's framework, facts, and essential judgements. The chief difference in historical approach is in the treatment of Richard himself. Vergil, with greater psychological subtlety but less dramatic force, allowed his hero-villain some uncertainties: he showed him in the course of his fall. For More, viewing his subject as a literary, not a real-life figure, Richard has embraced ambition and already fallen when the story opens.

Apart from this accepted, and fully evolved, basic account of Richard's life, what Pollard and others took to be 'oral traditions' in More's work fall into three categories. The first sort are the pieces of information that we know to be genuine, which are often used to give background verisimilitude, or made the basis for wider deductions (for example, Hastings and Catesby, or Mistress Shore's imprisonment). The second

---

[1] Above, pp. 45–8. Compare especially More (p. 71, ll. 18–21) 'in which inward war among ourself hath been so great effusion of the ancient noble blood of this realm, that scarcely the half remaineth'; with *Rot. Parl.*, VI. 240 'what discords, inward battles, effusion of Christian men's blood, and namely by the destruction of the noble blood of this land'; and More (p. 73, ll. 21–2) 'Whereby it may well seem that marriage not well made, of which there is so much mischief grown', with 'Therefore no marvel that, the sovereign lord and the head of this land being of such ungoodly disposition, provoking the ire and indignation of our Lord God, such heinous mischiefs . . . were . . . committed in the realm.'

are stories like those about Richard's birth, which More reports with a characteristic twist:

It is for truth reported that the duchess his mother had so much ado in her travail, that she could not be delivered of him uncut; and that he came into the world with the feet forward, as men be borne outward; and (as the fame runneth) also not untoothed.[1] Whether men of hatred report above the truth, or else that nature changed her course in his beginning, which in the course of his life many things unnaturally committed.[2]

One of More's recurrent jokes is to set up some such nonsensical story, throw doubt on it ('whether men exaggerate from hatred, or nature changed her habits'), and then draw from it a deduction in apparent seriousness, or use it as the basis for a jibe ('which would be appropriate, since he habitually acted against nature').[3]

The third type of More's 'traditions' embraces details or anecdotes that he almost certainly invented himself. One minor example is the looting of the queen's goods (above, p. 161), plainly deriving from no more than the play of a lively imagination and a stylist's desire to end a long sentence with a balanced antithesis between 'the next [nearest] way' and 'another way'. The inspiration for another such invention can be traced to the *Great Chronicle*, where, during the arrests at the Tower, Lord Stanley's face is 'rased with some weapon'.[4] *Rase* was a word very commonly used in connection with wild animals, and I think this is the origin of Stanley's dream of warning, 'in which him thought that a boar with his tusks so rased them both by the heads, that the blood ran about both their shoulders'.[5] Duly, in More's account, Hastings is beheaded and Stanley receives a blow, so that 'shortly as he shrank, yet ran the blood about his ears'.

But it is often difficult to tell whether, or how far, a particular matter is literary invention or genuine 'oral tradition'. The kind of problem that arises is illustrated by the story

---

[1] 'Exiens cum dentibus', Rous, ed. Hearne, p. 215.　　[2] p. 7.

[3] It has often been remarked that Rous states (at least in extant MSS., above p. 121 and n. 4) that Richard's right shoulder was higher than his left, and More reverses this. Was his memory at fault, or was he wryly aware that he too walked with the right shoulder higher, as Erasmus tells us? (R. W. Chambers, *Thomas More* (1935), p. 176.)

[4] p. 231.　　[5] p. 50.

of the merchant who plays a tiny part when the citizens comment on the proclamation of Hastings's treason.[1] At one extreme, we may think that this merchant was a real person,
possibly even More's maternal grandfather Thomas Granger,
or one of his friends, who remembered the incident and reported it faithfully in later years. At the other (taking into
account that in one of the Latin versions of his work More
entirely changed the comment of the schoolmaster and
dropped the merchant, and that in the second the citizens do
not appear at all), we are at equal liberty to guess that More
invented schoolmaster, merchant, all his versions of their
comments, and indeed the nature and gist of the proclamation
itself. Neither view of the matter is susceptible of final proof.
The one sees More as a historian, the other as a skilful writer
of fiction and interpreter of history, and for purposes of
argument I adopt the second whenever there is any doubt.

IV   MORE'S TREATMENT OF SOURCES

More did not hesitate to alter or embroider the historical
record in furtherance of his literary purpose. His treatment of
evidence is best demonstrated in his handling of the arrest and
execution of Lord Hastings, because the incident is especially
well documented in other sources. The account in the *Great
Chronicle* runs as follows:

And all this season was the Lord Hastings had in great favour with the said
protector and received of him many great benefits and gifts, as many other
noblemen did, and all to bring his evil purpose about. And thus, driving
and delaying the time till he had compassed his mind, upon the thirteenth
day of June he appointed a council to be holden within the Tower, to
the which was desired the Earl of Derby, the Lord Hastings, with many
other, but most of such as he knew would favour his cause. And upon the
same day dined the said Lord Hastings with him, and after dinner rode
behind him or behind the Duke of Buckingham unto the Tower, where
when they, with the other lords, were entered the council chamber and a
season had communed of such a matter as he before had purposed, suddenly
one made an outcry at the said council chamber door, 'Treason! Treason!'
And forthwith the usher opened the door and then pressed in such as before
were appointed, and straight laid hand upon the Earl of Derby and the
Lord Hastings, and incontinently, without process of any law or lawful
examination, led the said Lord Hastings out unto the green beside the chapel,

[1] pp. 53–4.

and there, upon an end of a squared piece of timber,[1] without any long confession or other space of remembrance, strake off his head. And thus was this noble man murdered for his truth and fidelity which he firmly bare unto his master. ... And in like wise should the Earl of Derby have been dealt with, as the fame after went, saving he feared the Lord Strange, the said earl's son, which then was in Lancashire, wherefore he was immediately set at his liberty without hurt, except that little his face was rased with some weapon when the tyrants first entered the chamber. Then was the Archbishop of York, Dr. Rotherham, and the Bishop of Ely, Dr. Morton, set in assurety for a time.[2]

Vergil has much more detail. In the manuscript, but not the printed texts, he says that the men hidden in the next room were Charles Pilkington, Robert Harington, and Thomas Howard (John Howard's son).[3] Richard was especially determined to destroy Hastings, 'whether it were that he feared his power, or despaired it possible to draw him to his side and opinion', 'before his purpose should be discovered to the residue, whom he did not yet fully trust'.[4] When Hastings, Rotherham, Morton, John Howard, Buckingham, and Stanley had gathered at the Tower, Richard said to them:

'My Lords, I have procured you all to be called hither this day for that only cause that I might show unto you in what great danger of death I stand: for by the space of a few days bypast neither night nor day can I rest, drink nor eat; wherefore my blood by little and little decreaseth, my force faileth, my breath shorteneth, and all the parts of my body do above measure, as you see', (and with that he showed them his arm) 'fall away. Which mischief verily proceedeth in me from that sorceress Elizabeth the queen, who with her witchcraft hath so enchanted me that by the annoyance thereof I am dissolved.' To these sayings, when no man gave answer, as making little to the purpose, William Lord Hastings, who hated not Duke Richard and was wont to speak all things with him very freely, answered that the queen deserved well both to be put to open shame and to be duly punished, if it might appear that by use of witchcraft she had done him any harm. To this Richard replied, 'I am undone, I say, by that very woman's sorcery.' Whereunto William made the same answer that before. Then Richard, to give a sign for them who were without laid privily for the nonce, spake with more shrill voice: 'What then, William, if by thine own practices I be brought to destruction?'[5] He had scarce uttered

---

[1] Fabyan, followed in one of More's Latin versions and the Grafton/Hall text, says 'which there lay with other for the repairing of the said Tower' (ed. Ellis, p. 669).

[2] p. 231.   [3] Hay, *Polydore Vergil*, pp. 204–5.   [4] (1844), p. 179.

[5] This is a slight misreading. The Latin (1534, p. 536) has 'Quid igitur Gulielme, sic tuis rationibus ducar ad interitum?' —'Well then, William, is it by your devices that I am led to destruction?'

these words when as they to whom charge was committed in that behalf issued, and with open assault apprehended all at once William Lord Hastings, both the bishops of York and Ely, and also the Lord Stanley. These three last were cast there into several prisons, but William Lord Hastings had scarce leisure to make his confession before his head was strick from his shoulders. So the Lord Hastings learned, by his own loss at the last, that the law of nature whereof the gospel speaketh: 'Whatsoever you will that men do unto you, do you so also unto them', cannot be broken without punishment. He was one of the smiters of Prince Edward, King Henry VI's son, who was finally quit with like manner of death. Would God such kind of examples might once be a learning for them who think it lawful to do whatsoever liketh them.[1]

More builds up the whole Hastings story to a central position in his narrative. Before considering his subsidiary scenes, however, let us look at what he does with the main Tower scene itself. He starts by making Richard arrive late, excusing himself pleasantly by saying that he has overslept that morning, and requesting a dish of Morton's famous strawberries.[2] This incongruous addition to the account has convinced critics of the authenticity of More's report of the whole scene. But this incongruity—the charming domestic contrast to Richard's terrifying change of mood that follows—could as well be the device of a creative imagination, and need have at most no greater connection with reality than More's possible recollection of the strawberry beds at Holborn when he was a lad and perhaps of Morton's pride in them. More, with the instinct of a dramatist, had to give dramatic expression to the change of mood he wished to convey. (Shakespeare, finding himself with still more time to fill in before Richard's re-entrance, makes the lords discuss the date of the coronation with absurd casualness: 'Are preparations well in hand?' 'Oh yes.' 'Well then, what about tomorrow?' 'Yes, that will do very well.' Stanley: 'Oh I say, chaps, my clothes aren't ready.')[3] More then makes a number of changes in Vergil's account. In Vergil, Richard accuses the queen dowager of

[1] pp. 180–1.

[2] A certain school of literary criticism might see this as an attempt to heap the sins of sloth and gluttony upon Richard's head. The oversleeping is more likely an ironic joke of Richard's: it is his victims who are caught napping.

[3] I am, of course, paraphrasing Act III sc.iv. Shakespeare is still more high-handed in Act II sc.i, where he makes Richard, in April 1483, inform a startled court of the death of Clarence (d. 1478).

bewitching him, and gives a case-book account of his symptoms, displaying his arm as proof that he is withering away.
The audience receives this with embarrassed silence, but
Hastings politely says that if the queen is really guilty, of course
she must be punished. Richard hotly asserts that she is indeed
guilty, and Hastings makes the same reply. Richard then turns
on him, saying that if the queen is not guilty, then Hastings
must be. More makes Richard's actions into a still more bitter
jest. In his version Richard shows the lords an arm which he
alleges has just been deformed by witchcraft, *but which they
know has been in that state from birth*. (The historical improbability
of this has often been pointed out, but historical fact is not at
issue. This is More's own dramatic invention.) More's Richard
accuses not only the queen but also (another of More's additions) Mistress Shore of witchcraft, and then, without retract-
ing the charge, includes Hastings in it. As far as we know,
More had no historical justification for introducing Elizabeth
Shore into the plot, and indeed he says explicitly that the
queen did not indulge in witchcraft, and that if she had, Shore's
wife was the last person to be her accomplice. More in fact
probably invents the whole charge, and then says it was a lie
of Richard's. Gairdner for one was taken in by this typical
ploy, and can be seen gradually persuading himself that,
whatever More says, More's story is likely to be true: the very
improbability of collusion between the queen and Mistress
Shore shows that there must have been something behind
the accusation![1]

More then takes from the *Great Chronicle* the description of
how Stanley was wounded, elaborating on it and introducing
(in the 1565 Latin version) the detail that he was injured by a
man named Middleton as a result of a private quarrel. This
may be a case of personal knowledge on More's part, at least
of a legal dispute between the two parties.[2] It is interesting that
Vergil's names of the attackers and More's do not coincide,
except that More implicates Thomas Howard elsewhere.
More then introduces a telling anecdote against Richard.
Hastings's execution was hurried because Richard swore that he
would not dine till Hastings's head was off, so that Hastings

---

[1] *Richard III*, pp. 69–70. Markham (*Richard III*, p. 100) expresses no doubts at
all. [2] p. 49 (Latin).

had to make short shrift, 'for a longer would not be suffered, the protector made so much haste to dinner, which he might not go to till this were done, for saving of his oath'. ('It would not be right for him to sit down at table before Hastings was dead. A pious man must not break his oath', says the Latin Arundel manuscript with heavy irony.[1]) Historically, there is just one thing wrong with this nasty addition to the story. Richard had eaten dinner some three hours before. Hastings was executed about noon, and the councillors must have dined about 9 a.m. in accordance with custom at the time. (According to Stallworth's letter of 9 June the council had met that day from 10 a.m. to 2 p.m. Among much other evidence for the time of 'dinner', cf. Thomas Betson's 'the clock smote nine, and all our household cried after me and bade me come down, come down to dinner at once.'[2] Whether More realized the discrepancy or not is immaterial: it decisively disproves his story.) The *Great Chronicle* says, indeed, that Hastings dined with Richard before the meeting, and whether this is true or not, it seems likely that More picked up the reference to dinner from this source, and adopted it as inspiration for his anecdote. When history is not fact but fictitious Truth, and there is no doubt of your villain's character, why not use an adroit invention to underline his wickedness? Richard comes in for similar treatment later, when More relates a story (which we are not meant to believe) that Richard was displeased with his nephews' summary burial in a vile corner, and comments 'Lo the honourable courage of a king, for he would recompense a detestable murder with a solemn obsequy.'[3]

More preceded his central scene of the arrests with a discussion of the reasons for Hastings's downfall. Principally he was in Richard's way and had to be sacrificed: 'Undoubtedly the protector loved him well, and loth was to have lost him, saving for fear lest his life should have quailed their purpose.' Professor Kendall's belief to the contrary, this is not a statement

[1] p. 128.   [2] *Stonor Letters*, II. 8.

[3] p. 86 and collations. The second part of the sentence is an addition in the Grafton/Hall text, possibly to soften the force of what might otherwise be taken as an aspersion on the honour of all kings, including the reigning one. Curiously enough, after More's death Henry VIII had his natural son, the Duke of Richmond, secretly interred, and subsequently scolded the Duke of Norfolk for carrying out his orders: Neville Williams, *Henry VIII and his Court* (New York, 1971), p. 149.

that Richard was greatly attached to Hastings and much distressed by the necessity of putting him to death.[1] When the
force of the conditional *saving* is observed, the sentence becomes
a sarcasm: 'No doubt the protector was very fond of him, and
would probably have been very reluctant to kill him, had he
not proved inconvenient at this point.' It is an exact parallel
to the sentence in More's initial description of Richard:
'Friend and foe was muchwhat indifferent where his advantage
grew; he spared no man's death whose life withstood his
purpose.'[2] To Vergil's account of the matter, however, More
adds his own suggestion that Catesby was involved, betraying
Hastings out of greed and hastening his death lest his own
double dealing should come to light. Hastings fell into the trap
because he trusted unwisely, and unwisely revealed too much
of the loyalists' plans.[3] More may or may not have had real
reason to suspect Catesby. Mancini mentions that the Duke
of Buckingham sounded Hastings about his support for Richard's claims to the throne,[4] but More might have heard a
story that cast Catesby in this role. He might, on the other
hand, have deduced Catesby's hostility from knowledge of the
growing territorial rivalry between the two men.[5] As a matter
of literary technique, it was a good idea to bring Catesby into
the story at this point if More wished to give him a major role
later; and his treachery to Hastings balances Ratcliff's execution of Rivers and the rest, and suggests the corruption rife
among the followers of an evil prince. Two things are noteworthy about More's treatment of the matter. He strongly
hints that Catesby double-crossed Richard as well as Hastings,
by pretending to have sounded him on his attitude without
doing so, but More declines to commit himself: 'But Catesby,
whether he assayed him or assayed him not, reported . . . '
This is much more telling than a flat statement about Catesby's

[1] *Richard III*, pp. 209–10. But the sentence could be read in this sense only if one
assumed that More approved of the 'purpose' of Richard and his supporters. The
Latin does say that Hastings is thought ('creditur') to have been dear to the protector but hated by Buckingham, although he stood in the way of both (p. 46).
[2] p. 8.
[3] This, I think, is the only suggestion in the literature that they had any specific
plans.
[4] p. 90.
[5] Cf. Sylvester's note, p. 214. The Latin text develops Catesby's portrait further:
p. 45, ll. 24 ff.

deceit. More also shifts the emphasis round from the loftier considerations of Realpolitik and feudal loyalty to motivations based in sheer ordinary avarice and ambition, as Tyrrell later acts from envy and Buckingham from a child's spited vanity.

To balance this realistic assessment of the personal conflicts behind Hastings's political downfall, More launches after the Tower scene into an account of the supernatural warnings which Hastings had received. ('Unlike what we should have expected in so wise a man', commented Gairdner naïvely.)[1] More's complex literary purpose is nowhere more in evidence than here. Partly he inserts the various omens (all of which he probably invented himself) because they were proper in a classical history—Hastings ought to have his Ides of March warning. They were also the right stuff of a traditional English chronicle. But having introduced them, More makes fun of them, in another variant of his technique of inventing a story just to knock it down again. He prefaces the warnings with a neat reminder of the ambiguity of such portents, and their place in the ageless debate about free will and foreknowledge: 'A marvellous case is it to hear, either the warnings of that he should have [a]voided, or the tokens of that he could not [a]void.' He then describes four incidents on the morning of Hastings's death. The first is Lord Stanley's dream, dramatically reported to Hastings in the early hours of the morning with instructions to flee at once. To this Hastings makes the sensible reply that if he is really in danger, flight will merely be taken as evidence of guilt, and in any case belief in dreams is plain witchcraft. Almost certainly, Hastings's attitude here was More's own, but More the artist is not going to resist the temptation to give a tincture of supernatural solemnity to his story by inventing the chillingly prophetic dream, which we have already seen come true. (It is like More to put his portents after the event.) The delicate balance of ambiguity is reinforced by the next incident: Hastings's horse stumbled twice or thrice on the way to the Tower.[2] Well, says More (who has invented this too), everybody knows this sort of thing

[1] *Richard III*, p. 67.
[2] Note that while in the *Great Chronicle* Hastings has dinner but no horse of his own, More reverses the situation.

can happen every day with no ill effects whatsoever; nevertheless it is well known that it is often a sure presage of disaster (!). The third and fourth events are then introduced more seriously to counteract this false suggestion of a deadly intervention by Fate. The next thing that I recount, says More, is not an omen but an instance of an enemy's cruel jest. One of the men who helped to trap Hastings went to fetch him to the meeting, and on the way they met a priest. The man (Thomas Howard, according to the Grafton/Hall version) interrupted Hastings's conversation, saying that there was no need to talk long, ' "You have no need of a priest yet", and therewith he laughed upon him, as though he would say, "Ye shall have soon." ' And finally, in the best classical manner, hubris helped contribute to Hastings's end. More gives him a last moment of ironic triumph, when he reminisces with his namesake the pursuivant[1] about their previous meeting at Tower Wharf at a time when he had been falsely accused of treason by Rivers, and gleefully hints that the tables have now been turned. More thus adroitly turns the emphasis away from his superstitious omens and back to the wellsprings of human conduct which he had previously explored. Between this section and the next, which is a matter of slapstick comedy with Richard and Buckingham donning their rusty armour (an idea probably taken from Fabyan's derisive description of the armour worn by Richard's northern troops),[2] More interposes a beautiful eulogy on Hastings:

Thus ended this honourable man, a good knight and a gentle, of great authority with his prince, of living somewhat dissolute, plain and open to his enemy and secret to his friend, [easy] to beguile, as he that of good heart and courage forestudied no perils. A loving man and passing well beloved: very faithful and trusty enough, trusting too much.[3]

There is violent contrast between this and the ensuing buffoonery. Comedy touches More's treatment of Richard for the remainder of the work; it is almost as though, with Hastings

---

[1] Hastings Pursuivant supplied cloth and ostrich feathers for Edward IV in 1480: *Privy Purse Expenses of Elizabeth of York; Wardrobe Accounts of Edward IV*, ed. N. H. Nicolas (1830), pp. 119, 125. This is possibly the John Walsh, alias Hastings, attainted in Henry VII's first parliament (*Rot. Parl.*, VI. 276; *C.P.R., 1485–94*, p. 134), and described in May 1485 as 'the king's servant John Walshe, alias Fawcon' (i.e. Falcon Herald): *C.P.R., 1476–85*, p. 522 and index.
[2] Ed. Ellis, p. 669.   [3] p. 52.

dead, chivalry and nobility of motive have died, leaving only
the vulgar pretence which More so often symbolizes, here and
elsewhere, as the posturings of a lout acting lord in a stage play.
Hastings's role in the work is not yet completed, however.
After Richard has appeared in his new persona as a villain of
burlesque, along with his stooge Buckingham (in a short front-
of-set scene, as it were) there is still the serio-comic matter of
the proclamation of Hastings's treason and the citizens' reaction, and the long description of Mistress Shore. This section
of the work concludes with the execution of Rivers and his
relations and supporters, dismissed rather cavalierly as good
men who suffered for the accident of their birth and their
loyalty to the young king. In the unfinished state of the work
at any rate, the Hastings episode is the central point, and
it is still more important if the view is accepted that in More's
original scheme the story was to end with Richard's accession.
More has chosen to invest Hastings with enormous literary
importance, carefully built up with surrounding details to the
main action. By making him the main subsidiary character
he has rather interestingly minimized the roles of Rotherham,
who appeared earlier in the story, and Morton, who will play
a part later. Stanley's role in Vergil and the *Great Chronicle* is
kept, but strictly subordinated to Hastings's part. (In the '1557'
text, indeed, More forgets to make any mention of the fate of
Stanley and the two bishops after their arrest at the Tower.)
Hastings plays not so much a historical as a symbolic role.

V   LITERARY CONSTRUCTION

At this point I should like to examine the construction of the
work from the beginning, with particular attention to the
various kinds of dramatic scene or set-piece which are inter-
spersed with the narrative passages that carry the story forward. The deliberately dramatic and highly elaborate construction of the whole thing makes nonsense of Rowse's vision
of More scribbling down the facts as they came to mind (quite
apart from the consideration that many of More's incidents
are not factual at all). Very roughly speaking, More's 'scenes'
fall into the categories of small scenes between two or
more characters (for example, that in which Bishop Rotherham is woken by a messenger from Hastings after the coup

at Stony Stratford), big scenes containing speeches or debate, sometimes mixed with action (as in the events at Stony Stratford and Northampton), and character sketches. Various kinds of portents also appear: the Pottier story, the warnings to Hastings, and (in the Grafton/Hall text) the 'G' prophecy cited by Vaughan at his execution. These different elements are very cleverly arranged within the historical framework of events to give variety of interest and pace to the narrative. If the construction is seen, in over-simplified manner, as a thread of narrative interrupted by such blocks of more theatrical material in the form of 'scenes', the work can be not incongruously described in terms of a five-act drama. In such terms, Rastell's 1557 text starts, after some preliminary matter, with portraits of Edward IV and then Richard. These are followed by the Pottier story, then Edward's death-bed scene, and then Richard's arguments to Buckingham and Hastings and others of the anti-Woodville faction, which drift imperceptibly into direct speech. The Grafton/Hall text, despite some awkward transitions (discussed below, Appendix, pp. 210–11) is constructionally superior, because the portrait of Richard (who is, after all, the subject of the book) comes first, followed by the death-bed scene, which is then balanced by the portrait of Edward. Richard's usurpation then gets under way with the portent of Pottier's prophecy, and Richard's machinations against the Woodvilles. More establishes the moral background of the work with Edward's death-bed reconciliation of the warring factions,[1] followed by his sermon against pride, ambition, and envy, and his exhortations about the political importance of charity and mutual trust, in accordance with nature and religious law. The theme of all that follows will be his brother's ambitious overthrowing of right order, his treachery, his subversion of religion, and his subsequent political downfall. Richard promptly sets his own purpose in motion by contravening Edward's precepts, and deliberately foments hatred for the Woodvilles by playing on the envy and ambition of the other lords. The first 'act', as it were, concludes with his triumphant seizure of the new king from the hands of his Woodville relations.

---

[1] Peculiar to More among the chroniclers proper, but vouched for by Mancini (p. 68).

'Act II' opens with the queen and her entourage fleeing to
sanctuary, and builds up to the very long and skilfully organized debates on the rights of sanctuary, and the cardinal's
successful attempt to wrest the young Duke of York from protection. The long scenes are saved from tedium, to a modern mind
less entranced with rhetoric and the niceties of legal or scholas-
tic debate than were More's contemporaries, and not at all
concerned with the privilege of sanctuary, by the touches of
human emotions and personality introduced. More, the advo-
cate of higher education for women, allows the queen to give
as good as she gets in the exchange, to the annoyance of the
men. For the over-all purpose of the work, the important issues
raised are the overriding force of law and religion over expedi-
ence, and the question of personal trust and loyalty, so that these
two themes of Edward's speech are reintroduced. There is an
extremely significant passage (replete with More's dramatic
irony) in Buckingham's speech in council.[1] In the course of a
rather complicated argument, which also serves to reveal the
duke's brash character, Buckingham says that the young prince
does not require the protection of sanctuary, because the privilege was designed to protect the wicked from lawful punishment, not the innocent from illegal persecution; 'Against unlawful harms, never pope nor king intended to privilege any
one place. For that privilege hath every place.'[2] Since the
prince is innocent, he is in no danger from the law and therefore
has no right to sanctuary, for his 'life or liberty can by no lawful
process stand in jeopardy'.[3] His safeguard lies in 'the king,
the law, and very nature'.[4] Buckingham's argument thus turns
law against justice. Richard's future actions will be a cynical
perversion of 'law and very nature', and the prince will fall
victim to his uncle's unlawful process because his innocence
is now depriving him of protection. The queen finally surren-
ders him, not because legal argument overcomes her private
fears (based on knowledge of Richard), but because she can
see no other way out—a More-ish comment, perhaps, on the
political advantages of force, and also on the futility of opposing
male argument about inessential questions of abstract law
against 'feminine intuition' and obstinacy.

[1] pp. 28–33.   [2] pp. 31–2.   [3] p. 33.   [4] p. 32.

'Acts III and IV' in More's scheme are devoted to the
further working-out of Richard's purpose by the killing of his
chief opponents. Richard's private betrayal of trust is now
accompanied by increasingly reckless public deception. The
big scene of 'Act III'—the scene at the Tower—this time comes
near the beginning of its 'act', and is followed by the supposed
portents of Hastings's death and the epitaph on him. After this
elegiac note, 'Act IV' starts with an abrupt change of mood:
a 'Shakespearian' introduction of a scene of comic relief. As
soon after the execution as Richard has had his mandatory
dinner, he and Buckingham enter in their new role of mounte-
banks, and Richard in effect says breathlessly to the Lord
Mayor: 'A dastardly attack has been made upon us. Pausing
only to eat dinner, we hastily donned the first armour we could
find and fought for our lives.'[1] The dinner has served already
to provide one joke; More now puts it to further comic use,
reiterating that 'after dinner' Richard also sent post haste for a
herald to issue his proclamation. The little scene with the mayor
is partly just light relief to break the tension, but it also contains three very important elements, which will come together
again throughout the last act. Richard and Buckingham now
play a conscious part in a performance of their own, which
they themselves conceive in a spirit of sardonic humour.
Their performance has an audience of citizens whose reactions
to it will be carefully observed both by actors and by More.
And More, having set these cynical puppets in motion, will
comment cynically from the wings on the buffoonery of their
actions, so that Richard becomes at once actor-manager in his
own comedy, and a comic character in More's.[2] Richard's
onlookers, too, are made to play responsible parts in More's
production.[3] The artificial nature of the comedy is underlined
by the Terentian quotation of the schoolmaster in the Latin
of the Arundel manuscript.[4] Noticing that the proclamation

---

[1] pp. 52-3.

[2] For a similar double vision, cf. *Utopia*, where More's character Hythloday
regales More-as-narrator with an unkind description of More as a hanger-on of
Cardinal Morton's (trans. Turner, pp. 54 ff.).

[3] For a more extended discussion of these aspects of the work, see A. N. Kincaid,
'The Dramatic Structure of Sir Thomas More's *History of King Richard III*', *Studies
in English Literature*, XII (1972), 223–42, which appeared after this chapter was
written.   [4] p. 131.

of Hastings's guilt and sentence had been drawn up well before the supposed crime took place, he quotes from the *Andria*: 'Haud satis commode divisa sunt temporibus, Dave, hec tibi': 'There is something wrong with the timing of your action, Davos.' Loosely translated the full passage runs: 'Remarkably prompt! She hastily goes into labour the minute I get to the house. My dear Davos, the timing of your little comedy is scarcely convincing! . . . Perhaps the cast are under-rehearsed?'[1]

The proclamation itself has considerable artistic function. C. S. Lewis castigated More's lack of taste in rehearsing its matter with 'conveyancing prolixity',[2] but the passage is a piece of stylistic parody, which exactly catches the tone of genuine proclamations of the time. More does not tamely say that the document was in proper form: he demonstrates so by purported quotation. Hastings is accused of treason against the king (a cruel irony, as he was in fact supporting him against the usurper), and so of offending against political order. There are further accusations of offences against moral order. Of both kinds of crime Richard himself stands convicted at More's bar. The proclamation carefully upholds the letter of the law— Hastings, it says, has been caught red-handed and the condemnation was subscribed by king and council (a flat lie). The spirit of the law is a different matter. By its very elaboration the document shows itself to be fraudulent, and as a judge Richard has done even better than the King of Hearts: the indictment, which is accusation, condemnation, and sentence all in one, preceded the alleged crime. The legal hair-splitting of the debates about sanctuary is thus a forerunner of the abuse of legal form in this *ante factum* justification for Hastings's murder, and both foreshadow Richard's seizure of the crown on the flimsy pretext of legal irregularities in the rival claim. More later explains at length 'upon how slipper a ground the protector builded his colour, by which he pretended King Edward's children to be bastards. But that invention, simple as it was, it liked them to whom it sufficed to have somewhat to say, while they were sure to be compelled to no larger proof than themself list to make.'[3]

---

[1] Terence, *Andria*, III. i. 16–19.   [2] *English Literature in the Sixteenth Century*, p. 166.

[3] p. 66. The absence of any offer to prove the case (above, pp. 47–8) must have been obvious to More as a lawyer.

After this scene, there is another sudden change of mood, and More reverts to Hastings's alleged accomplice, Elizabeth Shore.[1] There seems to be little or no historical evidence for their relationship. She was certainly arrested about the time of Hastings's execution, but not necessarily as his associate. Her arrest may have been in connection with the escape of Dorset, whose mistress she was officially said to have been. More, however (possibly on a clue from the *Great Chronicle*),[2] makes her the mistress of Hastings, and he makes Richard's proclamation lay stress on Hastings's notorious amours. His charming description of Elizabeth Shore then follows. This is not apparently very relevant to the history—'I doubt not some shall think this woman too slight a thing to be written of and set among the remembrances of great matters', says More himself—but More evidently thought it important. It is in all the versions of the work, but was progressively shortened from the long account in the earliest Latin text, where it certainly overbalances the narrative. Did More take a personal interest in her character and history, or does she have a real dramatic relevance? It is impossible to be sure, but if the *History* is to be treated respectfully as a skilled literary production, we shall not be justified in assuming that this character is introduced without literary purpose. Since she is not mentioned by Vergil, it is even possible that More coupled her name with the queen's in Richard's accusation of treason precisely so that he could discuss her at this later point. In three ways, in fact, the discussion of Elizabeth Shore seems to function as a bridge passage of one kind or another.

In the first place, the *History* is, necessarily for a man of More's time and habits of thought, concerned with sin, which naturally falls into the more concrete pattern of the Seven Deadly Sins. More did not, of course, intend it as a disquisition

---

[1] As Sylvester pointed out (p. 219), Mistress Shore's Christian name is not given by More or other early writers. She is first called Jane, as it now turns out incorrectly, by later dramatists. Nicolas Barker (in *Etoniana*, No. 125, reported in the *Times Literary Supplement*, 7 July 1972, p. 777) has found that she was Elizabeth, daughter of John Lambert, mercer, sheriff of London 1460–1. She petitioned for the annulment of her marriage to William Shore *c.* 1476, on the grounds of his impotence, and later married Thomas Lynom, solicitor-general of Richard III, who probably died in 1518.

[2] Her role is discussed briefly in Hanham, *E.H.R.* (1972), pp. 245–6. The *Great Chronicle* (p. 233) has her arrested after Richard's coronation.

like his *Four Last Things*, but it so happens that lechery will
play an important part in the next section, with Sha's attack
on the legitimacy of Edward and his sons, and Buckingham's
attack on Edward's reputation. Richard's posthumous attack
on Hastings's sexual morality, irrelevant enough to a charge
of treason, is thus dramatically relevant both to what follows,
and as a demonstration of Richard's hypocrisy. More, with his
habit of following an abstract statement by a concrete example,
sets up Mistress Shore as a personification of Lechery. Dis-
concertingly, he then writes a charming encomium on her
discretion, loyalty, and gentle generosity: '[the king's] favour
. . . she never abused to any man's hurt, but to many a man's
comfort and relief', and she was not greedy—can it be, suggests
More, that 'wanton women and wealthy be not alway
covetous'?[1] Lechery is, then, in plain contrast to the man who,
setting himself up 'as a goodly continent prince, clean and
faultless of himself, sent out of heaven into this vicious world
for the amendment of men's manners', murdered her lover
and put her to penance for loose living. This is very much in
accordance with the More of the *Four Last Things*. Lechery,
gluttony, and sloth contain the seeds of their own repentance,
but spiritual pride is almost incurable without God's special
mercy: 'In so far forth that I surely think there be some
who had, in good faith, made the best merchandise that
ever they made in their lives for their own souls, if they had
changed those spiritual vices of pride, wrath, and envy for the
beastly carnal sins of gluttony, sloth, and lechery.'[2] The
Christian image of the Magdalen was probably not far below
the surface for a contemporary reader, though where More
was not so clumsy as to make any overt reference we would
disturb the balance by stressing it. At least, in a history devoted
to Richard, Mistress Shore should have her memorial: 'Her
doings were not much less, albeit they be much less remembered, because they were not so evil.'

Secondly, by building up Elizabeth Shore so much, More
further adds to Hastings's stature and dramatic importance,

---

[1] p. 56. More's trick of multiple suggestion of motive, usually derogatory to his
characters, is here used to praise Elizabeth. The three reasons he advances for her
generosity are all to her credit.

[2] *English Works* (1931), p. 83 B–C.

and the effect of the whole passage about Elizabeth, and Edward's other favourites, is to give a gently idyllic impression of life at Edward's easy-going court. It therefore recalls the early part of the work, where Edward was described in glowing terms, and introduces what is to follow, where Edward will again play a large part. And thirdly, because More could say (in the earlier versions of the work, at least) that Mistress Shore was still alive, and could report eye-witness accounts of this survivor, the interlude has the further, perhaps fortuitous but none the less important, effect of bridging past and present, linking the historian and his readers with the real people behind his dramatic recreation of them, and lending actuality to his work.

'Act IV' thus has the constructional functions of recapitulation and preparation. It ends with a pithy character sketch of Ratcliff and the execution of Rivers, Grey, and Vaughan at Pontefract. More ties this in to the unity of his work by making it occur (unhistorically) on the same day as Hastings's death, and Hastings's gleeful anticipation of the Woodvilles' end was shown in the previous 'act'. The Grafton/Hall text greatly expands Rastell's 1557 text with a speech by Vaughan which provides a better climax to the section.

The fifth and final act in the account of Richard's usurpation contains, besides a necessary excursus into the history of Edward's marital affairs, which is made interesting by a lively exchange between Edward and his mother[1] (another of More's evenly matched battles between the sexes), the climax of three big scenes of oration. These are Sha's sermon, Buckingham's Guildhall speech, and the scene at Baynard's Castle when, by preconcert with Richard, Buckingham 'forces' him to accept the crown. More, like Vergil, avoids any suggestion of parliamentary involvement in this. Much of the detail in these scenes, like the speeches themselves, seems to be More's own invention. He surely concocted the comic business during Sha's sermon, when the play is disordered. Richard arranged

[1] pp. 61–4. For the contemporary reader this history had more interest than for us, since it touched the legitimacy of Henry's mother. More seems to avoid offence by setting up (and then demolishing) the false case that Edward's prior betrothal was to Elizabeth Lucy, not to the lady actually named by Richard's parliament. Contrast Vergil's treatment (above, pp. 128–9).

to arrive on cue, but feared to get there too early, and the preacher was afraid of reaching the point too late: the one delayed and the other hurried, and when Richard finally arrived his cue was past, and Sha had to stop, stumble, and say the important bit all over again and out of context. After all of which, as a modern public relations man might say, audience reaction was disappointingly negative. A variation is worked in the next scene. Again the citizens are stunned, partly by the force of Buckingham's eloquence, but far more by the enormity of his suggestions. He turns helplessly to the mayor to ask the reason for their stupidity, and the mayor suggests first that they haven't understood (so Buckingham makes a second speech), and then, ridiculously, that they are accustomed to be addressed by the Recorder. The Recorder, new to his office and much embarrassed by this unexpected duty, repeats Buckingham's words, being careful to emphasize that he acts only as an interpreter. Because More gives the Recorder's name and knew that he was newly appointed, the whole scene is thought to be authentic. But More, himself a city official, had every opportunity to learn the Recorder's name and circumstances, and one would suppose that if he had played such a part in the performance the city chronicles would mention it. Once again, the authenticity of More's picture is at best unproved. There is no evidence either for the part allotted to Buckingham as leader of the delegation to Baynard's Castle, when Richard is forced to accept the crown by the weighty argument of 'take it or leave it': 'which else, as every man may wit, would never of likelihood have inclined thereunto', says More, piling on the irony and making a triple pun on *like* 'wish' and *likely* 'probable', 'suitable'.[1]

In this comedy, the leading players all make fools of themselves. Richard and Buckingham are sheer figures of farce. Edmund Sha, the mayor, is led by pride and ambition to throw in his lot with the usurper and ends as Buckingham's stooge, and his brother Ralph Sha and Friar Penker pay for their roles as yes-men with their reputations. Buckingham's demagoguery plays on the self-importance of the Londoners as Morton will presently play on Buckingham's. Like Friars Sha and Penker, Richard has abandoned his honour, and becomes a

[1] p. 79.

Vice or Lord of Misrule: a despicable object whose sole remaining dignity is that he is aware of his own hypocrisy. At
first Richard and Buckingham are discomforted by the recep-
tion of their efforts to sway public opinion, but at the end they
are superbly in control and the clowning is a matter of deliberate deception. Buckingham concludes his speech at Baynard's
Castle like a priest leading the congregation in petition to the
deity: 'Then waxed he bold . . . finally to beseech his grace
that it would like him of his accustomed goodness and zeal
unto the realm, now with his eye of pity to behold the long
continued distress and decay of the same and to set his gracious
hands to the redress and amendment thereof, by taking upon
him the crown and governance of this realm.'[1] Richard is
much distressed by this suggestion, and voices scrupulous concern for his private honour:

For in all other nations where the truth were not well known, it should
peradventure be thought [he said] that it were his own ambitious mind and
device, to depose the prince and take himself the crown. With which infamy
he would not have his honour stained for any crown. In which he had ever
perceived much more labour and pain than pleasure to him that so would
so use it; as he that would not [and] were not worthy to have it.[2]

Nevertheless, Richard graciously forgives the lords for their
impertinent offer. In modest reply to Buckingham's prayer of
intercession, he adds that he has indeed done much to save
the realm recently, but the glory must be God's—he is referring,
of course, to the murder of five political opponents.

More gives the last word to the audience. This was all play-
acting, the citizens agree. All the same, it is dangerous to break
the illusion in such cases. The player-king has his henchmen
upon the stage who will avenge any attempt to recall him to
reality. 'And so they said that these matters be kings' games,
as it were stage plays, and for the more part played upon
scaffolds[3] . . . And they that wise be, will meddle no farther.

[1] p. 78.

[2] pp. 78–9. The Grafton/Hall reading of the last clause makes better sense syn-
tactically, in my opinion, than that of Rastell, which omits the *and*; i.e. '[Richard
spoke] as a man who did not want the crown, and one who was not worthy of it',
so weakening the force of the refusal by adducing his incapacity, and plainly asking
polite rebuttal.

[3] Sadly prophetic words, both of More's own fate and Henry's self-delusion,
as More must have seen the matter of church supremacy.

For they that sometime step up and play with them, when they cannot play their parts, they disorder the play and do themself no good.'[1] The further irony here is that Richard himself has usurped a part for which he had not been cast. He has disordered the play from the moment he started to disrupt the peace imposed by his brother Edward, and after the momentary triumph of his coronation, the comedy will turn to tragedy as he falls into ruin.

Unlike previous historians, however, More does not treat his subject exclusively as a kings' game. The importance of the citizens in these last three scenes is obvious. The audience for Sha and Buckingham was there historically, to be sure, but More gives it full weight, as befits a man who was long remembered for his justice to the common people, and who is shown by Shakespeare handling them as a trusted friend. More has brought the Londoners in as a kind of chorus before. He notes that they were happy to believe the official statement about the Woodville arms, their representatives welcome Edward V to London in a passage taken from a municipal chronicle, and two of them comment on the proclamation about Hastings. Finally Richard's audience becomes chorus and makes the last comment on the play. It is a slightly ambiguous comment, however. Richard's duplicity is abundantly clear to the onlookers, but (although Richard has just said, no doubt in bare-faced flattery, that no man can govern them against their will), they either cannot or will not interfere in events, and fall to arguing about the tangential question of whether Richard's pretended refusal of the throne was a matter of deceit, or proper form and decorum in the circumstances, like a bishop's formal refusal of office. This is a very shrewd comment of More's on the historical reality, though it also echoes the conclusion of Erasmus at the end of the corresponding passage in the *Encomium Moriae* about life as a stage play: 'It is the part of a prudent man, since we are only human, to prefer to see nothing out of the ordinary, and to go with the crowd, either blinking the facts cheerfully or embracing error in an affable spirit.'[2]

---

[1] p. 81.

[2] My translation. The Latin original is quoted in Dean, 'Literary Problems', p. 33.

The historical Richard did maintain that his accession was by popular acclaim, but he was plainly concerned by the possibility of riots against him, and he kept London under control at this period by a judicious threat of force and by confusing constitutional issues as far as possible. Under the determined leadership of men like Hastings and Morton the people might have prevented the usurpation. The more substantial citizens of the time had a deep horror of riot and sedition, however, and in this More and his contemporaries would have agreed. The whole question of the justice—and political possibility—of opposing a usurper by force is thus delicately adumbrated and left unsolved in the concluding words of this part of the *History*. But it might be claimed that More is the first person to give the people a due place in the writing of English history. Mancini, in somewhat similar vein, mentions that men wept in the streets over the fate of the princes, but in this case he was writing not so much *qua* historian as *qua* eye-witness. More's introductions of the citizens are a much more artificial device. The parallel with the ubiquitous citizens of Shakespeare's mature histories is obvious.

VI   THE CONTINUATION

I have treated the *History* as a historical drama in five acts, which has brought us up to Richard's acceptance of the crown. This plan is somewhat subjective, but my view of the form of the work was dictated by the divisions of the material as I saw them: I did not start with any preconceptions that the work might be made to fit the traditional framework of an Elizabethan play. The extant English texts, of course, continue further: to the beginnings of the Buckingham rebellion. What happens to my hypothetical 'act' and 'scene' elements in this continuation? The answer is that my scheme appears to break down entirely. There is really not enough of the continuation for us to be able to guess how More proposed to finish his *History*, but what there is of it falls into no such neat form as the preceding sections, and the style and construction alike are much looser. Throughout the work More's style changes with requirements of subject, so that the change in style is not conclusive argument that this second part was added later. (It is, on the other hand, sufficiently marked to have suggested that the first part was mere translation from Latin: see Appendix, p. 200.) There seems also, however, to be a more fundamental break in treatment, of the kind which Tillyard also observed in Shakespeare's *Richard III* at this point.[1] There is still some comedy in the treatment of Richard: he holds privy communication with his page in an appropriate spot,[2] and his scruples about the proper burial of a king's murdered sons do honour to the delicacy of his feelings.[3] But the torments of his conscience are a more serious matter.[4] There is plenty of satiric force in the encounter between Morton and Buckingham, but none of the tight cut and thrust of the debate between the cardinal and the queen, and little of More's earlier complexity of thought and syntax.

What does remain is the deliberate ambiguity of More's approach to history, notably in his masterly contribution to the formation of a 'mystery' about the death of the princes. In an appendix to his biography of Richard, P. M. Kendall has analysed More's account of the murder in detail, so as to bring out the improbabilities of the story.[5] Rather than rehearse these, I refer readers to Kendall's work (which should, however, be read with an awareness that many of the improbabilities were deliberate). The suggestion might be added that More could have taken the names of those he implicates, like William Slaughter and John Green, from the place where modern historians have found them—the grants of the reign.

Vergil, Rous, and the *Great Chronicle*, like Mancini and the Crowland chronicler, say explicitly that the exact fate of the princes was unknown. I hope I have by now shown that More could no more make such a disclaimer to knowledge than a novelist could plead ignorance of a central incident in his plot. What he does, in characteristic fashion, is to retail a version of events with names and places attached, explain

---

[1] E. M. W. Tillyard, *Shakespeare's History Plays* (1944), p. 209.   [2] p. 84.

[3] p. 86: 'He allowed not ... the burying in so vile a corner, saying that he would have them buried in a better place, because they were a king's sons.'

[4] Even here, however, More the historian feels obliged to account for his knowledge of Richard's intimate habits by a mock citation of 'such as were secret with his chamberers'. (Is this a sly reference to Vergil's researches among the *aulicos* of Edward IV (above, p. 132 n. 1)?) In fact the description seems to be based on Vergil's concluding portrait and on Sallust's description of Jugurtha's behaviour (Dean, 'Literary Problems', p. 28 n. 29).

[5] *Richard III*, Appendix I, pp. 398 ff.

that this is only one of many current versions, but 'it is hard to believe that it is not true', and conclude by saying that his informants had no particular reason to lie.[1] In other words, he omits nothing except the identity of his highly reliable sources, on whose credibility he contrives to cast a subtle doubt in the act of affirming it. Kendall, like other historians, fails to see the point of the subsidiary tale about the final disposal of the bodies. Its nature is brought out much more fully by an addition in the Grafton/Hall text:[2] 'For some say' that a priest of the innocent Sir Robert Brackenbury disinterred the bodies and put them, wrapped in lead, in a coffin of most precise description, and threw it into the mouth of the Thames at a precisely stated spot. 'This was the very truth, unknown by reason that the said priest died so shortly and disclosed it never to any person that would utter it.' Construe: 'this most circumstantial tale is undoubtedly the real exact truth of the matter—but it was never revealed' (except by some unexplained means to the historians who so carefully relate it). Similarly, it is 'very truth . . . well known' (to no recorder, apparently, save Thomas More) that Tyrrell and Dighton had confessed to the murder.

After this More adds one of his rare moral conclusions:

And thus . . . were these two noble princes, these innocent tender children, born of most royal blood, brought up in great wealth, likely long to live to reign and rule in the realm, by traitorous tyranny taken, deprived of their estate, shortly shut up in prison, and privately slain and murdered—their bodies cast God wot where—by the cruel ambition of their unnatural uncle and his dispiteous tormentors. Which things on every part well pondered, God never gave this world a more notable example, neither in what unsurety standeth this worldly weal, or what mischief worketh the proud enterprise of an high heart, or finally what wretched end ensueth such dispiteous cruelty. . . . King Richard himself, as ye shall hereafter hear, slain in the field, hacked and hewed of his enemies' hands, harried on horseback dead, his hair in despite torn and tugged like a cur dog.[3]

The passage is basically entirely serious, but at the same time More is indulging himself by reproducing the heavy alliterative style considered appropriate to such subjects by less sophisticated writers. Were it not in Rastell's 1557 text, we might ascribe the paragraph with certainty to Edward Hall, whose purple prose it might be parodying.

Why, after taking the project so far and lavishing so much care upon it, did More fail to complete the *History*? Did he lose interest, or abandon work (except for the revisions of the Grafton/Hall text) under pressure of other business? There is evidence for one or other of these hypotheses in the greater laxity of the new section after the highly concentrated writing of the first part. And it is a fact that More left many of his works unfinished. But various other, more literary, reasons could be adduced. More's account of the usurpation is an intricately crafted work which covers a short space of time at great length and with great richness of detail. It is also More's own unique blend of fact and fiction, and thirdly, it is, by the medieval definition of the word, a comedy because it ends happily for the central figure. Richard's reign was going to demand major changes in pattern. In Rastell's edition the story of the usurpation takes thirty-two and a quarter closely printed pages to cover the events of three months. A busy man might well quail at the thought of completing the work by describing the events of two more years, and the existing fragment of the continuation certainly suggests that More's treatment was not going to continue on the same scale or with the same intensity. The continuation would in any case have required a much wider canvas and larger cast. Where an account of the usurpation could be mainly confined to London, and the chief actors drawn from a small circle, the action of Richard's reign must be divided between England, Wales, France, and Brittany, and between two sets of characters: Richard and his supporters or secret opponents in England, and the entirely new circle of the Earl of Richmond and his entourage. All unity of place and action would have to be abandoned. And finally, the Earl of Richmond may have posed a tremendous difficulty. With the exception of Thomas Howard, Richard's supporters had mostly perished at Bosworth, or, like Tyrrell, been executed subsequently, so that they formed a safe basis for a work of imagination. More might well have felt obliged to stick more closely to fact in dealing with Henry's supporters. He would be still more limited in treating Henry himself. Could the father of the present king be readily worked, with fitting dignity, into a book that had been turning into something approaching comic history, with a buffoon for his opponent?

Alternatively, could Richard be given proper weight as a tragic figure in the presence of Henry? Probably if these objections did weigh with More, they were not very conscious considerations. In any case, it is plainly more difficult to write imaginary history about the more recent past, and for Tudor Englishmen the events which led directly to Bosworth and the Tudor accession were probably more real than the events which had led to Richard's accession two years earlier.

Unfinished as it was, More's work had tremendous success. In the first place it became widely known and influential through being incorporated in the successful chronicles of Grafton, Hall, and Holinshed, and was praised in the highest terms by such judges as Roger Ascham. (I hope I have shown, however, that it was unrealistic of Ascham, and much later Whibley,[1] to hold More up as a model for other historians.) In the second, it need scarcely be pointed out that More, through Hall, was the chief begetter of Shakespeare's Richard III. This study is not intended as literary criticism, so that I do not propose to pursue the relations between More and Shakespeare in detail. The most interesting thing about them is not the similarities, but the differences. Many of More's best scenes are not reproduced by Shakespeare at all. This is not surprising: brilliant artists on the threshold of a career commonly strive for originality at all costs. Shakespeare uses More's framework for part of the play, borrows some of his dialogue, and builds on his character of Richard as a gleeful hypocrite, but the stress on historical and moral continuity with the reign of Henry VI, and the Eumenides-chorus of vengeful queens which give *Richard III* so much of its power, are very un-Morelike.

It was thus the least authentic of the early accounts of Richard that had the greatest influence on subsequent opinion, whether positively on the orthodox, or negatively on those who require dogma to disbelieve. This success was due to its force as literature; a force which the author had achieved very largely by abandoning any attempt at literal realism and

---

[1] *Cambridge History of English Literature*, ed. A. W. Ward and A. R. Waller (15 vols., Cambridge, 1907–21), III. 335. Ascham and Whibley are both quoted by R. W. Chambers, *English Works*, pp. 28, 31.

concentrating on the superior illusion of reality that is the product of art. Paradoxically, the work's literary qualities have been underestimated because literary critics have thought of it as factual history, and historians, seduced by More's magisterial prose, have not disabused them. As a joke against historians, the *History of King Richard the Third* has indeed had a success brilliant beyond anything that its creator can have intended.

8   Conclusion

THE strongest plank in the platform of defenders of Richard III has been their insistence that 'Tudor historians' presented an untruthful picture of Richard and his reign. That erratic genius Horace Walpole went so far as to say of Henry VII in person that 'his reign was employed not only in extirpating the house of York, but in forging the most atrocious calumnies to blacken their memories and invalidate their just claim[1].' In milder form, this judgement has been adopted by the majority of twentieth-century historians, with perhaps some variation in what precisely is meant by 'Tudor historians'.[2] At the least, some reference to 'Tudor bias' has become obligatory, and J. J. Bagley can state flatly 'The Tudor historians were the real villains in the story. It is possible to plead that they were villains by necessity, but there is no denying that they obscured the truth so effectively that we can still only see Richard's reign through a glass darkly.'[3] Its present obscurity seems to me to be due far more to the lack of fifteenth-century records. It is in fact doubtful whether consistent distortion for political and dynastic ends can be charged against any of the historians here examined, with the possible exception of John Rous. The serious departure from truth occurred with Shakespeare, whose *Richard III* is a dramatic production (in line, it is true, with a moral 'Tudor' picture of history which Hall took up from Vergil) which nobody now would mistake for authentic history. For example, it is Shakespeare who turns crooked shoulders into a hunched back.

As for Henry VII and his supporters themselves, there is very little evidence that they took positive steps to blacken Richard's character. Even the *Titulus Regis* of Henry's first parliament passes rapidly over Richard's acts of tyranny, in contrast to the indictment of the rule of Edward IV rehearsed

---

[1] *Historic Doubts*, pp. 16–17.

[2] For a full discussion of changing views on Richard see A. R. Myers, 'Richard III and Historical Tradition', *History*, LIII (1968), 81–202, reprinted in *The Historical Association Book of the Tudors*, ed. Joel Hurstfield (1973).

[3] *Historical Interpretation* (Newton Abbot, 1972), I. 233.

to Richard's parliament in 1484. In some ways, indeed, Richard's contemporaries were severer critics than their sixteenth-century successors. Mancini's informants were at pains to explain to him how rudely everyone had been deceived by the usurper; the Crowland chronicler (and whoever he was, he was not John Morton or any other of Henry's fellow exiles of 1483–5) fails even to credit Richard with the remorse allowed him by Vergil and More, and the Spanish merchants who lent an avid ear to English gossip in 1485–6 heard little good of the late king, even from one of his captains. There is, it is true, one way in which the early Tudors may possibly have maligned Richard: it was simply not open to them to suggest that he had been a well-meaning man misled by evil councillors. And certainly if Catesby and Ratcliff really forced Richard to go before the public and lie about his earlier intentions with regard to marrying the Princess Elizabeth, this action by his advisers probably did nothing to enhance his reputation. But although these advisers come in for their share of obloquy from contemporaries, and were undoubtedly powerful as well as unpopular, the Crowland chronicler, who describes that incident, shows little sign of blaming them for the king's actions in general. Even Richard 'seldom dared go against their advice',[1] but he was a man 'of overweening mind' (*tam elevatae mentis*),[2] who 'was never sluggish, but carried out all his schemes swiftly and alertly',[3] or as Vergil put it, 'a man much to be feared for circumspection and celerity'.[4]

There were certainly distortions in the general Tudor picture, seen as a literary continuum, but few seem due to deliberate malice. One of the chief influences at work was the natural spread of stories such as the tale that Richard had murdered both Prince Edward of Lancaster and his father, Henry VI; and surmises, becoming more and more detailed, about the manner of death of the sons of Edward IV. In discounting these as authentic kinds of evidence in the foregoing discussion, I have probably laid less stress than is just on the importance of living informants. There must be a very great deal that was never put into writing at the time. And it cannot be denied that sometimes evidence may be handed down in verbal form over a surprisingly long period and with astonishing fidelity.

[1] p. 572.   [2] p. 567.   [3] p. 568.   [4] (1844), p. 200.

Unfortunately, however, no early Tudor writer attaches any piece of his evidence to an identified informant, so that the student is forced to distinguish only between written sources and what must be categorized as 'gossip', whether well informed or not. To discriminate further between the idle and the reliable becomes, in these circumstances, too much a matter of personal whim. Such gossip is valuable chiefly in reflecting attitudes. Thus Shakespeare makes the young Edward V discuss the role of oral history before his entrance into the Tower, allegedly built by Julius Caesar:

Edw. Is it upon record, or else reported
    Successively from age to age, he built it?
Buck. Upon record, my gracious lord.
Edw. But say, my lord, it were not registered;
    Methinks the truth should live from age to age
    As 'twere retailed to all posterity.[1]

The audience, of course, is intended to draw a parallel with the coming reputation of the listening Duke of Gloucester as Edward's murderer.

The more easily traced influences on the legend are literary ones, and perhaps (since history is a branch of literature) these are the more important. One minor concomitant of written history is the insertion of inadvertent alterations by new writers or copyists, so that tradition becomes accidentally expanded and diversified. A second source of growth is the conscious enlargement of detail for literary or dramatic effect, together with deductions about motive or circumstance. These, along with popular inventions, account for many of the embroideries which appear in the group of private and 'city' chronicles—the histories, that is, whose distortions cannot well be ascribed to any official policy. The third, purely literary, influence on the evolution of Richard's biography was the imitation of classical models by the more sophisticated writers like André, Vergil, and More. With André, imitation of the classics meant, harmlessly enough, the invention of high-flown orations, and comparisons like that of incidents in Henry VII's career to the labours of Hercules,[2] or Richard's rage

---

[1] *Richard III*, III. i.
[2] 'Les Douze Triomphes de Henry VII', ed. Gairdner, *Historia Regis Henrici Septimi*, pp. 133–53.

to the fury of the wounded Hyrcanean tiger or Marsian boar.[1]
Classical influence had a more subtle and more dangerous
effect on the work of Vergil and More. Too sophisticated to
plagiarize Seneca wholesale, they were nevertheless concerned with shaping history into a satisfying epic form, which
meant that there were certain conventions to be followed. It is
therefore hard to know whether their dissimulating and timor-
ous villain owes his being to authentic reports of the historical
King Richard or to the Emperor Tiberius as presented by
Tacitus, just as it is difficult to tell whether their manifestations
of Richard's tormented conscience depend on genuine information or a sense of what was proper to a bad man. It is
noteworthy that some of the most telling traits in More's
portrait of Richard may merely reflect Sallust's description of
Jugurtha.

Much, therefore, that is described as Tudor bias against
Richard may in reality derive from the urge to tell a good
story. As a small example of this process, one could cite the
emphasis on Edward IV's testamentary appointment of
Richard as protector of his son. The word 'protector' lent
itself to literary contrast with the notion of despoiler, and citation of Edward's will enabled historians to compare Richard to
the shepherd turned ravager. The Crowland chronicler, who
takes a modern interest in administrative and financial matters
and is not concerned to fit his characters to any legend, eschews
such embellishments and has the best title to be considered
a historian in the strictest sense, but even his account might
more accurately be compared to a statesman's memoirs.
He gives a succinct and pointed narrative, but these qualities
are achieved by a process of selection and compression. He is
careful to tell us only what he wishes us to know, and on questions which he seems well qualified to answer he often maintains
a dignified silence. Thomas More (and to a lesser extent,
Vergil) errs in the opposite direction of expansion. Sir Thomas
was writing at a much greater remove, about a man whose
story had already been laid down in its main outlines. He
undoubtedly exaggerated the villainy of his subject; it is
dubious, however, whether he did so from any specifically
Tudor bias; that is, whether he was the unconscious inheritor

[1] Ibid., p. 31.

of a Tudor view of history. It is most unlikely that he indulged in misrepresentation of the character and actions of a man whom he knew to be the undeserving object of propagandist lies. Indeed, he was plainly aware of the danger of both these sorts of distortion, and parodied their effects on other historians. But he was writing primarily as a literary craftsman, not as the investigator of historical evidence.

Given the straightforward story of the rise and fall of a wicked man, More, like Vergil, eagerly exploited the dramatic possibilities of his plot. More's treatment, however, not only sharpened the traditional account of Richard's career, but did so with decided malice. The explanation for this is twofold. More's early literary fame was as a writer of satirical verse, and contemporaries placed him with Skelton, Cornish, and Chaucer as a master of that genre.[1] In the *History* he put his gift for scurrility to joyous use, because he saw King Richard as a personification of that tyranny which he loathed with an intensely personal hatred. In his creative purpose, Richard became the symbolic figure in a moral story. This artificial role means that More's Richard is curiously hollow: a satirist's character exquisitely defined and demonstrated in action, but one that is less than flesh and blood.

In point of fact, it was Richard's actions that chiefly impressed his contemporaries as well. The most that can be certainly deduced about his personality from their accounts is that he exhibited no mental or physical peculiarities sufficiently striking to be recorded by serious historians. His personality was a political irrelevance: it was his deeds that made him disliked and distrusted by his subjects for a dangerous hypocrite. This does not mean that he was not an able and efficient administrator, with many of the qualities necessary for successful kingship, although there is not a great deal of evidence even on this point. His abilities were widely praised, and it is possible that, given time and luck, he might have obliterated the memory of his early treachery.[2] The very complaints of contemporaries about his financial measures may be a tribute to their success, since efficiency in financial

---

[1] *Great Chronicle*, p. 361.

[2] A striking modern example of such a recovery of prestige against great odds is furnished by Janos Kador of Hungary.

exaction is no guarantee of popularity; and the sense of deception that imbues contemporary reports of his usurpation shows that he had indeed been held in esteem before. But as it was, Richard's virtues proved insufficient. His unforgiven crime was not inefficiency, or unpopularity, or even, despite subsequent misplaced emphasis, the murder of his nephews. It was the boys' dispossession on grounds which were evidently not thought adequate by the country at large, and are certainly not presented convincingly in official statements like the Act of Settlement of 1484. As Richard II had alienated public opinion by wantonly barring Henry Bolingbroke from his lawful succession in the Duchy of Lancaster, Richard III had deprived his own brother's children of their inheritance. Such seizure of another's right was thought no less heinous for being relatively familiar, on a smaller scale, at a time when a man's title-deeds were among his most cherished possessions, whose loss or inadequacy could easily lead to the loss of his 'livelihood' to some strong or unscrupulous rival. If the age was violent, it was also acutely sensitive about violations of legal rights, breaches of social propriety, or abuse of trust.

In the Latin hexameters which conclude its account of Richard's reign, the *Crowland Chronicle* refers to those who have entered the place of power by a back door, 'confounding themselves and their cause together by confusing private desires with public good. Neither birth nor experience nor military valour can suffice to make such a man a real king thereafter.'[1] Usurpation, once committed, plainly tended to colour all subsequent views of Richard in minds to which usurpation and tyranny were synonymous. But this attitude was being taken long before the accession of Henry Tudor, and indeed did much to make that possible. The old revisionary thesis of Buck, Walpole, and Markham is enticing but the evidence will not sustain it. Mancini and the Crowland chronicler, the only observers who have left a detailed record of their impressions, give independent accounts of how Richard reached power by a coup carried out with the greatest foresight,

---

[1] p. 577. A reference is probably intended to John 10: 1–5, 'He that entereth not by the door into the sheepfold . . . the same is a thief and a robber. But he that entereth in by the door is the shepherd of the sheep. . . . And a stranger will they not follow, but will flee from him.'

cunning, and economy. The historian may make some allowance for a dramatic element in their narratives, but he cannot dismiss them as liars. Any interpretation of Richard's career which rejects their evidence belongs, like Kendall's *Richard III*, in the realm of fiction. And as Walpole himself pointed out, repetition of a hypothesis does not make it fact:

There is a kind of litterary [*sic*] superstition, which men are apt to contract from habit, and which makes them look on any attempt towards shaking their belief in any established characters, no matter whether good or bad, as a sort of prophanation. They are determined to adhere to their first impressions, and are equally offended at any innovation, whether the person, whose character is to be raised or depressed, were patriot or tyrant, saint or sinner. No indulgence is granted to those who would ascertain the truth. The more the testimonies on either side have been multiplied, the stronger is the conviction; though it generally happens that the original evidence is wonderous slender, and that the number of writers have but copied one another; or, what is worse, have only added to the original, without any new authority. Attachment so groundless is not to be regarded; and in mere matters of curiosity, it were ridiculous to pay any deference to it. If time brings new materials to light, if facts and dates confute historians, what does it signify that we have been for two or three hundred years under an error? Does antiquity consecrate darkness? Does a lie become venerable from its age?[1]

In course of time, Walpole's light-hearted exposition of a heretical thesis hardened into a new orthodoxy. Since 1768 'new materials' have indeed come to light. They prove his thesis wrong, and his acute description of blind devotion to old dogma must now be turned against the fanatics of his own party.

[1] *Historic Doubts*, pp. 1–2.

Appendix   The Texts of More's
History of King Richard the Third

I   RASTELL'S TEXTS

SIR THOMAS MORE was executed in 1535. Twenty-two years later, in 1557, his nephew William Rastell printed a collection of his English works as a pious and affectionate memorial. Rastell's well-known preface to the incomplete 'History of King Richard the Third' runs

> The history of king Richard the thirde (unfinished) writen by Master Thomas More than one of the under-sheriffs of London: about the yeare of our Lorde, 1513. Which worke hath bene before this tyme printed, in hardynges Cronicle, and in Hallys Cronicle: but very much corrupte in many places, sometyme havyng lesse, and sometime having more, and altered in wordes and whole sentences: muche varying fro the copie of his own hand, by which thys is printed.

Eight years later again, in 1565, a copy of More's Latin version of his *History* was printed at Louvain, with an editorial comment that the English equivalent, 'ab eodem authore quam elegantissime conscriptum', had been available in England for several ('complures') years, and that the Latin text here presented, having been written as an exercise, was unpolished and incomplete.[1] The 1557 version takes the story to midway in a conversation between Buckingham and Morton when the latter was the duke's prisoner at Brecknock. The 1565 Latin concludes neatly enough with the coronation of Richard, so that it is the history of his usurpation alone. It is complete within these limits, and in 1557 Rastell had filled in gaps in his English manuscript by translating from this Latin version, or a manuscript close to it.[2]

Rastell (who died in Louvain shortly before the publication of the Latin, but seems the most likely person to have prepared the edition)[3] was apparently unaware of the existence of a second Latin version of the *History*, also by More, which today survives in a

---

[1] Quoted in *English Works* (1931), pp. 190–1.

[2] Sylvester (Yale *Works*, II. xliii ff.) argues that Rastell did not work from the manuscript which served as copy for *1565*. I am not greatly convinced by his argument, since it appears to rest substantially on the translation of a single word and Rastell's text could have contained variants.

[3] Sylvester, however, proposes John Harris.

manuscript in the College of Arms—MS. Arundel 43.[1] This is
much closer, especially in matters of style and wording, to the 1557
English version, but less complete than the 1565 Latin, since the
manuscript breaks off (apparently because the final pages are
missing) at the point where Buckingham is about to offer Richard
the crown, and it shares an omission with *1557*.[2] This manuscript
appears to depend on an English version close, but probably prior,
to the English version presented by the 1557 print, and antedates
the Latin version of *1565*, and an interesting feature is that the
copyist, who was not More himself, 'inserted at the time of writing,
over words that remain uncancelled, a large number of synonymous
alternatives, which are not consistently adopted in the printed
edition. It might be a fair copy of an author's draft.'[3] Thus,
while Rastell was probably right in saying that his 1565 version
was never revised further, he evidently did not know that it was
itself a detailed revision of an earlier text, and so not as rough and
carefree as he believed.

One of several rather sterile debates about More's *History* concerned the question of which came first, the English or the Latin
(1565) version. The answer—that the Latin is basically a translation from the English—was decisively supplied when the Arundel
manuscript was first properly examined by the editors of the volume
in the projected series of More's *Complete English Works* which
appeared in 1931. But some confusion still lingered. One contri-
butor, W. A. G. Doyle-Davidson, was inclined to think that More
wrote his first drafts piecemeal in both languages, working now on
the English and now on the Latin version,[4] while the author of the
'Philological Notes' to the volume, Professor A. W. Reed, proceeded
on the assumption that the Latin of the Arundel manuscript was
earlier than any English version.[5] Both views are unconvincing.[6]
One cannot deduce too much about More's methods from his
(unsound) advice to his children to draft in English what they wished
to say in Latin,[7] but it is evident that the Anglicized constructions

[1] Printed in Yale *Works*, pp. 96–149.   [2] Ibid., p. xxxvi.

[3] *English Works*, p. 50. *1557* retains one such uncancelled variant, along with its
alternative: Yale *Works*, p. xliii.

[4] *English Works*, p. 52.   [5] Ibid., pp. 191–4.

[6] Sylvester's more recent arguments for the view that More composed his work
in separate blocks, sometimes in English and sometimes in Latin (pp. liv–lix) are
no more compelling. Especially, there is no reason to suppose that because More
translated literally from the writings of others he would feel obliged to do so when
adapting his own work (pp. lvii–viii). Sylvester pertinently emphasizes that such a
method of dual composition as he postulates is otherwise unheard of.

[7] *The Correspondence of Sir Thomas More*, ed. Elizabeth F. Rogers (Princeton,
N.J., 1947), pp. 256–7.

and idioms in the Arundel manuscript were occasioned by such a process of literal translation. Many of the alterations in *1565* were made in the interests of a more elegant and classical Latin style.[1] The argument advanced by Doyle-Davidson (apparently relying on Reed) for the priority of a Latin text in some instances is mainly a philological one that is untenable. Doyle-Davidson refers to 'words and phrases [in the English] that demand a previously existing Latin, without which they could not have occurred, or, in fact, even be understood'. Page 191 of the edition cites five of these words or phrases which are allegedly unintelligible without reference to a Latin original. If the editors had consulted the *Oxford English Dictionary* they would have found that all are recorded in English use about More's time.

The second piece of evidence which is supposed to show that the English was, in effect, a translation of the Latin is 'the sudden and striking change, after the Latin stops [i.e. after Richard's accession], in the style of the English, which now hurries on vividly and dramatically where before Latin habits of thought had imposed some restraint'.[2] There are, however, other possible explanations for a change in style. One is that the author returned to the work after an interval of time; possibly, in More's case, after more practice in writing English. My own view is that Rastell's English manuscript contained a finished version of More's initial composition, which had covered only the usurpation and was used as a basis for his two translations into Latin, and a continuation which had been added at a later date. All we know about the manuscript is that it was in More's own writing, and that it was defective in that in three places matter seemed to be missing which Rastell supplied from the Latin. We do not know, and Rastell probably did not know, at what approximate date either the *1557* or the *1565* manuscript was compiled, and there is no reason to suppose that the '*1557*' text was really earlier than the '*1565*'. (Rastell's approximate date of 'about 1513' need mean only that a family tradition—twenty-two years after More's death—remembered More's interest in Richard III at the period when he was under-sheriff.) More quite plainly was an author of restless mind who liked tinkering with his work— the sort of writer whom publishers hate to let loose on page proofs— and the three versions of his book so far discussed bear ample evidence of his habit of adding and rewriting. It is therefore quite likely that the *1565* Latin translation went only as far as the coronation because it was made at a time when More had taken the English version no further, and that Rastell's *1557* manuscript represented a

---

[1] *English Works*, p. 52.   [2] Ibid., pp. 52, 189.

later stage in the work. I have already (Chapter 7) suggested other, literary, grounds for thinking that it was More's original idea to cover only the events of the usurpation.[1]

The three versions so far considered—Rastell's 1557 English version and the two Latin redactions, Arundel 43 and *1565*—have a number of salient points in common. They make the same mistakes in calling Lord Hastings 'Richard' instead of 'William' and the Duke of Buckingham 'Edward' instead of 'Henry'; they confuse the Archbishops of Canterbury and York at one point; and *1557* and *1565* at least were evidently composed when Thomas Howard was Earl of Surrey and before he became third Duke of Norfolk, i.e. between 1 February 1513/14 and 21 May 1524.[2] It is possible that all three versions avoided giving dates for the events in their narrative. Rastell inserts blanks at various points in his English version, and it is usually taken for granted that these were in his manuscript, so that his retention of them in print shows his scrupulous fidelity as editor. Such blank dates occur quite commonly elsewhere, both in manuscripts and printed works. But one is a little suspicious of Rastell in this case, because in the description of Richard's coronation which he had to translate from More's Latin, he says (inaccurately) 'When he hadde begonne his reygne the   daye of June, after this mockishe eleccion, than was he crowned the   day of the same moneth.'[3] This apology for dates, however, appears in neither of the extant Latin versions. Did Rastell, with the publisher's fondness for dates, however vague, that has been noted previously, himself insert these and other incomplete dates into More's work?

It is rather misleading to describe either the Arundel manuscript or *1565* as a 'translation' of the English text of 1557. In a sense they are largely independent author's drafts: that is to say, More felt quite free to add or omit passages in each version. The most obvious example of this is the description of the scene of the Hastings proclamation. *1557* has the detailed account of how the elaboration of the document made it plain that it had been compiled in advance: 'So that upon the proclaming therof, one that was scole master of Poules of chaunce standing by, & comparing the shortnes of the time with the length of the matter, said unto them that stode about him "Here is a gay goodly cast, foule cast awai for

---

[1] This theory was also raised by Sylvester (p. li): 'More may once have planned to end [his] first draft with Richard's successful attainment of the crown'; but he had difficulty reconciling it with his views on the date of the Grafton/Hall version.   [2] Yale *Works*, p. 3.

[3] Facsimile, *English Works*, p. 67. The passage has been edited in the Yale text (p. 82).

hast!" And a merchant answered hym, that it was writen by profecy' (p. 54, ll. 9–13). The schoolmaster's comment on this case of 'execution first then verdict' involves a complicated More-ish pun on various senses of *cast*: an ironic comment that 'the judicial condemnation has been botched by hurried production';[1] 'it's a fine prophetic piece of work: coming true so quickly makes it look ugly, though'; or 'good try; pity it was spoilt by over-eagerness'. The merchant digests this, and then repeats the joke less subtly: 'It was second sight.' This could not be translated easily into Latin, and in the Arundel manuscript the schoolmaster finds an apt quotation from Terence and the merchant disappears. The 1565 Latin has neither anecdote. Such reworking of the original material exemplifies on a small scale the technique of additions and changes in plan which J. H. Hexter has been able to detect and demonstrate in the two parts of *Utopia*.[2]

II THE GRAFTON/HALL TEXTS

As Rastell mentioned in his prefatory note to the 1557 edition of the *History*, another version had already become current in Richard Grafton's 'Continuation' to *The Chronicle of Jhon Hardyng* (first edition January 1543 n.s., second edition (similarly dated) *ante* December 1546)[3] and Edward Hall's *The Union of the Two Noble and Illustre Fameleis of Lancastre and Yorke*, also published by Grafton (first edition 1548, second edition 1550).[4] We have already had

---

[1] More elsewhere used the verb *cast* in the sense 'condemn'. An equivalent sense of the n. is not recorded, but seems a possible meaning here.

[2] J. H. Hexter, *More's 'Utopia': the Biography of an Idea* (Harper Torchbook, New York, Evanston, Ill., and London, new edn. with epilogue, 1965).

[3] Quotations from Grafton's text are from the second edition, issued 'Ex Officina Richardi Graftoni' (S.T.C. 12767), the miscalled 'Hardyng I' of the *English Works* and Yale *Works*. The primacy of the edition issued 'In Officina Richardi Graftoni' (S.T.C. 12768) is evident both because it contains numerous mistranslations from Vergil's Latin which are corrected in S.T.C. 12767, and because the Houghton Library of Harvard contains a so-far-unrecorded variant of S.T.C. 12768 in which two new folios have replaced the original ff. cvii-cviii (sigs. Oo ii and Oo iii). In other copies these contain an egregious mistranslation which describes Edward Stafford, 3rd Duke of Buckingham, executed for treason in 1521, as eldest son of Henry VII. It is likely that this political blunder in the first issue caused Grafton's imprisonment in April–May 1543.

[4] The 2nd edn. is here cited, from the facsimile issued by the Scolar Press (Menston, 1970). It is illogical to refer to these works as 'Hardyng' and 'Hall', and rather misleading to use merely the dates of the first editions, in view of my contention that '1557' preceded '1543' in composition. I therefore term them 'Grafton' and 'Hall', despite the fact that Grafton, as publisher, was technically responsible for both. In general references to the texts I shall use the abbreviation 'G/H', and cite Rastell's version as *1557*.

occasion to notice the way in which Grafton and Hall severally made use of Polydore Vergil's *Anglica Historia* for their compilations. Although Grafton, Hall's friend and executor, must have known of Hall's parallel work when he produced his edition of Hardyng with its continuation, their translations of the same material from Vergil seem to have been made independently, initially at least.[1] Something rather similar apparently happened with their sections on Edward V and the early part of the reign of Richard III. Both abandoned Vergil's account for Sir Thomas More's, but reverted to it when More's came to an end. While Hall embroiders freely on Vergil, in the case of the More text until near the end his only important addition (i.e. of matter not in Grafton) is the anecdote about Burdet and the 'Crown' which he inserts into Buckingham's speech at the Guildhall.[2] When More suddenly ends, Grafton goes straight back to Vergil but Hall continues the dialogue between Buckingham and Morton in inferior imitation of More's style and at excessive length, and introduces surprising new material of his own.[3] But where he had a text of More before him, Hall like Grafton followed it scrupulously.

The Grafton/Hall text of the *History of King Richard the Third* differs substantially from Rastell's 1557 version. Apart from printers' and copyists' errors (of which *1557* also has its share), these may be summarized and discussed under six heads.

1. Dates have been inserted (taken mainly, it appears, from Fabyan), names have been corrected, and material has been updated, e.g. Thomas Howard II is described as Duke of Norfolk, and Dighton and Shore's wife are said to have died—the latter in 1526 or 1527.

2. In two places matter omitted in the More manuscript of *1557* is also missing in G/H. A third gap in *1557* is now filled with a lengthy account of Richard's coronation, taken from some other source.

3. There are certain important alterations that concern the writer and the general scheme of the work. In the earlier editions of Grafton and Hall (but not in those that appeared after

---

[1] Grafton's second edition has occasional alterations which bring it closer to Hall's text.

[2] Yale *Works*, p. 70, collations. But Hall departs from both More and Grafton by interpolating material from Vergil and the *Great Chronicle* (or its source) between the murder of the princes and Buckingham's *rapprochement* with Morton. He indicates clearly that this is not by More.

[3] e.g. Richard's oath to Buckingham that he would honourably provide for his deposed nephews (sig. bb.5), and Buckingham's chance encounter with the Countess of Richmond (sig. bb.6).

1557) occurs the famous and puzzling statement that Edward IV's last illness 'continued longer then false and fantasticall tales have untruly and falsely surmised, as I my self that wrote this pamphlet truly knewe'.[1] On the other hand, More's reference to his projected authorship of further works which occurs in *1557*: 'yf we hereafter happen to write the time of the late noble prince of famous memory king Henry the seventh, or parcase that history of Perkin in any compendious processe by it selfe'[2] is changed in G/H to a reference to 'the life of the noble prince kyng Henry the .vii. in the processe of Parkyn'.[3] And *1557*'s account of the quarrel between Edward IV and Warwick is replaced by 'therof ensued muche trouble and great bludshed as is declared before in the story of Edward the .IIII.'[4] The claim to special knowledge about Edward's illness has little significance, and certainly need not imply that either scribe or author was present at his death-bed. It could have been written by More, either because he had some information on the point or as one of his jokes. On the other hand, it may be noteworthy that Grafton deleted the sentence after the appearance of Rastell's version, with its attack on the authenticity of his text. It is more interesting that whoever was responsible for producing the text shared by Grafton and Hall knew that it was to form part of a larger history covering the reigns of both Edward IV and Henry VII, and that the history of the latter was not written by More.[5]

4. There are numerous additions to the text of *1557*, of much the same nature as those that appear in the Latin versions. One example occurs in the conversation between Hastings and the pursuivant of the same name. *1557* concludes with Lord Hastings saying '& I never in my life so mery, nor never in so great suerty' (p. 52, ll. 12–13). G/H continues: ' "I praye God it prove so", quoth [the pursuivant]. "Prove?" quoth he, "doubtest thou that? Nay, nay, I warraunt the!" And so, in maner displeased, he entered into the Towre, where he was not long on live, as you have heard' (ff. lix^v–lx). Another example shows the lawyer precisely filling in details in his case (words in italics are alterations and additions that appear in Grafton's text):

---

[1] Grafton, f. xxxiiii. The false version had been disseminated most vigorously, perhaps, by Skelton's poem, which was subsequently incorporated into Sackville's *Myrroure for Magistrates* (1559) as 'How king Edward, through his surfeting and untemperate life, sodainly died in the mids of his prosperity'.

[2] pp. 82–3. [3] Grafton, f. lxxx^v. [4] Ibid., f. lxvii^v.

[5] I do not think that Grafton's failure to credit More with the authorship of the *Richard III* necessarily implies either ignorance or suppression. He does not name Vergil as the author of the rest of his material, although he evidently took it from the printed book that bears his name. Hall duly acknowledged both sources.

Ye maye not *from* hence take my horsse fro me, *if I stale hym not nor owe you nothyng. Then foloweth it that you maie not* take my childe fro me; he is also my warde. For as *farre as* my lerned counsell sheweth mee, syth he hath nothing by discent holden by knightes service, *but by socage, then* the law maketh his mother his gardaine. (p. 38, ll. 27–30; G. f. liii)

Longer additions concern, for instance, the execution of Rivers and Vaughan (whose last speech Sylvester thinks was probably More's composition),[1] and there are new statements, as that after the execution of Hastings Richard proclaimed that his nephew's coronation was deferred until 2 November (an evident error of fact).[2] There are few notable omissions of passages, except that the description of Mistress Shore has been cut down a little (*1557*'s description in turn is much shorter than that in the Arundel MS.).

5. There are a large number of minor changes in wording and sentence structure. Not all of them are common to both Grafton and Hall, and where the texts diverge, it is often Hall who is closer to *1557*. These changes will be discussed presently.

6. A major rearrangement of material takes place at the beginning of the work. This is also discussed below.

Doyle-Davidson[3] reduced these six heads to three main categories: '(a) certain additions, (b) a rearrangement of the paragraphs of the opening pages, (c) a large number of small verbal differences throughout.' He continued:

(a) can quite definitely, we think, be defended as improvements, and are probably due to Grafton; (b) is rather a problem, there being no apparent reason for the change; (c) form the great bulk of the collations, and can only be described as gratuitous, in no way defensible, and probably, we think, no fault of Grafton's.

In other words, on this view the G/H text is an edited version of a curiously corrupt derivative copy of Rastell's manuscript. R. S. Sylvester has a more complicated theory: that the G/H versions stem from an early More draft which antedated both Rastell's manuscript and the extant Latin versions.[4] He can thus conveniently attribute certain favoured passages and readings to More, while labelling other variants 'degenerate'. I think this theory raises far more difficulties than it solves. I would propound an entirely different explanation, namely that the bulk of the changes in G/H, whether described as 'improvements' or 'gratuitous' and indefensible, were added to a copy of the *1557* version by More himself.

---

[1] Yale *Works*, p. xxiv. Quoted above, p. 121 n. 2.
[2] Grafton, f. lxiii^v.   [3] *English Works*, p. 222.
[4] See especially Yale *Works*, pp. xxvii–viii.

III THE RELATIONSHIP OF THE FOUR MAIN TEXTS

Rastell, possessing two manuscripts which he knew to come from his uncle's own hand, and faced with a version from another publisher which differed considerably from his own, very naturally concluded that the differences were due to corruptions in the course of transmission of unauthorized copies. (As a rival printer, he would probably be inclined to overlook the fact that in some places the 'corrupt' text gave better readings than his own.)[1] It has already been pointed out that Rastell mistook the position with regard to his Latin manuscript because he knew of no other version. I think he similarly misunderstood the alterations in G/H, and has consequently imposed a false view of them. I would suggest for the four extant main versions of More's *History* the following stemma, in which all the versions represent redactions by the author himself.

Lost original English draft
(usurpation only)

Latin version in Arundel MS.

Latin MS. printed in 1565

Rastell's English MS., with usurpation and added matter on Richard's reign (= *1557*)

Revised MS., source of Grafton/Hall texts

The original draft probably dealt only with Richard's usurpation, and coincided for that period very closely with Rastell's English manuscript, so that the Arundel manuscript and *1557* also largely coincide. *1557* shows some alteration of the original draft, as translated in the Arundel manuscript, however. For example, it shortens the charming but disproportionately long description of Mistress Shore, and omits some of Arundel's details about Hastings's execution. *1565* is a reworking of Arundel—the only version of the *History* that More brought to a state in which it was publishable on its own. This (like Arundel) concluded with Richard's attainment of his ambition, and at the time More may have regarded it as concluding his excursion into English history. Some time after completing this second Latin version, however, More seems to have renewed his interest in the subject of Richard III and the problems of historiography (was he spurred to further work when Vergil began revising his *Anglica Historia*?), and to have formed the more ambitious project of expanding his work into a history of the rise and fall of Richard and perhaps the reign of Henry VII as well. He therefore

---

[1] Cf. below, p. 212.

looked out his English draft and continued the story with an account
of the murder of the princes and the beginning of the Buckingham
conspiracy, mentioning in passing his intention of describing Richard's fate (p. 87, l.4) and of writing either a separate work on Perkin
Warbeck or a general life of Henry VII. Again, however, he
stopped and put the work aside. It was a fair copy of the draft at this
stage that came to William Rastell.

In support of this contention that the manuscript of *1557* was a
copy containing material written at two different periods we must
look at Rastell's editing of it. As I have said, at three places Rastell
found gaps in his text and thought it necessary to fill them with
passages translated from the Latin of *1565*. The last of these cases
is relatively straightforward: the manuscript was apparently defective (was a page missing, or had More deleted matter which he had
not yet replaced?) at the place where Richard's accession and coronation should have been noted.[1] Rastell had therefore to insert a
translation to avoid a hiatus in the narrative. The other two cases
are different. The first occurs in the middle of the debate between
the queen and the cardinal.[2] Rastell's interpolated passage deals
with the birth of the king, Edward V, in this same sanctuary. It is
a clever addition to the argument, but the text runs smoothly
without it, and in the English, but not the *1565* Latin, as Sylvester
has pointed out,[3] the story is given later. Was there a lacuna in the
manuscript (such gaps occur in the Arundel manuscript),[4] an
indication that a deletion had been made, or a mark indicating that
further missing material should be added; or did Rastell simply
observe material in the Latin that was lacking in the English?
He does not say. His second interpolation in point of order is more
interesting.[5] It deals chiefly with Richard's subversion of the Duke
of Buckingham after both princes were in his power. (Rastell also
supplies from the Latin an opening phrase and the first part of a
concluding sentence which are necessary to the main narrative
but were apparently not present in his English exemplar,[6] and
he mistakenly makes the Archbishop of York Lord Chancellor.)[7]
Part of his insertion reads, ungrammatically,

Although I know that many thought that this duke was privy to al the
protectours counsel even from the beginning,[8] and some of the protectours

---

[1] pp. 81–2.   [2] p. 39.   [3] p. 206.   [4] Sylvester, pp. xxxv–vi.
[5] pp. 42–4.   [6] The G/H texts show no sign of disruption at this point.
[7] He does not 'correct' the Latin, which does not say that Cardinal Bourchier
was chancellor, as Sylvester supposes (p. 211).
[8] Compare Vergil, ed. Ellis (1844), p. 174; 'as is commonly believed' Richard
disclosed his plans of usurpation to Buckingham at Northampton before seizing
Edward V.

frendes said that the duke was the first mover of the protectoure to this matter, sending a privie messenger unto him streight after king Edwards death, but other again which knewe better the suttle wit of the protectour deny that he ever opened his enterprise to the duke untill he had brought to passe the thinges before rehersed. (pp. 42–3)

Now in this case Rastell has officiously inserted material that had no place in his author's new scheme. When he translated this passage from the Latin, he failed to notice that there was very good reason for omitting it from an English version that continued further: the story about the secret messenger, which More had rejected in the Latin as a false invention of Richard's supporters, he now introduced at a later point as a truthful account: 'as I have for certain bene enformed' (p. 88). I have shown that the literal truth or otherwise of such accounts was of little interest for More's artistic purposes, but he was too careful a craftsman to contradict himself so blatantly in the same manuscript.[1] It is, however, typical of him to juggle round with the same story in successive versions like this. The question of Buckingham's motives and the nature of his association with Richard is still an unsolved problem for historians, and it fascinated More, especially when he had to incorporate Buckingham's rebellion into his expanded narrative. The Arundel manuscript, accidentally or deliberately, omits the discussion of Buckingham's relations with Richard altogether. The 1565 version inserts it between the accounts of the extraction of the young prince from sanctuary and the arrest of Hastings, as a reintroduction of Buckingham and an explanation of his forthcoming role in obtaining the throne for Richard.[2] *1557* (with this inserted by Rastell) later prefaces its account of the *entente* between Buckingham and Morton with a description of how Buckingham had offered his services to Richard immediately after the death of Edward IV (pp. 88–9), and the G/H text (retaining a brief recapitulation at that point) transfers this description to its logical place, before Richard's seizure of Edward V.

This treatment of the Gloucester/Buckingham relationship in successive versions suggests strongly that Rastell's manuscript was defective for the reason that the author had himself deleted material from it in the process of revision: it was an interim draft.[3] The transfer of the passage in the G/H version in turn suggests the author's further reworking of material: the G/H

[1] I cannot agree with Sylvester (p. 210) that the two accounts are compatible.
[2] pp. 42–4.
[3] Similarly *1565* (p. 82) has at the end a description of Richard clutching his dagger and constantly glancing about him 'like one ready to strike back', which parallels a later passage in the 'continuation' in *1557* (p. 87) and G/H.

version derives from another, and later, of More's working drafts. Different commentators will concede that different alterations in G/H constitute improvements on *1557*, but the consensus of opinion is still that G/H is 'a garbled version' of *1557*, and that *1557* uniquely exemplifies More's authentic work.[1] There are historical reasons for the persistence of this opinion: Rastell's authority, and the fact that although the Latin Arundel manuscript had long been known, it was first properly examined and collated for the 1931 edition of the *History*. As a consequence perhaps, the editors themselves had not become so familiar with the idea that More was a compulsive rewriter that they could take the further step of seeing the G/H text as yet another authorial revision. The seed from a new discovery commonly takes long to germinate.

IV   TEXTUAL CHANGES IN GRAFTON/HALL

The important rearrangement made by G/H in the opening paragraphs of More's work can best be illustrated by a summary of G/H which divides the material into numbered blocks. Italicized matter represents connective links which are not in *1557*. Roman numerals in square brackets show the order in *1557*.

Edward V began his reign on 9 April 1483. But within three months his uncle killed him. First we must learn their lineage.

[II]   1. Richard Duke of York had three sons. . . . Portrait of the youngest, Richard. Richard is said to have killed Henry VI and possibly connived at the death of his brother Clarence. This, however, is matter for conjecture, like the point at which he started to aim at the throne.

Before relating Richard's wickedness we must mention an example of Edward IV's beneficence.

[IV]   2. Edward's death-bed reconciliation of his friends.

[I]   3. Edward IV reigned 22 years. . . . He left the following children. . . . Portrait of Edward. But he left his sons an unnatural protector in their uncle Richard.

Who obviously (to some) plotted their deaths in their father's lifetime, because

[III]   4. Pottier immediately prophesied on Edward's death that Richard would be king. To return to the history, Richard now fomented strife with the Woodvilles.
5. The Duke of Buckingham conspired with Richard right after Edward's death.[2]

---

[1] R. W. Chambers in *English Works*, p. 27.
[2] This (the story denied in *1565* and Rastell's insertion) appears in *1557* at a point close to the end of the whole narrative.

This rearrangement of material has rightly puzzled critics who assume that it was done by Grafton. There was no obvious reason for an editor to disturb the order, especially when to do so meant writing new connecting links, and Grafton seems in fact to have been a faithful printer, and one unlikely to tamper with the work of a famous and highly respected author like More. In the first edition of his continuation of Hardyng's chronicle he printed non-sensical mistranslations from Vergil; he left unchanged statements by More about Edward IV that directly contradicted statements which he had taken from Vergil; he repeated the anecdote about the 'G. following E.' prophecy, which was also in Vergil's material; and, like Rastell, he preserved a clumsy repetition that most editors would have removed—the two comments on Hastings's relations with Elizabeth Shore: 'savyng it is sayd that he forbare her for reverence towarde his kyng, or els of a certayne kynd of fydelitee towarde his frend' (f. lvii^v), and 'whiche . . . yet he forbare, either for a pryncely reverence or for a certayne frendely faithfulnesse' (f. lxii).[1] He also seems to have retained copyists' errors in his exemplar: for instance both Grafton and Hall have (with slight variation in spelling) 'wherfore either is there peril, ner none there is deede, or if any be it is rather in goyng' (G. f. lviii^v; H. sig. CC. ij), where *1557* has, evidently correctly, 'wherfore either is there no peryl (nor none there is in dede); or if any be, it is rather in going' (p. 50). It is therefore unlikely that Grafton would have made major and inexplicable changes in the ordering of his text. These changes are, on the other hand, ones that might well occur to an author. One of them—the transfer of matter concerning Buckingham—was made in connection with a problem which had demonstrably bothered More in earlier stages of revision. The others seem similarly to be made in an attempt to find the best order for rather intractable material. It is possible that *1557* already contained at least one change from More's original draft. On the second page of the text in the *1557* edition (Yale, p. 6) More says that Edward IV died leaving his sons to the protection of their uncle Richard, who bereft them of their dignity and their lives. He then promises a description of the villain who is the subject of his book: 'It is therefore conveniente sommewhat to shewe you ere we farther goe, what maner of manne this was that coulde fynde in his hearte so much mischiefe to conceive.' But the next sentence starts, not with the expected 'Richard Duke of Gloucester', but with 'Richarde Duke of Yorke'; that is, it embarks on an abrupt account of the lineage of the Duke of Gloucester and his brothers. (The Latin texts follow

---

[1] More himself omits the first occurrence in the two Latin translations.

suit.) G/H, far more logically, puts this paragraph at an earlier point. It also describes the death-bed scene of Edward IV at an earlier place than *1557*, which inserts it very late, after Richard's actions on Edward's death have been discussed. So far, so good: the reviser had put his material into much better chronological order. But he then found himself in difficulty, because the paragraph that dealt with the history of the York family had ended with speculations about the point in time at which Richard had started to think about usurping the throne, and had commented that such speculation was idle: 'But of al this pointe is there no certaintie, and whoso divineth uppon conjectures maye as wel shote to farre as to short' (p. 9). In *1557* this led on to the anecdote about Pottier (introduced by 'Howbeit this have I by credible informacion learned') and Pottier's prophecy (a 'conjecture' in another sense of the word): 'Then wyll my mayster the Duke of Gloucester bee kynge.'

For chronological reasons the G/H reviser wished to introduce Edward's death-scene at this place, so he held back the Pottier story and inserted it later, after the passage describing Edward IV's reign and the deceptive protection given his sons, which he had displaced from its position at the beginning of *1557*. This was a rather clumsy manoeuvre, but it enables us to make a very interesting observation on the reviser's methods. In the earlier version, as I have said, the story occurs immediately after the remark that it is useless to found guesses on conjectures (baseless interpretations or prophecies). It there concludes with 'But nowe to returne to the course of this hystorye' (p. 9). In the new version, the remark about conjectures had appeared long before, and had then been annotated 'but this conjecture afterward toke place (as fewe doe) as you shall perceive here after'. The reviser therefore now reverts to it with 'And first to shewe you, that *by conjecture* he pretended this thyng in his brothers life, ye shall understand for a truth that in the same night that Kyng Edwarde died, one called Mistelbrooke . . .' Then, to emphasize that this anecdote is of a distinctly shaggy variety and designed to demonstrate the sort of absurdity involved in 'conjectures', the reviser concludes 'But now too returne to *the trewe historie* . . .' (ff. xxxviii–xxxviii^v).[1] He similarly makes fun of another story later in the narrative. In *1557* More (probably as light relief from a serious subject, and to give substance to his intended jibe about Richard's desire to give his nephews kingly burial) relates that 'they say' that a priest of Sir Robert Brackenbury's reinterred the bodies of the princes and died without revealing the place (p. 86). G/H adds another, fuller, version, and makes it quite explicit that it is nonsense:

[1] My italics.

For some say that Kyng Rycharde caused the priest to take them up and close them in lead and put them in a coffyne full of holes hoked at the endes with ii. hokes of yron, and so to cast them into a place called the Blacke Depes at the Themes mouth, so that they should never rise up nor be sene agayne. This was the very trueth unknowen by reason that the sayd priest died so shortly and disclosed it never to any person that would utter it. (f. lxxxii^v)

If More did not furnish these alterations to his own text, someone else was taking remarkable liberties. He also had the same impish sense of humour, because he goes out of his way to preserve More's indications that his story of Pottier's prophecy is fatuous, and makes clear that his own contribution to the tales of the princes' murder (complete with careful description of the coffin) is a barefaced lie.

Whether the verbal changes in G/H are an improvement on *1557* or inept alterations is largely, perhaps, a matter of taste. The more useful question is whether they are of a kind probably made by an editor or copyist, or by the author in person. Some are obvious misreadings by copyists, like 'as the south wind' for 'as the sea without wind' (p. 44, l. 26). There are similar mistakes, by printer or copyist, in Rastell's text: 'hee shall not, If I aske' (p. 38, l. 24) for 'he shall not. Note, if I aske' in G/H; 'bene a slepe' (p. 47, l. 5) for 'bene a sleper', or 'estemed no slight' (p. 34, l. 27, note) for 'estemed not slight', just as Rastell omits a crucial phrase, supplied by G/H and here added in italics, in 'And the mischief that he tooke, within lesse then thre yeares of the mischiefe that he dyd *in thre monethes be not comparable*' (p. 87), or in 'of more learning then vertue, of more fame then lerning, *& yet of more learnyng then trueth*' (p. 58). It certainly cannot be argued that all verbal changes in the text are due to the author—copyists and printers have undoubtedly taken a hand. I would suggest, however, that the deliberate changes are too many (there is scarcely a sentence without some alteration) and too competent to be the work of a hack editor, and not thoroughgoing enough to be made by a plagiarist or adapter. There is a further significant thing about them. American publishers commonly give their authors' manuscripts to a copy-editor who is at liberty to suggest extensive changes in style and wording. The author who checks through these alterations by a second person will almost invariably find that some have seriously distorted his meaning. This is not the case with the changes in G/H. They may simplify a construction, add new information, substitute a synonym,[1] expand

[1] e.g. *1557*, p. 38 'Suppose he could not aske it, suppose he woulde not aske it, suppose hee woulde aske to goe owte', which becomes in G. (f. liii) 'Suppose he could not aske it, & thynke he would not aske it, and ymagene he would aske to go out'.

a story or an argument, or clarify a point, but they do not (except in the case of obvious literal errors which usually occur in one edition and are corrected in the others, or in cases where Grafton and Hall diverge) show such inadvertent misunderstanding of the earlier text. This seems strong evidence that they were made by the original author.

The bulk of the alterations, in my opinion, are therefore the emendations of a style-conscious author going over earlier work and striving for greater clarity and more elegant phrasing.[1] One of the clearest examples of such an improvement occurs in the description of Richard, where the earlier text has 'hard favoured of visage, and suche as is in states called warlye, in other menne otherwise' (p. 7). Grafton has 'hard favoured of visage, suche as in estates is called a warlike visage, and emong commen persones a crabbed face' (f. xxxiii). It seems small compliment to More to suppose that another man had to make this excellent amendment to the flat 'in other menne otherwise'. Similarly, *1557* has 'For men use, if they have an evil turne, to write it in marble, and whoso doth us a good tourne, we write it in duste' (p. 57). G/H reduces this to the more epigrammatic 'For [men] use to wryte an evil turne in marble stone, but a good turne they wryte in the dust' (f. lxiii). And for one of very many instances of simplified constructions, compare *1557*: 'his hors twise or thrise stumbled with him almost to the falling, which thing albeit eche man wote wel daily happeneth to them to whom no such mischaunce is toward, yet hath it ben of an olde rite and custome, observed as a token often times natably foregoing some great misfortune' (p. 50) with Grafton 'his horse that he accustomed to ride on, stombled with him twise or thrise almost to the fallyng, whiche thyng although it happeth to them dayly to whom no mischaunce is toward, yet hath it bene as an olde evil token observed as a goyng toward mischief' (f. lix).

According to Sylvester, simplification is one of the three scribal vices—'simplification, modernization, vulgarization—that inevitably occur when an author's manuscript is passed from hand to hand, copied and recopied over a fairly extended period'.[2] Perhaps, but authors have themselves been known to simplify and modernize, not necessarily for the worse. It is equally common to find copyists confusing their matter. The copyists allegedly responsible for the

[1] It is true that G/H sometimes blunts the edge of the *1557* text; notably it destroys the subtleties in the discussion of Richard's earlier deeds (above, p. 157). This change, however, is in line with More's increasingly uncompromising attitude to Richard as the work progressed. Possibly, too, he now had in mind a wider and less sophisticated readership than his private circle.

[2] p. xxiii.

degenerate state of the G/H text not only produced felicities worthy of More himself, but appear to have read his mind to an uncanny degree. Where *1557* has '& somme yet drewe to them that holpe to carrye a wronge waye' (p. 21), G/H has '& some caried more then they were commaunded to another place', which is both clearer and closer to the Latin versions, 'nec deerant . . . qui alio quaedam quam quo destinabantur efferrent.' For *1557*'s 'and made a short shrift, for a longer would not be suffered, the protectour made so much hast to dyner, which he might not go to til this wer done for saving of his othe' (p. 49), G/H has 'made so muche hast to his diner, whiche might not go to it tyl this murther were done, for saving of his ungratious othe'. In the Arundel manuscript More had similarly stressed Richard's impious piety: 'ne protector non satis tempestive pranderet cui non erat phas ante discumbere quam ille occubuisset, videlicet homo pius ne pegeraret' (p. 128). Is there not a More pun intended on 'ungracious' and 'grace before dinner'? Were there really two men involved with the text of More's *History* who had this habit of playing about with an idea and dressing it in different forms of words?

V   HALL'S VARIATIONS

So far I have treated the texts of Grafton and Hall as essentially the same. There remains to be considered the problem posed by the discrepancies between the two, because, as Sylvester has pointed out, there are puzzling instances where Hall departs from Grafton's reading and gives one that is much closer to *1557*. These make it quite clear that Hall's text was not a transcript from Grafton's print. The plainest case is in the following set of parallel texts from the dialogue between the cardinal and the queen. *1557* has:

'I mynde that he shalbe where I am till I see further. For I assure you, for that I se some men so gredye . . . to have him, this maketh me much the more farder to deliver him'. 'Truely, madame', quod he, 'and the farder that you be to delyver him, the farder bene other men to suffer you to kepe hym, lest your causeles fere might cause you ferther to convay him'. (p. 37)

Grafton reads:

'I mynde he shall bee where I am till I see further, for I see some menne so gredy . . . too have hym, whiche maketh me muche more afraied and scrupulous too deliver hym'. 'Truely, madame', quoth the cardynall, 'the more afraied that ye bee too deliver hym, the more other menne feareth too suffre you too kepe hym, leaste youre causelesse feare might cause you farther too conveighe hym'. (f. lii)

And Hall:

'I mynde he shalbe where I am till I see further, for I se some men so gredy
. . . to have him, whiche maketh me much more further and scrupulous too
deliver hym'. 'Truely, madame', quod the cardinall, 'the further that ye
bee too deliver hym, the further bee other menne too suffre you too kepe
hym, leaste your causelesse feare myght cause you farther to conveyghe
hym'. (sig. BB.5)

Here Hall shares most of Grafton's wording, but Grafton's text
changes the old-fashioned and ambiguous *farder* (i.e. more fearful)
to 'more afraied'. Hall, or his exemplar, like Sylvester and the editors of the 1931 edition, has misunderstood *farder* as meaning
further, a mistake helped by the earlier occurrence of *further*.[1]
Hall could not have produced such a reading from Grafton's text:
it could arise only from one that retained the wording of *1557*.
(Grafton, in the same way, could have modernized the wording of
1557, but would be unlikely to deduce the correct sense from Hall.)
  Sylvester thought that the 'corrections' made in Hall as against
Grafton, i.e. these cases where Hall is closer to *1557*, 'would point
to the descent of both manuscripts [of Grafton and Hall] from a
common ancestor, with Halle's copy (perhaps edited by himself)
descending through a lesser number of intermediaries'.[2] I would
agree with this estimate in general, but I think some of the divergencies can be explained more precisely, if we hypothesize that both
Hall and Grafton descend from a manuscript like the Arundel
manuscript or the manuscript of Vergil's *Anglica Historia*. In other
words, from an author's working draft, in which some of the earlier
text was retained uncancelled, and second thoughts and alternative words and phrases were inserted.[3] In such a manuscript,
More's corrected draft of the passage just quoted might have had:

I mynde ~~that~~ he shalbe where I am till I see further for

~~I assure you for that~~ I se some men so gredye
              whiche   afraied & scrupulous
to have him ~~this~~ maketh me much ~~the~~ more farder to deliver
                        ye cardynall   more afraied
him. Truely madame quod ~~he and~~ the farder that you be
              more other menne feareth
to delyver him the farder bene other men to suffer you
to kepe hym

  [1] The Latin leaves no doubt of the meaning: 'horreo . . . pertimescis . . . alij
magis metuunt.'   [2] p. xxii n. 1.
  [3] It is noteworthy that in the Arundel MS. both main text and additions are in
the hand of the same copyist (not More): see above, p. 199. This copyist himself
introduced evident errors.

From this, different copyists could readily derive different readings. There is a variation of similar significance between *1557* and G/H at Yale p. 9, ll. 20–22 (Grafton f. xxxviii^v; Hall sig. AA. iiij). *1557* reads: 'were it that the duke of Gloucester hadde of olde foreminded this conclusion, or was nowe at erste therunto moved'. Grafton has: 'wer it that the duke of Gloucestre had of olde sore practised this conclusion, or was before tyme[1] moved there unto.' *Practised* is a reasonable synonym for *foreminded* ('plotted' for 'planned'). It was probably interlineated over *foreminded*, and a scribe adopted the substitution. But he apparently thought that *practised* was intended as an alternative to the simple verb *minded* alone, and so read the prefix *fore-* as the adverb *sore*, and retained it (rather inappropriately) to modify *practised*.[2] A like explanation can be given of the passages in *1557* (Yale, p. 38, ll. 8–10), Grafton (f. lii^v), and Hall (sig. BB.5). *1557* has: 'Troweth the protector (I pray god he may prove a protectour) troweth he that I parceive not whereunto his painted processe draweth? It is not honorable . . .'[3] Grafton gives: 'Troweth the protectoure (I praie God he maie prove a protectour, rather then a destroyer, where unto his painted processe draweth. Is it not honourable . . .' Hall has: 'Troweth the protector (I pray God he may prove a protectour, rather then a destroyer, where unto his painted processe draweth) y^t is it not honourable, y^t the duke byde here?' Here a copyist (or reader) seems to have observed the insertion 'rather than a destroyer', but thought it was meant to supersede 'troweth he that I perceive not', so that the latter phrase was dropped to the detriment of the sense. In this case Hall has attempted to make some sense by altering the punctuation, but Hall or a printer also seems to have misunderstood the first occurrence of *y^t* as the abbreviation for *that*.

The relationship between the work of Grafton and Hall in general is hard to establish, and has only peripheral importance in the present discussion. Grafton's role as a publisher of new texts has been underestimated. But there seems to have been collaboration between the two men. It is not clear whether it was Grafton who inserted the passage dealing with Richard's coronation into More's work, to be subsequently copied by Hall, or whether More's manu-

[1] 'Before time' ('prematurely') for 'nowe at erste' seems to be one of the few cases where the sense is altered. But did the reviser intend 'nowe before time', i.e. 'now prematurely' (because there were still two heirs living)?

[2] It should be said, however, that 'sore myndeth' occurs on p. 49 H of *1557* (facsimile in *English Works*), and in G/H, so that it is just possible that *foreminded* is here a misprint of Rastell's.

[3] The Latin has 'Adeo me protector (qui superos precor ut protectorem se probet) stupidam arbitratur, ut quorsum eius phalerata tendat oratio non sentiam?'

script also already contained this addition, made perhaps by a further, anonymous, editor, before derivatives came to Grafton and Hall. Nor is it clear who tailored More's work to fit it into a more extensive chronicle (above, p. 204). If, as seems almost certain, Grafton took his annals for the years 1509–12 in the continuation to Hardyng's chronicle from the *Great Chronicle of London*, he can be shown to have edited his sources to such a limited extent. But he did not indulge in more serious alterations.

VI   DATING

I have argued that More at first intended to write only about Richard's usurpation. This general stage of his composition is now represented by the portion of William Rastell's manuscript covering the usurpation, by the draft Latin translation (the Arundel manuscript) in the College of Arms, and by the finished Latin translation printed in 1565. (It seems most likely, in view of its completed state, that this latter was the 'Chronicle of More's making of Richard III' that Sir Geoffrey Pole lent George Crofts before 1538,[1] but Pole may have had a manuscript of one of the English versions: possibly even that which came to Hall.) The manuscript eventually published by William Rastell in 1557 was a composite one, containing what might be renamed 'More's "Usurpation of Richard III" ', with some gaps where the author had removed material in the course of revision, and a continuation started later when More decided to write a history of the whole reign. Rastell's manuscript was in More's own hand, and Rastell concluded that it represented More's final working-up of the *History*. I have argued that it did not: that it was only the second stage in a three-stage process. More returned for a third time to his *History*, had a copy made of the 'second stage' (*1557* version), and started to work this up with additions and revisions. From this later working draft the G/H texts derive.

Some dates might be proposed for these different stages on a highly conjectural basis. Rastell's 'about 1513', it is now generally agreed, could be applied literally only to More's inception of the work, and seems early even for that. *1557* and *1565* (but not the Arundel manuscript, which leaves a blank at this point) refer to Thomas Howard II, who was created Earl of Surrey 1 February 1514 and succeeded as third Duke of Norfolk 21 May 1524, as Earl of Surrey, so that they must have been completed between 1514 and 1524. If More relied on the printed edition of Fabyan's *Chronicles* (Pynson, 'February 1516'), rather than on a manuscript copy, or on one of Fabyan's sources, for Edward V's civic welcome in *1557*,

---

[1] *English Works*, p. 41.

and for the detail that Hastings was beheaded on a log of wood meant for repairs, in the Arundel manuscript and *1565*, the date of all three can be narrowed to between 1516 (or 1517, depending on whether Pynson started his year on 1 January or 25 March) and 1524. It will be noted, however, that this rests on an assumption which is by no means proved. The statement in the Arundel manuscript that Mistress Shore is now a woman of seventy is scarcely helpful, though Sylvester tries to make something of it.[1] She could well have been much younger than Edward IV. We now know that she married Thomas Lynom, who probably died in 1518.[2] More's descriptions of a woman friendless and in beggary do not suggest that she had a husband still living, but this may be entirely a matter of artistic licence. Further scraps of evidence are no more conclusive. Professor Hay suggested that Vergil's manuscript of the *Anglica Historia* to 1513 was completed by the spring of 1514, and that he then left it in Italy until his next visit in 1516–17.[3] If this were the only copy available, More must then have seen it either in 1513 or after 1516.[4] Later, in 1521–4, Vergil reworked his manuscript for publication.[5] Did his renewed activity encourage More to continue his *History*? Or, to the contrary, did the execution of Edward Stafford, Duke of Buckingham, in May 1521 (to which More refers movingly in *The Four Last Things*)[6] cause him to break off the extended narrative about that time? Buckingham's death, if this is applied strictly, would furnish a *terminus ad quem* for the second main stage of composition (i.e. the continuation after Richard's coronation as it appears in Rastell's edition) of May 1521. The Latin versions, which I have suggested represent the first stage of planning, would have been completed sometime before this. But there is no real need to suppose that More threw down his pen on receiving the news of the execution. The parallels between the fate of father and son, if they really struck him as an obstacle, could have occurred to him at any subsequent time.

These various imprecise indications of possible date, taken together, could suggest that More wrote the first part of his *History* about 1518–19.[7] The second part, as it appears in Rastell's edition, may have been written as late as 1524, but was perhaps started—and then abandoned—about 1520–1.[8] Unless such alterations were

[1] pp. lxiv–lxv.
[2] Cf. above, chapter seven, p. 179 n. 1.   [3] *Polydore Vergil*, pp. 10, 14, 80.
[4] The later date becomes the more likely if one accepts C. H. Clough's suggestions in *E.H.R.* LXXXII (1967), 776–7.
[5] *Polydore Vergil*, p. 82.   [6] *English Works*, p. 86.
[7] Sylvester proposed 1516–18 for Rastell's complete text (pp. lxiii–v).
[8] G. R. Elton has shown that at least until Oct. 1525, when he had exchanged the

made not by More but by Grafton in the 1540s (which I consider
to be unlikely), the Grafton/Hall text contains indications that
More was working on it—that is on the third stage of his book—
after 1527. Mistress Shore is now said to have died 18 Henry VIII
(i.e. between 24 April 1526 and 23 April 1527),[1] and the reference
to Katharine of York (died November 1527) has been changed to
suggest that she is no longer alive.[2] Thomas Howard I, having died
in 1524, is now identified as participating in Hastings's downfall.
Less certainly, the absurd story about the disposal of the princes'
bodies (above, p. 212) may derive from John Rastell's *Pastime of
People* (1529) (above, p. 104): the resemblance extends even to the
citation of a place known as 'the Black Deeps'. Equally, More could
have seen his brother-in-law's manuscript before publication,
Rastell could have taken the story from More, or both used the same
source.

Sylvester[3] canvasses a hypothesis that the source of the Grafton/
Hall versions (which he takes to have been an *early* draft by More)
might have come to Hall through John Onley, a close friend of the
official, Sir Richard Rich, who confiscated the books which More
had in the Tower in May 1535; 'Yet it is hard to believe, given the
corrupt state of the Hardyng–Halle versions, that such a degenerate
text[4] could have remained in More's hands as late as 1535.' Whatever may be the truth of the speculation about the Onley/Rich
connection, I suggest that Sylvester's stated objection is fallacious.
The source of the Grafton/Hall texts was not an early but a late
draft by More, and the texts are not degenerate and corrupt (except
in so far as they contain the usual copyists' and printers' errors),
but embody the author's own last corrections. It is thus not at
all improbable that the manuscript was still in More's possession in
1535. Whether he would actually take to the Tower, when accused
of treason, a manuscript dealing with a king's wicked deeds and
subsequent downfall, is debatable, but he might have been working
on it as late as the 1530s. Busy as he was (and evidently reluctant
or unable to complete the work), he may have found occasional
relaxation in revising the existing text of what was to prove his
English masterpiece. The resultant untidy manuscript could very
well have produced many of the variant readings in the texts of
Grafton and Hall.

---

undertreasurership of the Exchequer for the chancellorship of the Duchy of
Lancaster, More's official duties were not so overwhelming as some of his hagio-
graphers have liked to suggest: 'Thomas More, Councillor', *St. Thomas More:
Action and Contemplation*, ed. Sylvester, p. 95.
[1] p. 55, collation.   [2] p. 3, collation.   [3] Yale *Works*, II, Appendix, p. 276.
[4] That is, the source of such a degenerate text.

Index